Troubleshooting SQL

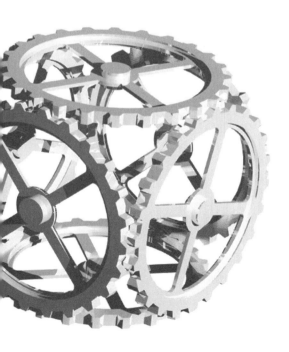

About the Author

Forrest Houlette started his professional career as a linguist who focused on the writing process. His academic work led him to create computer programs that modeled the writing process. Five years ago, seduced by the lure of writing software, he left academics to become a computer consultant. In that role, he has taught courses for Learning Tree International, worked with a variety of clients, and written several computer books. He lives and works in Louisville, Kentucky.

About the Contributors

Steve Juntunen is a consultant focusing on databases and mobile computing applications, technologies, and implementation practices. Steve's experience deals with the analysis, design, installation, and support of numerous systems for finance, manufacturing, and healthcare companies throughout the world.

Paul Nielsen has been a programmer since 1979 and has focused exclusively on database development since the early 1980s. Paul co-authored a book with Peter Norton in the early 1990s and has been a contributing writer to various programming and database books, as well as a technical editor for Access Advisor Magazine. He has spoken at several computer conferences including Microsoft Tech-Ed and ICCM. Recently, Paul was the data modeler and SQL Server developer for a team that built an MRP/II Inventory system. Currently, Paul publishes www.IsNotNull.com, a free weekly newsletter for SQL Server developers, and is a SQL Server trainer with Learning Tree International. He also volunteers development and training efforts for organizations that help third-world countries, and is involved with a SIM-TEC, a computer literacy program in West Africa.

Troubleshooting SQL

Forrest Houlette

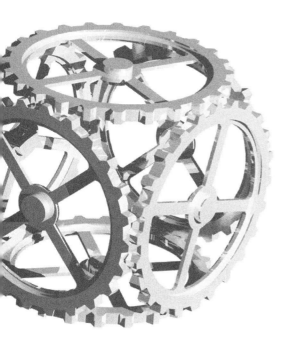

Osborne/**McGraw-Hill**

New York Chicago San Francisco
Lisbon London Madrid Mexico City
Milan New Delhi San Juan
Seoul Singapore Sydney Toronto

Osborne/**McGraw-Hill**
2600 Tenth Street
Berkeley, California 94710
U.S.A.

To arrange bulk purchase discounts for sales promotions, premiums, or fund-raisers, please contact Osborne/**McGraw-Hill** at the above address. For information on translations or book distributors outside the U.S.A., please see the International Contact Information page immediately following the index of this book.

Troubleshooting SQL

1234567890 FGR FGR 01987654321

ISBN 0-07-213489-5

Publisher	Brandon A. Nordin
Vice President & Associate Publisher	Scott Rogers
Acquisitions Editor	Ann Sellers
Project Editor	Jody McKenzie
Acquisitions Coordinator	Tim Madrid
Contributing Authors	Steve Juntunen, Paul Nielsen
Technical Editor	Kevin Heslin
Copy Editor	Robert Campbell
Proofreader	Susie Elkind
Indexer	Karin Arrigoni
Computer Designers	Lucie Ericksen, Tara A. Davis
Illustrators	Lyssa Wald, Michael Mueller
Series Designer	Roberta Steele
Cover Series Designer	Greg Scott
Cover Illustrator	Eliot Bergman

This book was composed with Corel VENTURA™ Publisher.

To everyone who pulled together to get this one finished. I owe you all more than I can ever express. Thanks for coming through when I needed you.

Contents at a Glance

Contents

Introduction

This book is about troubleshooting SQL. SQL is a different kind of programming language because it is declarative rather than procedural. Instead of writing code that undertakes grabbing each record from a database and processing it, SQL allows you to say SELECT * FROM MyTable. The query processor has to figure out the procedure for getting the data. You don't even get involved in the process.

Because of its declarative nature, SQL is difficult to troubleshoot. You have no interactive debugger. You do not have a well-developed error object that gets populated with information about the error. You may not even get an accurate description of what line in the code caused the error.

As a result, you have to be fairly clever about setting up your troubleshooting environment. That's what this book is about.

About This Book

My father is fond of reminding me that my Franklin ACE 1000 contained more memory than the mainframes he worked on. His stories are akin to the "when I was a kid" stories that involve walking ten miles to school in the snow drifts, but they have instructive points. When you start working with SQL, you have all the debugging advantages that my father had when he walked ten miles through the snow drifts to feed punch cards to his mainframe. Which is to say, you have to view your program as a black box that takes input in the form of a SQL statement and gives very little output. You get to divine what goes on inside from the scant information that comes out.

SQL is a wonderful language for defining databases and manipulating data. It has been standardized, so you can expect the bulk of the statements to be implemented consistently on any SQL-compliant database. The SQL standards do not say anything about debugging facilities. Which is to say, you get the opportunity to be very clever about building a debugging environment. And you should see this as an opportunity, not as a setback.

If you ever worked with punch cards while programming a mainframe, then you have all the debugging skills you need to troubleshoot problem SQL queries. Since the odds are that you haven't, however, you may want some pointers so that you can get oriented to the mindset necessary. This book provides you with that orientation. Not that I wish to reveal that I am old enough to have used punch cards. It's just that I offer my advice without talking about walking ten miles to school in snowdrifts. (I grew up in Southern California.)

This book covers all that you need to know to effectively troubleshoot SQL queries. It shows you how to set up a SQL debugging environment. It shows you best programming practices. And it steps you through working with common types of queries, offering insights about debugging along the way.

Who Is the Book For?

This book assumes that you know some SQL. You should be familiar with framing queries using SELECT, INSERT, UPDATE, and DELETE. You should also be able to distinguish the FROM phrase from a WHERE clause, and you should be able to distinguish between the work done by a HAVING clause and the work done by a WHERE clause. If you pass this test, you are ready for this book. If you don't pass, you will want to have a book like my *SQL: A Beginner's Guide* (Osborne/McGraw-Hill, 2000) handy, because you may wish to review the basics of SQL programming before you jump into the chapters on using specific SQL statements.

This book is for any SQL programmer who wants to become more efficient at working with SQL. SQL programmers can easily find ways to waste time. Recently, I was debugging a report that seemed to deliver the wrong data. I ran a copy of the production report and ran the query behind it against the production database. I compared the results, and, sure enough, there was a problem. The report wasn't printing all the data. I ran a copy of the report against the test server, and I executed the query against the test server. The report printed all of the data in this environment. Now, before I tell you that I spent the better part of a day before I found the problem, if you can see what I missed, then I will allow that you may not be a member of this book's intended audience.

However, if you are like the majority of us, including me, you need to know I spent the better part of a day comparing the settings in the report template and the query outputs in the test and production environments. I could find no change that would make the production report print the data that returned from the production query. And then about quitting time, it came to me. The production report was printing the test data. This book is about providing you with such vicarious experiences so that you don't spend a day like I spent. And, just for the record, I have not met a SQL programmer who didn't need more experience.

How to Use This Book

To benefit from this book, you need to start with Chapter 1 and read it straight through. Because of the anecdotal nature of the experience you gain, it will be hard to treat this book as an encyclopedic reference. It isn't the type of book for looking up basic SQL syntax, although that information is here. This book has lots of information about SELECT statements, for example, that come from experience writing such SELECT statements. You will pick up on this information better if you read the book straight through.

As you read through the book, you should mark certain sections. You might see how to write a SELECT in a certain way to solve a particular problem that you encounter frequently. Put a Post-it note on that page so that you can find the example again easily. What you really want to do is to create your own index by tagging the pages that contain your most frequently encountered problems. And, of course, you want to write in notes about the problems you have solved. In this manner, the book becomes your compendium of SQL programming experience.

Chapter Breakdown

The book is split into three parts. Part I covers building a functional development environment that allows you to troubleshoot SQL queries effectively. Part II looks at basic SQL statements, reviewing syntax and usage, but also discussing complex uses of each statement. Part III covers more complex problems and includes material that addresses platform-specific SQL development for the major SQL databases.

The chapter-specific contents are as follows:

▶ Chapter 1, "Choosing a Troubleshooting Environment," looks at the debugging environments available, and how to choose one.

▶ Chapter 2, "Using Best Practices," gives a detailed look at SQL programming best practices and how to employ them.

▶ Chapter 3, "Preparing Your Troubleshooting Environment," is a guide to creating your own effective working environment.

▶ Chapter 4, "Creating Databases," follows on from the previous chapters and looks at the best process for creating databases, since many problems you might troubleshoot are actually design rather than programming problems.

► Chapter 5, "Normalizing Tables," is a guide to designing tables for use with SQL queries. It focuses on showing how table design choices can create problems down the line for SQL programmers.

► Chapter 6, "Using Data Types," looks at the common problems associated with data types and their implementation in SQL databases.

► Chapter 7, "Selecting Data," is a fundamental look at using the SELECT statement, with a look at a common form of a complex SELECT statement.

► Chapter 8, "Inserting Data," gives information about the INSERT statement and walks you through common problems that can arise when using it.

► Chapter 9, "Updating Data," is a guide to the UPDATE statement, with information about the common problems it can cause.

► Chapter 10, "Deleting Data," gives information about using the DELETE statement, probably the most dangerous statement in SQL. It shows you how to protect yourself from the risks associated with deleting data.

► Chapter 11, "Grouping and Aggregating Data," looks at the aggregation functions and the use of the HAVING statement.

► Chapter 12, "Using Joins," gives detailed information about creating joins and the common uses for joins.

► Chapter 13, "Using Subqueries," is a guide to writing queries within queries and how to work around the performance problems that subqueries can create.

► Chapter 14, "Using Views," offers some insight into the use of virtual tables, as views are often called. This chapter discusses common scenarios for best exploiting this tool.

► Chapter 15, "Triggers, Stored Procedures, and Parameters," discusses creating procedures on the database server, probably the most common task for SQL programmers. This chapter shows how to use SQL to squeeze the best performance out of your database programs.

► Chapter 16, "Transactions," analyzes transactions, a database's means of maintaining data consistency. You learn how to create and exploit transactions in optimized queries.

► Chapter 17, "Using Cursors and Exceptions," takes up the topic most associated with speed of response in any database program. Cursors are slow, but this chapter shows you how to use them effectively, and it shows you how to raise exceptions to monitor the work the cursor is doing.

▶ Chapter 18, "Trees," shows how to work with tree data structures as represented in a database. This topic gives you experience with advanced SQL, as well as showing you how to work effectively with a common data structure.

Conventions Used in This Book

All SQL keywords appear in ALL CAPS. This makes them stand out more clearly, although the language itself is not case-sensitive.

-1 `Examples and code are displayed using a fixed-width font.`

SQL syntax statements [and/or reports and other output] are formatted using the same fixed-width font.

NOTE

Notes, formatted like this, include additional information about a particular topic.

DESIGN TIP

This highlights an item that promotes better programming practice and usually identifies a better way of approaching an existing piece of code.

DEBUGGING TIP

This gives a strategy that helps you to spot common bugs quickly.

Contacting the Author

Feel free to contact me with comments and suggestions about this book at forrestw@bellsouth.net. If you want to see what I do with the rest of my life, surf to my Web site at http://www.writeenvironment.com. There is, after all, an old picture there so that you can see what I look like.

You will find that I can be fairly conversational. I really do enjoy hearing from you.

Laying the Groundwork

OBJECTIVES

▶ Select a troubleshooting environment

▶ Review Query Analyzers

▶ Review graphical design environments

▶ Make practical choices about tools

▶ Learn about several best practices

▶ Discover simple techniques for optimizing queries

▶ Learn practices for protecting data

▶ Plan the objects you need to have ready to use

▶ Plan the systems you want available to you

Choosing a Troubleshooting Environment

IN THIS CHAPTER:

Query Analyzers

Graphical Tools

Development Environments

Facing Reality

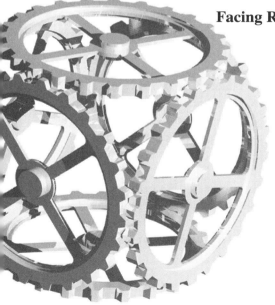

To troubleshoot Structured Query Language, you have to accept that you are starting from a weak position. SQL is a language implemented by database designers. IBM invented SQL, but the first commercial version originated with the Oracle database. Oracle beat IBM to market with the first implementation.

Relational database theory states that you must have a means of defining the nature of your data, now commonly called a *data definition language (DDL)*. DDL allows you to describe data types and to organize them into the named columns of a table. You must also have a means of manipulating data, now commonly called a *data manipulation language (DML)*. DML allows you to retrieve data, sort data, and summarize data. At the time IBM created SQL, the database was running on a mainframe and was taken care of by people who specialized in database management.

The nature of this cadre did not really require that the language exceed the capabilities of any other programming language of the day. Keep in mind that the people who took care of the database were comfortable programming in languages like FORTRAN and COBOL. Almost all of them had experience using punched cards to submit program statements, and getting a printout of errors on green bar paper after the program had been submitted for a run in batch mode. The error reporting this group was used to consisted of a line number and a suggestion about what might be wrong. Usually this descriptor simply read "syntax error." They were supposed to know the syntax so that they could spot the error.

In a certain sense, because of its origin, SQL does not incorporate extensive debugging support. Because of its nature, moreover, SQL does not lend itself to extensive debugging support. SQL is typically not compiled on the machine where you create the query and submit it for processing. In most scenarios, the query has to be submitted to a database server, the physical computer where the database software resides, for compilation. At best, what resides on the client computer where you frame the query is a syntax checker. This tool can tell you that you have failed to enclose a string value in quotes, for example, but it cannot tell you whether your query can actually compile. To run a compile of a SQL statement, you must execute an operation known as a SQL Prepare, passing the SQL statement itself as a parameter. When you prepare a statement, the database client software passes the statement out to the database server. The compiler at the database server compiles the statement, preparing it for execution.

As a part of this process, the compiler will optimize the query. The optimizer takes into account facts like the number of processors on the database server, and it prepares a query execution plan that divides the query into schedulable units and assigns them to processors appropriately. While the compiler can perform great

Many SQL Tools Hide Details

Many SQL tools hide the implementation of compiling SQL statements. Often, you just execute the query. The Open Database Connectivity API, as a counterexample, offers three functions: SQLPrepare, SQLExecute, and SQLPrepareAndExecute. SQLPrepare compiles the query, SQLExecute executes a compiled query, and SQLPrepareAndExecute undertakes both operations. Gupta's SQLWindows, a SQL programming environment for Windows, offers all these options. Microsoft's ActiveX Data Objects (ADO) mentions none of these options. Proprietary database tools like Microsoft's Query Analyzer mention nothing about the steps they undertake to run a query, and they can connect to the database using a variety of connection APIs. Keep in mind that the database engine, no matter what explicit steps you perceive you are taking, compiles the SQL statement and executes it. Some SQL environments, like Microsoft Access, allow compilation to take place on the client side. Others require that compilation take place on the server side. You may not be aware exactly what steps take place in the background behind your tool. Just rest assured that compilation followed by execution is the norm for SQL environments, even though the environment might hide the details of the implementation.

tasks, it cannot provide extensive interactive debugging support. It is limited to passing back the results of the compilation to the database client software.

To execute a SQL statement, you must first execute a SQL Prepare, and then you pass the prepared statement to a SQL Execute operation. SQL Execute is the equivalent of executing an executable file. To invoke such a service in MS-DOS, you simply entered the name of the executable file at the command prompt and pressed the ENTER key. Under other operating systems, you typed **Run** at a command prompt and pressed ENTER. SQL Execute operations are similar.

This operation causes the query to execute according to the plan developed by the compiler. During execution, you can encounter errors as well. Fatal errors will return some sort of an exit code. Logical errors, however, will provide no error information. Logical errors return data, just not the data you expected to return. When you execute the statement, you can get back one of three results: the data you expected, the data you didn't expect, or an error code. In the latter two cases, a debugger is of little use. You are either learning about a fatal error that would have crashed a debugger too, or you are learning that you asked for the wrong data from the database, the classic problem of expecting the database to recognize your intentions rather than what you actually wrote in the SQL statement.

If you wanted to run a SQL statement with all the advantages of a symbolic debugger, you would have to be running your statement at the database server, or you would have to work in a networked environment that could support real-time passing of debug information back to the client. Both of these possibilities are unrealistic. To work on the database server itself, you have to violate all sorts of security restrictions. No one in their right mind will let you experiment on a production database server in this fashion. First, crashing the server, a realistic possibility while troubleshooting, is not popular among those who need to provide data on a 24 × 7 basis. Second, allowing someone that level of control over a single server, either production or development, is a security risk. To debug against a database, you need administrative privileges, and allowing any programmer that level of control is asking for security trouble. At the least, the server may be subtly corrupted by the development effort. As the scenario escalates in levels of severity, you can imagine viruses propagating across the network with administrative privileges.

DESIGN TIP

No matter what your circumstances, you should always use a development server, rather than a production server, on which to develop and test your queries and procedures. A common error is to execute a query against the wrong database. My current client maintains 80 different databases on a production server, and they also do development against an 81st database on the same server. While it is good that the development database is kept separate from the production databases, in this client's configuration, a developer could easily execute a query against a production database by mistake. I was recently asked to sanitize the data in the test database by changing social security numbers and addresses. I did this at the end of the day. I could easily have been tired and could easily have forgotten not to set the active database before writing and executing the query. Imagine the consequences of UPDATE CriticalTable SET SSN = '123456789' executed against the wrong database!

Creating a network that would support SQL debugging has always been cost-prohibitive. For starters, when SQL was first created, practical networking was in its infancy. As the technology that Xerox did not want began to leak out of the Palo Alto Research Center, networking was available to the masses, but the network could easily be overwhelmed by the amount of traffic required for troubleshooting. Because of these facts, SQL was developed without this kind of debugging support.

With gigabit Ethernet and recent hardware advances, such a debugger is theoretically possible. But the mold for SQL debugging was cast long before.

When you create SQL statements, therefore, you can expect to have all the debugging support that you would have if you were writing your first FORTRAN program in 1978. For those of you who don't date that far back into the history of computing, you would have been using a shared mainframe computer. Woz had not even created the Apple I yet. Every program statement you created resided on a punch card, which limited your statement to about 80 characters in length. When you wanted to test your program, you carried your card deck to the computer center and gave it to a technician who ran the deck through a card reader. On a good night, given your limited access authority, you could expect your job to return a printout in about three hours. Then you read the printout carefully looking for sources of error. Normally, you needed to add print statements to reveal the values of variables or the intended output at any given moment in the program. Then you resubmitted your job, and you waited another three hours for your new printout, this time with the revealing error information.

Why do I raise this specter at the beginning of a book on troubleshooting? For a very simple reason: most SQL databases do not provide much more feedback than this scenario captures. When you are writing SQL statements, you need all the skills that I had to develop when I was in graduate school in 1978 and writing FORTRAN programs. If you are used to an integrated development environment with a debugger that allows you to step through subroutines and functions, watching the values of expressions along the way, you will be traumatized when you attempt to debug SQL. You just won't have that level of support.

Unfortunately, that's the bad news. Fortunately, I have good news. This book is about developing the skills you need to troubleshoot SQL successfully. It makes no difference whether you are dealing with a single query against a database, or with an extensive SQL procedure that is composed of several statements. To troubleshoot SQL effectively, you have to realize your limitations. Those limitations define your operating environment. You cannot watch the value of a variable change within a loop if you have no capability to implement watches. However, you can work around almost every limitation that SQL imposes on your operating environment. You just have to be creative. You have to think like a programmer from yesteryear. You have to outsmart the system that you have been given to deal with.

So how do you outsmart SQL? The simple answer is that you lie, cheat, and steal. The remainder of this book will explain the significance of that statement. The realistic answer is that you choose your tools carefully, and that you understand your tools in minute detail.

Query Analyzers

To create SQL statements, you need an editor. Any text editor will do, as Figure 1-1 shows. You could use Notepad, Brief, Multi-Edit, or any other available text editor to create the statements you will execute against your database. And many people take this approach. However, using a plain text editor deprives you of many features that you might like to have.

For example, if you use Notepad or a similar editor to create SQL statements, you have no means of executing those statements from your editor against the database. As a result, you must write some sort of a program that will open the text file that Notepad creates and run it against the database. The debugging support that you receive in this situation is sub-minimal. At best, if your statement returns an error, you can only guess at its cause. You are likely to be facing errors such as an ActiveX Data Objects recordset returning a value of –1 as the record count. This value means "I could not determine the accurate count of the records in the recordset at this time." If you spend much time working with ActiveX Data Objects, you quickly learn that

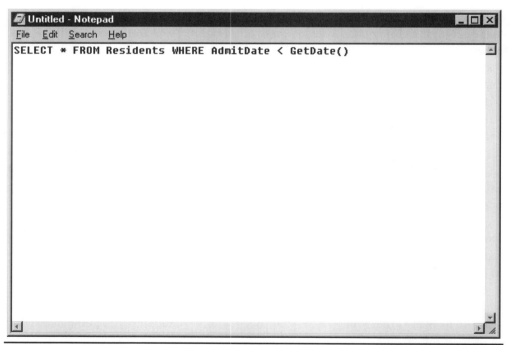

Figure 1-1 *A text editor used to create SQL statements*

the record count property on the recordset object routinely returns –1 as a value. You might begin to wonder, therefore, whether this object can ever count its records.

If you have gone this route of using a text editor and a program to develop your SQL queries, you know that debugging SQL is hell from this point of view. What you might prefer is an editor that can enter queries, execute them, and return results to you, all from the same windowed interface. Most database vendors will offer you such a product. Microsoft calls its offering a Query Analyzer, and this is as good a generic term as you might find for all such products. You have an editor, and typically the editor will color-code the SQL syntax. Keywords are blue, strings are pink, functions are gray, and what have you. The main advantage this color-coding gives you is that you can tell when you have used a keyword of a particular kind and when you haven't (see Figure 1-2). Avoiding the use of keywords in certain situations is extremely valuable.

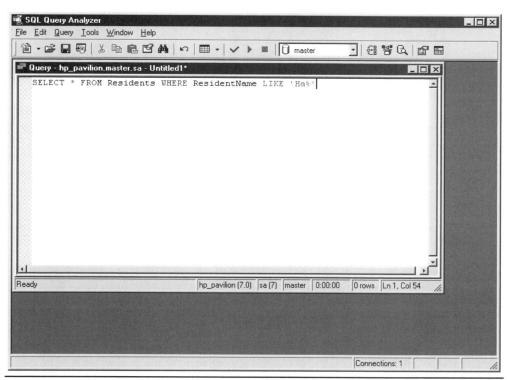

Figure 1-2   *An example of color coding in a query analyzer*

DESIGN TIP

SQL and the databases that implement it often allow you to exercise various options that are inadvisable. When you see a warning not to do something, have trust that someone else has already been bitten by that particular bit of foolishness. Just because you can do something with SQL in a database does not always mean that you should do it.

For example, no table column name should ever be the same as a SQL keyword. You might want to abbreviate the description field for your record as DESC, but doing so simply causes you headaches, because DESC is the SQL keyword for a descending sort order. To reference your column name, you will always have to resort to a workaround. In the various dialects of SQL, the solution varies. Some require that you enclose the column name in square brackets, as in this example: [DESC]. Other dialects require that you use double double quotes to delineate the column name, as in this example: ""DESC"". And many databases will accept several variants of the syntax for compatibility's sake, but only if the query is issued from a program. If you issue the query from the database vendor's query analyzer, you must use the proper syntax. Having a tool that will point out the syntax issues to you with color coding is extremely useful.

DESIGN TIP

Sometimes the implementation of SQL syntax varies within a given database. Microsoft's SQL Server 7.0 will accept a semicolon as a terminator for a SQL statement when the query is issued from the Query Analyzer or from the stored procedure building utility. The view building utility, however, will not accept the semicolon.

Query analyzers are very useful tools. They combine a text editor with features like color coding with the capability to submit queries to the database for processing. Executing a SQL statement is a matter of clicking a Run button. Such tools allow you to run groups, or batches, of statements, and even multiple batches of statements in sequence. You can build very complex SQL programs using these tools because of this flexibility.

In addition to being able to build and execute queries, you can get information back about the state of your query. For example, such tools provide a client-side syntax checker. By clicking a button, you can get a report of whether you have violated any syntax rules of the SQL implementation you are using. In addition, the tool is able to receive information back from the SQL Prepare or SQL Execute operation. Errors reported by the compiler appear in a status area of the tool's window. You will get error messages associated with line numbers.

While virtually every database vendor provides such a product for use with its database, you need to think carefully about whether such products will meet your needs for query development. Yes, they provide cool features that help with troubleshooting, color coding chief among them. However, all of these products are notorious liars in other respects. Most of them purport to tell you, for example, the line on which an error occurred in your SQL statements. What they don't tell you is that the editor's definition of a line and your definition of a line might differ.

For example, it is a common practice to format SQL statements in an editor so that each column name in an INSERT statement appears on a single line in the editor. The values in the VALUES clause are formatted one to a line as well. As a result, you have an easy time matching the column name to the value inserted into the column (see Figure 1-3). This approach is well and good, except that many query analyzers, Microsoft's among them, seem to count complete SQL statements as lines and not the lines in the text file as lines.

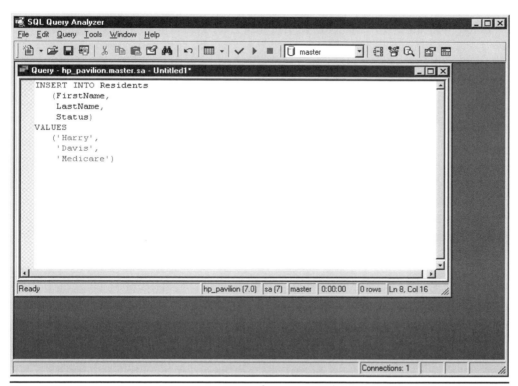

Figure 1-3   *Formatting an INSERT statement for easy reading*

What you face, as a result, is a query analyzer that reports an error on line 2. If you look at line 2 in the text file, you cannot find the error. Your failure to find the error is directly related to the fact that the editor is counting lines in SQL statements differently from the way you do. As a result, you literally have to guess about where the error is, because the line you see is not the line the query analyzer counted.

DESIGN TIP

The best way to solve the problem of a misreported line number is to create more lines. If you create a new line before the error in the code, the line number reported for the error should increment. If you create the new line after the error, the line number reported will not change.

So the tools your database vendor provides can be cool, but they can have their problems. They are, after all, free with the database, so what do you expect, perfection? Actually, you could expect more than you typically get from the free tools that database vendors provide. But such is the state of such tools.

If you are really serious about developing queries and applications in the SQL language, you need to consider other options. In doing so, you enter the realm of third-party applications, and in this arena you must be careful of your needs as opposed to the technology the vendor is poised to deliver.

Graphical Tools

The next level up from free tools is a group of graphical tools for developing databases. In general, these tools fall under the rubric of business graphics applications, and they seek to deploy a series of graphical methods for describing databases that you might wish to create. These tools allow you, for example, to create entity-relationship diagrams that describe database tables. You can then click a button or a menu item to generate the table from the diagram. Visio is an example of such a product. An example of one of its diagrams is shown in Figure 1-4.

To create a diagram, you use the services of the tool. Visio, for example, allows you to drag and drop any particular element from a tool palette onto a diagram. If you have a database diagram in progress, you select the Entity tool in the tool palette, and you drag it onto your diagram. You then have available an object that can represent a table. Double-clicking on the object allows you to fill in the object's properties, as shown in Figure 1-5.

Within the graphical tool, you can use the properties sheet to fill in the details of your table. You can define the name of the table, you can define the names and properties of columns, you can define primary keys, you can create indexes, you can

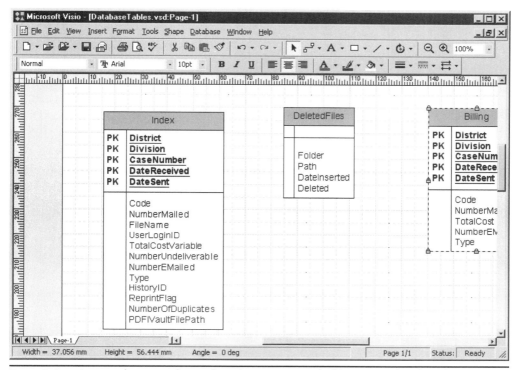

Figure 1-4   *A typical entity-relationship diagram provided by a graphical tool*

create triggers, you can create check constraints, you can create extended attributes, and you can create notes about the elements you have added to the table under the graphical environment. Saving a Visio object causes the graphical tool to create the table, and to apply the constraints to the table that you have defined in the graphical environment. Visio installs the Microsoft Data Engine (MSDE) on a computer that does not have another database installed, and uses MSDE as the server on which to create the database elements you have described in the diagram.

NOTE

Graphical tools of this type typically implement DDL only. You need another tool, such as a query analyzer, to work with DML.

Graphical tools can be highly seductive. They can lead you to determine easily which entities (that is, data elements) you must describe, and they will cause you to define tables in quick and easy diagrams that capture the relations among the data

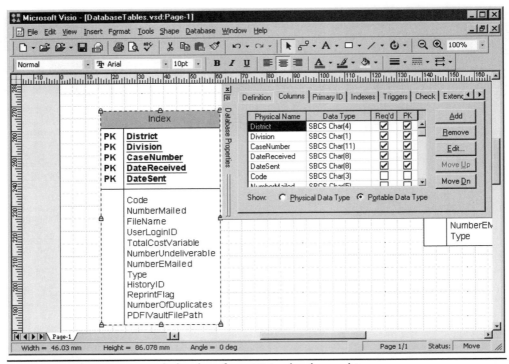

Figure 1-5   *The properties dialog box for a Visio database object*

elements you must organize. Most tools offer several alternative methods of diagramming a database. In addition, they easily allow you to try out "what if" scenarios about how to organize your data elements. Rearranging entities is a matter of dragging and dropping among table diagrams. Investigating different referential integrity constraints is a matter of a few clicks to change the possibilities. If you do not want to use a local database to house the tables, you can generate scripts that can be run on any database. In addition, the tool will provide a set of data types that are generic among databases, and translate them into the specific data types associated with a given database when creating the scripts.

Another advantage of graphical tools is that they can typically reverse-engineer an existing database. If you have ever been handed an existing database and been told to figure out its structure, you will find this feature very useful. Magically the table structures and constraint architecture reveal themselves. To get answers about what type of constraint a particular line in the diagram represents, you need only to click on the line. Some sort of a dialog box will appear that reveals the nature of the constraint.

However, graphical tools have a mind of their own. For example, you can define a table in a graphical tool that will not achieve physical existence in the database. All you need to do is to define a database table that does not meet the expectation for primary key constraints. What kind of table might this be? The table type is very straightforward. It is a bridging table. Its purpose is to link one set of records to another. Microsoft's Pubs example database, which ships with SQL Server, has a table in it that links authors to book titles. The table contains foreign keys: the author key and the title key, specifically. While the table requires uniqueness of pairings between a given author key and a given title key, it must be able to tolerate multiple pairings of authors and titles, because any given title may have more than one author. Visio, however, insists that such a table must have a primary key to be created.

Another example of a table that might not get created is a table that can hold duplicate records. For example, you might need to delete a table of files. In this case, you need the file path and the date the file was scheduled for deletion in the table. You probably do not care whether you might have duplicate records in the database table that describe the same file. You are going to loop through the table and execute delete statements against the file system to remove the files that are no longer relevant. Your table will link one set of columns to another, and your table will not use a primary key. However, if you try to create this table using a Visio diagram, you will not be able to do so. Visio tables must have a primary key, no matter what the database designer intended for the table.

Graphical tools, despite such minor issues, have tremendous advantages for those working with SQL database design. Reifying the design of a database is a difficult conceptual task. Approaching the task from the point of view of a set of CREATE TABLE statements is next to impossible. You have to create some sort of a diagram, or a series of lists, or some set of objects. You have to convert an undifferentiated list of data elements into an organized structure, and this conversion is what graphical tools are designed to facilitate.

NOTE

Business graphics tools that support database development are typically not very expensive. They run the same price as an office suite, and they may even be packaged along with an office suite.

Development Environments

Graphical design tools are a boon to database designers, and you might wish for a complete development environment that provides graphical support for database design along with debugging support for those developing queries and stored procedures. Such tools do exist, and the offering from Embarcadero is a good example (see Figure 1-6). These tools come at a premium license price, however, since they offer a great deal of functionality.

So what do you get out of a database development environment? First, Data Definition Language is implemented using some sort of a diagramming tool. When you design a database, you acquire a list of data elements and organize them into tables using a drawing tool. Once you have defined tables as entities, you will define the relationships among tables using graphical lines that represent relationships including foreign key constraints, uniqueness constraints, and so forth. From this

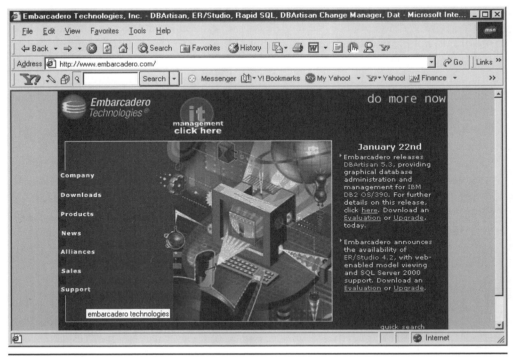

Figure 1-6 *The Embarcadero web site demonstrates the types of tools that you can get to help with SQL debugging.*

diagram, you can either generate a database on your server or generate the SQL scripts to run on the server. Maintenance of an existing database is a matter of revising the diagram and propagating the changes directly on the server or generating SQL scripts that will make the changes when you run them on the server. The Data Definition tool will also reverse-engineer a database, and it can usually import database diagrams from other sources.

Data Manipulation Language will be implemented as an editor with several debugging features. You can expect to find the normal color coding and feedback about errors. However, you also get many advanced feedback features that display information about the database as you work on your queries. For example, it is nice to know the size of a table when you start to frame a stored procedure. The way you might extract information from 11,000 rows might be completely different from the way you might approach 11,000,000 rows. Tools like Embarcadero's provide a list of tables in a window pane, and the number of rows in each table appears next to the table name. Yes, you can extract that information for yourself by issuing SELECT COUNT(*PrimaryKeyName*) FROM *TableName* against the database. But to do so, you need a separate editor window, you have to run the query, and you have to run the query each time you need an answer. Having this information available to you on demand in a convenient list is very handy.

The real advantage of the advanced environments is that you get much more information at your fingertips, to use a Microsoft cliché. The additional information makes working with a database much easier. Once you experience such an environment, you won't want to use anything else. They are very seductive.

However, even in such an advanced working environment, you still will not have an interactive debugger of the sort that you find in integrated development environments for writing programs in languages like Basic or C. Database servers just don't typically provide that level of access to information about SQL statements. You get a lot of aids, though, that make the lack of such debugging support much more tolerable.

Facing Reality

As is obvious if you research the market, you have a wide range of tools to use when developing databases and writing queries and procedures in SQL. The tools that you choose determine the nature of your working environment and the level of troubleshooting support you will have. A question every development shop has to face is just what kind of environment they will invest in. How we answer this question also determines the nature of this book.

Right now, as reader, you are probably looking to me as author for a recommendation. I'm afraid you are looking to the wrong person. I could easily say that you should invest in an advanced development environment. However, for many companies, such an environment is overkill. Average clients of mine are maintaining only a few databases. They were designed using tools available several years ago. Tables don't change often, and when they do, the changes are minor. The major activity necessary to database maintenance is writing and maintaining appropriate queries for extracting information. In this situation, an investment in an advanced environment could be overkill. The tools that come with your database are probably sufficient for the job. Remember, we are talking about a licensing fee on the order of $750 per developer. And to keep the tools current, you are probably looking at annual upgrade fees. Companies with slim profit margins on the information technology products they offer might see such an investment as exorbitant. For large companies, the price escalates with the number of developers. You need to see clear benefits that justify the investment.

When is the investment justified? When you maintain lots of databases for lots of different clients, and you need to rapidly prototype databases to meet client needs and deliver a high grade of maintenance support. Such an operation might be within a single company, serving many client departments, or it could be an outsourcing agency that meets the data needs of many companies. The average reader of this book, however, is not likely to work in this situation.

Most of us have to work with limited budgets, and within departments that hedge on database client licenses to reduce the cost of making the data available. Another $7,500 to outfit the developers with tools is the rough equivalent of a file server with a version control system and an Internet connection license for the database. Odds are that most of us would rather have a secure place to store code and enough licenses to make the Web-delivered data available to clients. Cool tools can at times be a luxury.

My advice on choosing tools is always to get the best tools for the job at hand. However, my experience with companies and database development tells me that you are more likely to get Visual Studio, Delphi, or PowerBuilder so that you can write client programs than to get a set of specialized database tools. As a result, I am choosing to write this book from this average point of view. You can do a lot of good work with the free stuff that comes with your database. And SQL debugging is roughly the same in any environment, precisely because you never get the equivalent of a symbolic debugger.

Having looked at our options, considered some recommendations, and faced practical reality, let's get on to practical methods for debugging SQL.

Summary

In this chapter, we have looked at the issue of what tools to use when writing SQL queries and procedures. We've examined three options, and we've looked at making practical choices among those options. We have also chosen a strategy for explaining how to troubleshoot SQL in this book.

Using Best Practices

Best practices are details that annoy every programmer, akin to documentation. When we were trained as programmers, we were taught to document religiously, accurately, and understandably. If you have ever taken over another programmer's project, you know full well that even good programmers don't adhere to their training on documentation.

Because the detail work like documentation is both very important and very likely to be done poorly, a doctrine of best practices has evolved within the programming community. We would all like code to be maintainable and reusable. Those dreams have rarely been realized. Microsoft Press has published at least one book on the subject of how to write such code the Microsoft way. Other design tools, such as Universal Markup Language and Interface Design Language, have been created to help make objects and their interfaces more standard, self-documenting, reusable, and easy to maintain. Best practices are, at the least, someone's opinion of what makes code better. By "better," we don't mean easier to write. Most programmers grump about the extra typing and detail work that adhering to best practices requires. The code that is written according to best practices has a longer useful life, however, than code not written in this manner. Thirty days after the code is written and the entire team has moved on to another project is when the results of best-practice programming kick in.

Best practices can be reduced to a few principles that have effects that propagate throughout your code. A practical articulation of these principles is as follows:

- ▶ Make your code self-documenting.
- ▶ Make your code readable.
- ▶ Undertake all actions explicitly.
- ▶ Given the choice between the cryptic and the verbose, be verbose.
- ▶ Include narrative comments.
- ▶ Stick to supported options.

Going down the list, you probably have no gag reactions to any of these. In implementing these guidelines in practice, however, you probably have a lot to learn. And because you are an individual, you will probably find the need to vary from the guidelines at least from time to time.

Some shops deal with the need for programming in this style by writing detailed standards to which all programmers must adhere. I have seen standards sheets 30 pages long and, quite frankly, feel that such detailed standards are a waste of time.

Best Practices Prevent Problems

If you want your database and all the SQL surrounding it to run twenty-four hours per day seven days a week, you have to help yourself achieve that goal. Best practices are about helping yourself in this way. On database servers, things happen that are not readily explainable. Processes can run wild, for example, eating up clock cycles but doing no useful work. How they get started may seem to be a mystery, but weak coding is often the starting place for such problems. If you adhere to best practices in designing your database and your SQL queries and procedures, you give yourself a fighting chance at achieving the 24 × 7 goal. To meet this goal, you have to beat all the demons that hide in systems and militate to cause problems. So, imagine yourself as the one called in at 2 A.M. to resolve a crisis that involves procedures other people wrote. You are under pressure because down time is money, and you have to struggle to get the beast back up and running. You encounter procedures that reduce all table names to one-character aliases that make no sense. You have to untangle nested joins and nested cursors to work out what is happening. At times like this, you meet many of the demons that militated to cause the problem you are facing. They usually have a well-intentioned human face at most other hours. Best practices help them to have that same well-intentioned face at times of great stress. They also help you to achieve short times to solution when problems arise. You want to develop a team culture that encourages adhering to best practices.

You spend more time looking up details about how to express your code more than you do writing code. I think the goal of best practices is not to create lockstep standards. I think the goal of the doctrine is to create some basic guidelines that leave room for individualism. Personally, I believe successful coding is that which any other programmer can pick up and follow by reading the code alone. In the SQL database arena, good code is any procedure that makes immediate sense when you read through it. A good database design is one that does not leave you sorting through lists of cryptic names trying to figure out how to extract the judge's name from the judge table while querying from the case table. You should not have to learn what a Run_ID is, and why it is different from a Batch_ID, or a Record_ID, or a Program_ID. These matters should be self-interpreting as you read the code.

Achieving this sort of goal is not difficult. Actually, it takes very little discipline. You just need an appropriate point of view.

A Guided Tour of Best Practices

So how do you translate the best practices guidelines just articulated into programming reality? Let's take each principle and look at how it might translate. Remember, we are not creating the standards document to end all standards documents. We are trying to create a SQL database environment that is easy to work in and that promotes effective troubleshooting. So we are seeking a balance between standards and working style.

Make Your Code Self-Documenting

All code has certain elements in common, names among them. One of the most frustrating practices to encounter is naming conventions. Elements must have names. They can have cryptic names, or they can have readable, self-interpreting names, or they can fall somewhere in between.

From the point of view of databases and SQL, you want to fall more on the side of the readable and self-interpreting.

At one time, "self-interpreting" meant including the object's type embedded in its name. This convention arose when you were using a command line to list a set of all objects in the database. Under these circumstances, you wanted to see _TAB attached to every table name, and _SP attached to every stored procedure. You needed to have a way of differentiating among database objects.

These days, however, we have graphical tools that we use to interact with databases. Objects of like types are grouped together in a graphical tool, so that to see the tables you select the table list, to see the views you select the view list, and so forth (see Figure 2-1). Because we have these organizing tools, you may feel less pressure to include object type information in an object's name. Doing so, however, is never wrong.

DESIGN TIP

There is at least one case where including object type information in the name is very helpful. If you are using a version control system like Visual SourceSafe or PVCS, having the object type in the name allows you to scan a list of items in a version control tool and tell immediately what the object is.

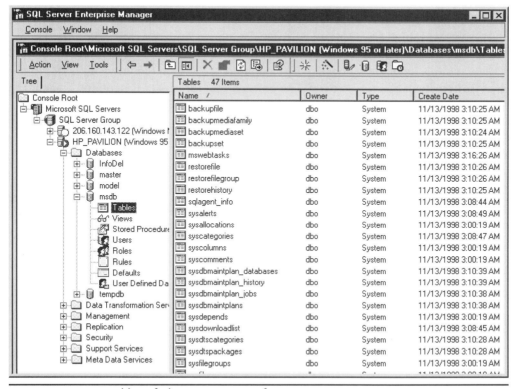

Figure 2-1   *A sorted list of objects in Microsoft's Enterprise Manager*

It is more important, however, to give your objects meaningful names. We have escaped the 8.3 naming convention, and so you can use names of reasonable length to describe your objects. And if you think about it, you can reasonably differentiate object names by choosing appropriate naming conventions so that you don't have to add type information in the name. You can therefore focus on functional description in choosing your names. You want to include at least one word in the name that describes function. The other words need to identify relevant relationships.

Consider the common elements that you have to name in your database. The most common are tables, constraints, triggers, views, users, roles, and stored procedures. Each of these has its own interesting set of functional and relationship requirements. If you name them carefully, you can look at the object and know what it does. Let's look at each in turn.

Tables

In databases, tables are containers. Literally, they contain rows and columns. However, the combination of columns in a relational database implies that the items in the columns have a relationship. The columns are associated into a table because they participate in this relationship. The most critical functional description associated with a table is the name of this relationship. The functional word in a table name, therefore, ought to be the name of the relationship. This word should be a noun, and it should name the most salient feature associated with the relationship that associates the collection of columns into the table.

I have worked with clients recently who manage nursing homes and bankruptcy courts. In both of these arenas, there are many self-obvious entities that must be described by columns in a table. For example, each nursing home itself is an entity, and the most salient feature of a nursing home is its physical facility. If you ask anyone what a nursing home is or where one is, they will describe a facility. Because of the saliency of the facility, any database that contains information about a nursing home must describe the physical facility as a part of the database structure. Residents live in rooms, these rooms have attributes, different personnel work in different rooms, and different activities take place in different rooms. Any database describing a nursing home must have a table that collects items of information about the physical facility.

What might you name this table? Any number of possible names come to mind. One client used the name "Facility." However, the name you choose needs to reflect the context in which the database is used. If I were writing a database to serve a single nursing home, I probably would not choose the name "Facility" for this table. I would choose another term that reflects the understanding of those who use the database. Inevitably, those working in the facility have names for the physical plant. They might call it the "building," or the "physical plant," or the "structure." They may refer to it as something that reflects their interaction with the elements of the structure, such as the "floor plan." I would choose a functional word for this table name that reflects both the nature of the item and the way the users refer to it. I could call it the "blueprint" or the "site elevation," but I doubt some other programmer following in my footsteps could understand what I was talking about, and I doubt that any of the users who might consult this program could figure out what I meant either.

In a company that manages multiple nursing facilities, "building" or "physical plant" probably make no sense. Names like "facility" make more sense, because they can denote a collection of things, and companies that manage multiple nursing centers have collections of nursing centers. If they manage only nursing centers, I might choose "nursing center" as the name. However, companies that support long-term care often have other types of facilities. There are long-term care hospitals, outpatient facilities, and so forth. Naming under these circumstances forces you more toward the generic "facility" rather than toward a more specific term.

In table naming, therefore, your choice of names needs to reflect the business logic of the organization that uses the database, the ordinary speech of the users that use the database, and the practical logic of database design. In most cases, using a single noun or compound noun, such as "airship hangar" or "Statue of Liberty," is sufficient for naming a table. Tables typically represent entities, and their names should describe the entities they represent. Clearly name tables after the entities they represent. If you make certain that your table names reflect the ways users talk about their business, the entity names should be self-describing to anyone reading your work.

Some tables, however, do not represent entities. They can represent relationships between or among entities. For example, in the bankruptcy industry, you often must track relationships between courts, debtors, and creditors. You can easily imagine having a creditors table to contain information about the creditor entity. You can easily imagine having a debtors table to contain information about the debtor entity. You will also need a way to link the two. You need to know how to relate a single debtor to his or her many creditors. A common practice is to use a table that contains one entry that pairs the ID of a creditor with the ID of a debtor for each such pairing. Such tables are often said to *bridge* between entities. You can select all the creditors for a debtor by using a query like this:

```
SELECT * FROM Debtor_Creditor WHERE Debtor = 'Some Debtor'
```

You can easily construct a similar query to identify all the creditors for a given debtor. It looks like this:

```
SELECT * FROM Debtor_Creditor WHERE Creditor = 'Some Creditor'
```

In showing this example, I have given away my naming convention for tables that capture relationships. I typically use a pairing of the two (or more) entities that participate in the tables. I link the names of the entities with underscore characters to build the complete table name. When you look at such a name, you can easily say that this is a table that links X entities, as indicated by the number of nouns in its name.

In naming tables, the basic rules for best practices are the following:

▶ Select table names based on the possible names for the entities involved.

▶ Use nouns for table names.

▶ Make certain that the names make intuitive sense within the culture of those who use the database.

► Express relationships captured by tables by linking the names of the entities linked by the table.

Within tables, columns have to be named. Columns represent discrete items of information about the entity named by the table. They also typically do not represent relationships. Because of these facts, a column name should be a noun that names the item of information it represents. It should be a noun that reflects the way users talk about the item of information, and it should reflect salient features about the item of information. For example, you could name the column that contains the Colonel's Secret Recipe "Q12345," but no one, including the Colonel, would know what this means. Name your columns something salient, like "Secret_Recipe."

DESIGN TIP

Facts about the items stored in your database may change significantly over time. As a result, choosing names that reflect the specifics of current details may not reflect reality as the business changes. My long-term care client started out in the business of serving ventilator patients in hospitals. They now serve a more general population in a variety of long-term care situations. Naming their facilities "Ventilator_Units" would not have served their business goals. You need to focus on names that might serve long-term business goals.

Naming Practices and Underscore Characters

Somewhere in the history of database creation, someone became enamored of the underscore character. Typically, all names in a database use an underscore where you would use a blank space if you were writing in any human language. Using the underscore makes names readable, because you can tell where to break the words. This convention arose when we used all caps in all of our names (because we had no choice in character sets). Most of us don't date back that far in computing, but there was such a time (1969?). Underscores have an almost religious following in SQL code. However, another convention that relies on upper- and lowercase characters has gained favor. Under this convention, you capitalize the first letter of each word in the name, as in "ThisIsATableName." This convention does not have as devout a following. You may find shops where someone will have heated discussions with you for not using underscores. Both conventions, however, are equally functional. Use whichever convention suits your corporate culture.

Constraints

Within a database, *constraints* limit what you can do. They state limits like "you must have this key in another table before you add it to this table." Or, they can state limits like "all pairings in this table must be unique." You can accept default naming conventions like "PK_30205," or you can create more meaningful names. More meaningful names are much better when troubleshooting at two in the morning during a crisis.

You need a word in a constraint name that describes what the constraint is by type. Constraints come in several common types. For example, you might have the following types:

- ▶ Primary key constraints
- ▶ Foreign key constraints
- ▶ Uniqueness constraints
- ▶ Check constraints

Each type of constraint has a different meaning. A *primary key* constraint prevents you from adding duplicate values for a primary key to a table. The primary key serves to uniquely identify rows in a table. Because of this fact, you should never have duplicate values for a primary key. *Foreign key* constraints state that a key value must exist as a primary key in some other table before it exists in this table, or it must exist as a uniqueness constraint in some other table before it exists in this table.

Uniqueness constraints state that a set of column values in a table must be unique, or that a pairing of column values in this table must be unique. You cannot have duplicate values in columns that are governed by the constraint.

Check constraints state that the value of a column must match a pattern, as "(XXX) XXX-XXXX" for a telephone number.

If you allow your database to impose default names for constraints, you will have a hard time imagining what PK_0390078 refers to when you see it in a list of constraints. You might be able to interpret the "PK" as meaning "primary key," but you will have no idea what table it applies to. Random numbers, while they guarantee uniqueness for the name, rarely allow you to understand what the name refers to.

Constraints refer to relationships among data elements and should bear names that reflect those relationships. A primary key constraint, for example, describes the relation of one row to another in a table. A uniqueness constraint also describes a similar relationship, but it guarantees uniqueness not in terms of the value of a key, but in terms of the pairing of data elements. Foreign key constraints describe a relationship between a data element in one table and a data element in another table. Check constraints describe a relationship between data being entered and data being stored.

Constraints can be easily named in self-interpreting ways. Use a two-letter abbreviation to identify the nature of the constraint: PK for primary key, FK for foreign key, CK for check, UN for uniqueness. Then use the name of the table to which the constraint applies as the second element of the name. A primary key constraint for the Facilities table would therefore be named PK_Facilities. In the case of foreign keys, where two tables are involved, name the second table as the third element of the constraint name. A foreign key between the Facilities and Residents tables would have the name FK_Facilities_Residents. Where two tables are involved, make the second element of the name the table where the primary key resides and the third element of the name the location of the foreign key. Finally, for constraints like check constraints that have a functional role, add a final element to the name that describes its function. A check constraint that guarantees the format of a phone number, for example, might have this name: CK_Facilities_FormatPhone.

Triggers

Triggers are SQL code attached to tables that fires when a threshold action—an INSERT, UPDATE, or DELETE—takes place. The action can affect the table to which the trigger is attached, or it can affect other tables in the database. Because of these facts, triggers should be named much like constraints. I use the prefix "tr" to mark a trigger, since there is nothing inherent in a trigger's nature to distinguish it from a stored procedure. The second element of the name should be the table to which the trigger is attached.

After establishing that this code is a trigger and that it is "owned" by the table to which it is attached, you need to consider the trigger's function. What does it do? Are you deleting references in other tables because something was deleted here? Are you inserting something in another table to record who updated a record? Are you conducting a parallel insert to protect critical data? Can you express this function in a word or two? You want to include this expression as a part of the name. Finally, if other tables are affected, you should include some description of what these other tables are.

The description of other tables may need to be sweeping rather than specific. It is theoretically possible for you to do a SELECT INTO using a five-table join that creates a temporary table. Putting all six table names into the name of your trigger would be useful, but it also makes the name of your trigger genuinely unwieldy. As with any naming convention, you have to balance practicality of use with self-documentation. Ninety-character names are hard to use. You may find that the functional description is sufficient. However, it is useful to know what other tables are affected, and it is useful to know when you look at the name, because other documentation will be somewhere else not readily available when you need it. You really want to try to characterize the output or range of what is affected if a single table name won't do the trick.

Views

Views are virtual tables. They are not materialized until demanded. Although they are stored as database objects, they are not stored in the same way as tables. Views typically have different functionality than the tables they are related to. For example, a view may be read-only. It may or may not be updatable. Views may contain very stable data that is always present in the database, or they may calculate data that is present in the database only as long as the view is in use. Because of their different nature, views need to be distinguished from tables. As a result, I use the prefix "vw" to start the name.

Views typically do not exist to present data from a single table. If they do present data from a single table, they present it for a different purpose than the table presents the data. Database administrators often use views to keep consumers and programmers away from the actual tables. If I let you query against a view, I can be very certain that you won't accidentally damage my data in the table. I will let you look at the data and do whatever you wish with the data, but I will keep you away from the setting where you might do a DELETE without a WHERE clause.

The case I am building is to name views after their function. After the "vw," you should express the function of the view. For example, "vwFirstAndLastSurveyDates" conveys what you might find in the view and gives you a sense of what its purpose is. When you see the name, you know what is there; you can make reasonable predictions about who is using the data, and what they use it for. One other element can be useful in a view name, and that is the name of a procedure or other view that consumes the data, if there is one. Often you will scan a list of views and wonder if one of them is in use anymore. You can always execute a stored procedure or use the graphical management tool to discover the view's dependencies, but it is nice to know when you see the view. Then you don't have to search for the answer, or get lost in momentary confusion as you troubleshoot a problem because you thought you knew what this view did, when you really don't remember.

Users

Every shop has a convention for naming users. First initial and last name, or two zeros and initials and last name (so that you can use 01 and 02 to distinguish among people who have nonunique names). The basic point is that you need a convention that makes user names predictable, so that users can remember their own logins, if nothing else.

With databases, however, you may have more users to think about than interactive users. Often programs have logins embedded into them. That way, the program can attach to the database without having to prompt a user for a login name and password. Such logins are very useful for programmers who write programs that use embedded SQL. However, such logins do open an attachment point that, if anyone knows what it is, allows them in, often with privileges that you would prefer they not have. The usual purpose of the program is, after all, to shield users from direct access to the database.

Programmatic logins should get a special naming convention. If you are scanning logs for unusual behavior, you want to be able to tell which logins represent programs and which ones don't. This convention allows you to spot unusual activity just a little more easily. A simple convention is to prefix "p_" to such logins.

Other types of users that you may wish to distinguish are administrators, and users whose privileges exceed the ordinary. Again, what you are trying to do is to improve your ability to spot the unusual trends that identify potential security breaches.

All users need to have passwords. Passwords should include at least one nonstandard character and at least one number. These features make dictionary lookup programs work much harder to guess a password. Upper- and lowercase characters drive users crazy when they try to log into the database, but they do improve security. Special-purpose logins, like those for programs, should have long and complex passwords. The reason they should is that no one is going to type this password, and you want it to be especially difficult for a programmer to remember—especially one who has left the company.

DESIGN TIP

A very good practice to encourage among programmers is to allow the password and login name used by a program to be set easily, from either a command line or a graphical interface. When someone leaves a company, it is very good practice to change the passwords on accounts that person had access to. If you change the password on a programmatic login and you have to recompile the program to change the embedded password, keeping to this security practice can be very difficult. Often the change management process makes recompiling and redistributing a long and complex set of steps. Better to allow an administrator to make a simple change in a dialog box.

Roles and Groups

Databases group users together for convenient administration. These groupings are called *roles* or *groups,* depending on the database. Privileges can be granted to entire groups, rather than to each individual user in the group, simplifying user management. Whatever privileges the group has, its members have.

Most databases provide you with some built-in groups, and you can do nothing about their names. For groups or roles that you create, however, you need a naming convention. A general convention for all contexts is difficult to specify. A good rule of thumb, though, is to name the group after its function. If these are users of one database program, naming the group the name of the program plus "users" is sensible. If these are users who share a role within the company, name the group after that role. Seek out names that allow you to identify what those users do, and roughly what access they have. You want to know what the access is when you look at the group name. You are giving yourself that quick sense of what security is in force when you see the group mentioned in a log. The less you have to remember at such times, the more effective you will be in making administrative decisions.

Stored Procedures

If you are a SQL programmer, you will work a lot with *stored procedures,* saved queries that do lots of interesting work for you. One of the daunting tasks for anyone working with a database is staring at a long list of stored procedures trying to figure out what they do. The only organization most databases provide for this list is alphabetical. As a result, careful naming can make your life much easier as you work with the database.

Having listened to other programmers tell tales and having made some very bad decisions myself about stored procedures, I've developed a suggested naming convention that I think is really helpful. Start the name of the stored procedure with a prefix that describes its basic action. Use the following list to get you started, and add to it as you find procedures that have more complex actions:

- ▶ sel for SELECT
- ▶ up for UPDATE
- ▶ ins for INSERT
- ▶ del for DELETE

You may find it useful to develop prefixes for actions like sorting, calculating statistics, hashing sensitive data to create test tables for test databases, and so on. Whatever you develop, keep the list as short as possible, and make sure that all administrators and programmers know what the conventions are. You want them used and observed.

Use the remainder of the name to tie the stored procedure to its usage. I write most of my data access programs in Visual Basic, and most of my stored procedures are invoked by some function or subroutine in a program. As a consequence, I have developed a naming convention that tells me how to get to the code that invokes the stored procedure. After the prefix comes the name of the calling program. After the program name comes the name of the module in which the code invoking the procedure lies. After the name of the module comes the name of the function or subroutine that actually calls the stored procedure. Then, if more than one stored procedure is invoked by that subroutine or function, I add a sequence number to tell me which invocation in the code this one is. When I look at a stored procedure named this way, I know roughly what action it undertakes, what program issues the call, and where in the program to find the call. You may wish to include the name of the table involved, or some sweeping description of the tables involved, if you want to know the target of the action. I consider this optional myself, and I include the target only if the name is not so long that I consider typing it into code unwieldy.

Other types of naming conventions are useful to employ. Sometimes a program is not the user of the stored procedure. It may be a database process itself, like a scheduled maintenance procedure. Or it may be another stored procedure. In this case, I substitute the name of the process or stored procedure for the program name, and I use a sequence number to help me locate what step in the process or procedure makes the call. As you can see, you might need to extend the convention to cover many different scenarios. The main point is to tell yourself what code is the main consumer of this stored procedure, and how to find where it is invoked easily.

Variable names in stored procedures deserve some comment. Variable names are perhaps my greatest pet peeve as a programmer. A long time ago, there was AppleSoft BASIC, and because the entire language had to fit into a single ROM chip and work with very limited memory, the language allowed only two characters for variable names.

Among microcomputer programmers, the tradition of short, cryptic variable names was born. There are some traditions, however, that need not be perpetuated, and this is one of them.

Recently I had to perform maintenance on a program that was written by a guy who believed that you should have to struggle with the code to understand it. He used one-character variable names, and as a consequence the cost of having a consultant come in to do maintenance on this program was considerably higher than it should have been. Let's do the math to illustrate the point. Average billable hours went to this company at $55 per hour. It took eight hours just to figure out what this piece of code did. That time cost the company $440. Keep in mind, all that happened during that time was that the consultant read the code and traced its thread of execution. It took two hours to make and test the change, time billable for a total of $110. If we assume that self-documenting code could have reduced the research time by half, the cost for making a minor change to the program drops by $220. The point is that self-documenting code reduces the cost of owning a software system considerably. Variable names figure into that cost reduction as a significant factor.

Two basic rules of thumb allow you to create variable names that do not impede development and maintenance. First, identify the variable type within the name. The most common way of doing so is to include a one- to four-character prefix in the name that identifies the type. An integer variable, for example, might be named intCounter. Second, make the rest of the name descriptive of the variable's function. A string that you use just for temporarily holding information, for example, might be named strTempStorage.

Avoid using a single variable for multiple purposes. Consider a stored procedure that defines a variable named intCounter. A very confusing scenario is one like the following. In the top section of the procedure, intCounter is used to count the number of times a condition is met within a while loop. In the middle section of the procedure, intCounter is used to count the number of times a while loop executes. Then at the bottom section of the procedure, intCounter is used to count the number of records meeting a condition. You can easily lose track of what the value of intCounter should be at any given point in the execution. This scenario is especially confusing when intCounter is a parameter that is passed by reference or it is a return value. You must remember that you will have at your disposal only primitive debugging tools. Using multiple, single-purpose variables helps you to divine what is going on inside your procedure when it provides outcomes that you do not expect.

As you work with SQL, you might notice that SQL offers lots of data types. SQL Server, for example, offers at least char, varchar, nchar, and nvarchar for strings. Do you need prefixes for each of these data types? One answer to that question would be that yes, you do. If you take this approach, you will always be able to tell what type you are dealing with, and you will be less likely to pass a char data type to a stored procedure that requires an nchar data type, as many of Microsoft's built-in stored procedures now do. Another answer, however, is that so much detail makes programming inefficient. It is enough to know that you are dealing with string data, and strings pretty much are strings. Most databases don't have such sticky requirements on their built-in stored procedures, and so you are better off working with a generic prefix rather than spending your time meticulously typing the right prefix for each specific data type. Most SQL programmers I know take this approach.

As you think about naming conventions, the most important factor is to focus on reducing cost of ownership along two dimensions, original development time and maintenance time. Building elaborate standards for names can increase original development time. Programmers get confused about whether that one is a char or an nchar, so they spend lots of time looking up details rather than writing code. They also spend lots of time correcting mistakes in their code. On the other hand, some time spent on the development side drastically reduces costs on the maintenance side. You need to find a balance between the two. Generic prefixes for multiple, similar data types is an example of a compromise that balances the requirements for reducing costs on both programming tasks.

Make Your Code Readable

All of us hate having to open up a procedure that we did not write and finding a file filled with lines that run together and make no sense. If you have never had the experience, all you need to do is open a text file delimited with line feed characters in Windows Notepad. Notepad does not interpret the line feeds as an instruction to start a new line on the screen. All of the text runs together with a strange black square showing where each line ends (see Figure 2-2).

This simple example shows why you need to make your code readable. If everything runs together as in our example, you have a hard time catching spelling mistakes, syntax errors, and any other momentary lapse in typing that keeps a procedure from running. A common mistake, for example, is forgetting to enclose a string value in single quotes when you assign that value to a column. The error returned will vary depending on the context of the mistake. Finding such an error in hopelessly tangled lines of code is difficult.

The guiding principle of making code readable is to use white space strategically. SQL does not care where lines begin and end when they are presented in the editor's screen. The SQL parser easily finds a statement's beginning and ending in terms of its grammar. Some databases require you to terminate SQL statements with a semicolon to assist the parser in finding the end of a statement. The benefit to you as a programmer is that you can freely arrange your statements in the editor to make them more readable, improving your chances of spotting details that have gone awry.

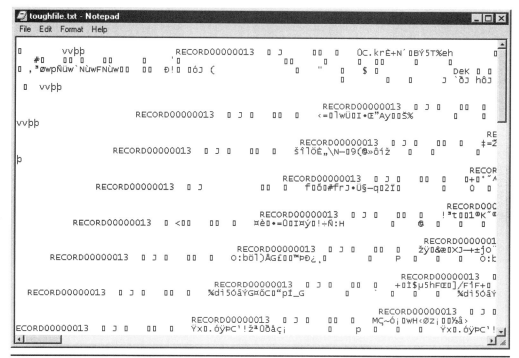

Figure 2-2   *An example of a hard-to-read file*

Here are some common conventions that make code more readable:

▶ Write SQL keywords in all capitals. Doing so allows you to immediately distinguish the keywords from other elements, such as column names and data values.

▶ Write column names as they are spelled in the database. If your database administrator has used all capitals for column names, see if you can use a different convention for capitals in your code. You probably can, unless a nondictionary sort order is in force. Capitalize the first character of each word in the column name, for example, and you can readily tell column names from SQL keywords.

► Use a vertical layout for column lists. Many programmers place one column name per line, making the column list a pancake stack of column names. This convention works well unless you have a large number of column names to include. When you have large numbers of column names, placing more than one on a single line helps to improve readability, because you can find the rest of the SQL statement somewhere on the same screen as the column list. Try to avoid requiring horizontal scrolling to read parts of the SQL statement. You have an easier time remembering the whole function if you scroll vertically to see different parts of it than if you scroll horizontally. Mixing the two is not a recipe for success.

► Match values being assigned to columns by position on the screen. If you have a list of nine columns you are inserting to, you should have a list of nine values. SQL requires that the values be in the same order as the columns; otherwise, you will assign the wrong value to a column. As you lay out the SQL statement in your editor, you should match the layout of the values to the layout of the columns. If you have three lines with three columns each on a line, you should have three lines of values with three values each. Doing so helps you to match which value gets assigned to which column easily.

Figure 2-3 provides an example of a properly formatted SQL statement.

DESIGN TIP

At least one programmer in my acquaintance recommends placing the BEGIN keyword on the same line as the IF keyword. In cases where you have multiple levels of indentation in your code, this convention reduces the level of indentation by one, helping you to achieve the goal of avoiding horizontal scrolling.

Undertake All Actions Explicitly

Often you have multiple options for how to perform a single task. When you write embedded SQL using Microsoft's ActiveX Data Objects (ADO), you can find several examples. You can open a connection to a database and execute a query using any of three different objects: the connection object, the command object, or the recordset object. Each method seems equivalent and should be equivalent. In an early version of ADO, however, sometimes executing the connection and query from the recordset object had different effects from executing the connection and query from the command object. What was happening is that the other two objects were being created implicitly for your program's use, even though you saw yourself as

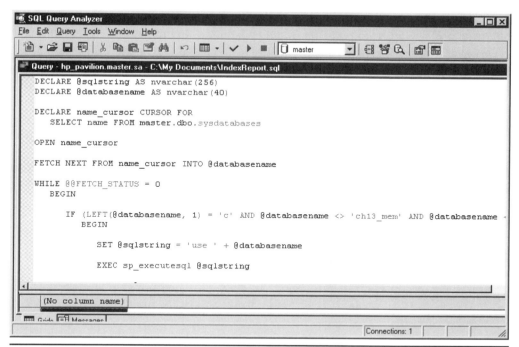

Figure 2-3   *An example of using white space and typing conventions to make your code readable*

using one object in the program. The details of the implicit creation did not match your intentions in executing the connection and query from the single object. The moral of this tale is to create and manage all three objects yourself, because then you know for certain what they are doing.

SQL often provides shorthand methods for accomplishing goals. SELECT INTO can create a table for you and populate it with data. It replaces a CREATE TABLE, and an INSERT that uses a subquery to extract the data. Both are pretty much equivalent in terms of execution time. However, the second method is more explicit than the other. You reveal all the steps necessary to take the action. When you are doing maintenance, the steps will be present in the code. Their presence reminds you of what actually goes on in your SQL procedure.

Why does the explicit reminder help? Coding explicitly reduces the cost of maintenance by reducing the mistakes you make when debugging because your attention is diverted by the problem. You are seeing the code that is present when you are in this mode, not the code that got shorthanded. You have greater difficulty remembering that a table got created in the background on the fly at such times.

Seeing that the table is created explicitly in the code reduces the demand on your attention and helps you to focus on finding a solution. In most cases, being explicit does not carry a performance penalty. If it does, you should use the faster form and write narrative comments to remind yourself about what steps are implied. This technique balances the requirement for explicitness with the requirement for speed.

Include Narrative Comments

Speaking of narrative comments, you should include narrative comments in your SQL code to help both others and yourself to understand what the code does. Some shops have elaborate headers that you are required to fill in, including the name of the procedure, its function, the parameter values it receives, the parameter values it sends out, and the value it returns. Other items might be included as well, such as the date written, the date last modified, and the author's name. Such headers can be useful, but they are often not updated when the code is modified. Such updates are often the last thing on a programmer's mind.

I think you ought to insert comments that are highly functional as a priority as you write the code. Headers are useful, but I can see the list of in and out parameters at the head of any stored procedure.

Stick to Supported Options

When you write programs, you always will be tempted to use things you find that are not covered in the documentation. You might find a stored procedure that isn't explained. If you are using a database API to connect to the database and submit your queries, you might find an undocumented function call that seems very useful. You can experiment with these features and discover what they do. And as long as you work only with your current version of the database as it is implemented on your operating system, you might be just fine.

The problem with this approach, however, is that undocumented features come and go. Any product vendor reserves the right to abandon that feature at any time, as well as the right not to implement the feature on all platforms. So that little tweak you might find in the Windows version may not work on the Linux version. When you port your program or queries over to the other system, you might suddenly find you have more work than you expected to do.

If you select the right licensing option, you may find that you have the source code for your database. (Borland's Interbase product, for example, is free, and you get the source code with the free download.) Possessing the source code provides a sense of security. If you need to tweak the program, you can do it, right? My response is that yes, you can. But you also have to realize that in customizing any implementation of a program as large and as complex as a database, you are marrying yourself to your customizations, and possibly only to the version you customized. If you want to move to the next version, you have to reapply your customization, if, in fact, it is still valid within the new source code.

Magazines, books, and newsletters within the computer industry love to tell you all about the tips and tricks that software designers don't want you to know about. The SQL community has its own such publications, and you can find out more than you ever wanted to know about how to shave clock cycles off query processing. Just keep in mind as you read the hype that you don't want to force yourself into a box that is self-limiting and that provides no path forward to the next version. Almost any API has functions in it that are provided for backward compatibility only, and which should be abandoned in programs currently under development. Relying on a particular version of an implementation or a particular customization could make all the code you write a one-time implementation of your program logic.

DESIGN TIP

SQL, because it is standardized, does not provide you with as many hidden features as other programming languages or application programming interfaces. However, you must keep in mind that only a part of a database's SQL language has been standardized. Loops, for example, are not a part of the current SQL standard. The way you write a loop in Oracle is not the way you write a loop in SQL Server. When you have to work across different databases, you want to stay with the most common elements across SQL implementations, so that you have less work to do when you move a query from one database to another.

Optimizing Queries

Everybody wants their data returned from the database quickly. You can probably find no end of advice about squeezing every last ounce of performance out of a SQL database by optimizing your queries. In general, query optimization is a matter of letting the query optimizer component of your database engine do its job. Each database vendor invests considerable effort on providing an optimizer that works well. After all, you will not choose a database that offers poor performance. The query optimizer encapsulates all sorts of general rules about how best to run a query. It is more likely to make good decisions about how to provide the best performance than you are as a programmer.

However, there are some general principles that apply to framing queries in the first place that can help you to get better performance. First, consider the need to collect information from more than one table in a single query. In general, you have two ways to collect this information. You can *join* the tables, an operation in which the recordset returned contains records selected from both tables by virtue of an equality between a column in one table and a column in another. When the database creates a join, the query optimizer chooses a technique for reading the two tables that provides the fastest data retrieval. If one table is large and the other is small, for example, nested loops are typically used to reduce input/output operations while providing a fast scan through the rows of the two tables. On two large tables, the query optimizer uses a hashing algorithm that improves the efficiency of scanning through large sets of rows. Because databases implement such algorithms to maximize the efficiency of join operations, joins typically provide quick response times.

Your other method for retrieving information from multiple tables is to use *subqueries*. (A subquery is a query nested within a query.) While query optimizers have algorithms for maximizing the efficiency of subquery operations, subqueries can often lead to a situation where the nested query must return before the parent query can execute completely. Linear dependencies of this sort can introduce delays. Because of this possibility, if you have a choice between using a subquery and a join, choose the join.

NOTE

As we discuss optimization here, keep in mind that we will revisit this topic in each subsequent chapter. Here we will consider general options that any SQL programmer needs to consider in writing just about any query. We will look at more context-specific strategies as we take up each chapter topic.

Second, when you look at query performance, consider the effects on query performance of using indexes. Unindexed tables, especially large unindexed tables, are slow to scan. The data is sorted in no particular order, and search strategies that apply without an index are the least efficient. Applying indexes to columns used for joins or frequently used in WHERE clauses will improve your query performance. If you do not have permissions to build indexes, therefore, make sure that your database administrator knows what your needs are.

In general, you can build two types of indexes, clustered and nonclustered. A *clustered* index selects the sort order for data storage, so only one clustered index can be applied per table. *Nonclustered* indexes do not affect the storage order of the table but serve to provide efficient searches for values within the column that has the index applied. In planning indexes, you want the clustered index to be on the column most likely to be searched by a WHERE clause and most likely to be invoked in an ORDER BY phrase. Apply nonclustered indexes to the other columns you frequently use in joins or WHERE clauses.

DESIGN TIP

In working with indexes, rely on your database tools to help you out. Some databases provide tools that help you interpret usage statistics to reveal which columns need indexes of which type.

Third, when you work with views, keep in mind that views must materialize before they can be used. That is, the virtual table has to be created in memory before you can do anything with it. If you have a choice of working with a view or a table, therefore, querying directly against the table is likely to provide superior performance. In addition, keep in mind that where views depend on other views, the same linearity dependencies can appear in the execution plan for your query. If a large view must completely materialize before a dependent view can materialize, you will be waiting for one operation to complete before the other can start. Lots of memory and multiple processors cannot completely work around such dependencies. If you can avoid views that reference other views, you will probably squeeze greater performance out of your SQL code.

Fourth, if your query uses cursors, see if you can find a way to write it without using cursors. A *cursor* is an object that references rows in a recordset. Creating the object takes time, and using the object to retrieve rows adds overhead to the operation of your query. If you have to use a cursor, keep in mind that the more features the cursor has, the more overhead it requires, and the slower it performs. Forward-only cursors are faster than cursors that allow you to scroll back through the data because they require less overhead and do not have to keep track of previous rows once they are out of scope.

Fifth, be careful of loops. If your application uses a loop that executes a SQL query multiple times, moving the loop from the application to the query will improve query performance.

For the application to run the query, it must make a round-trip to the database server for each pass through the loop. If the loop is within the query, you pass the query to the database server in a single trip, and you retrieve the results in a single trip. In addition, the query optimizer component of your database can work out an optimization plan for the loop. This plan will probably provide better response than the repeated execution of single queries.

Finally, while you must rely on the database engine's query optimizer, don't be afraid to second-guess it. However, make your second guesses only when performance is absolutely substandard and you have to boost it. Queries allow optimization hints (to be covered in other chapters) that you can apply to alter how the query execution plan is built. In general, supplying optimization hints usually does not help the situation. There are moments, however, when trying something nonstandard might improve performance. If you are stuck in a mire of substandard performance, try the hints. Keep a stopwatch in hand. And choose the form of the query that performs best.

There is always a low-tech way to reveal query performance. Insert this statement between the steps of multiple statement queries:

```
PRINT GETDATE()
```

All this statement does is to output to your query tool the current date/time stamp. If you do the time math, you can at least figure out what steps consume the most time. Other tuning tools provided by your database vendor might give more sophisticated information. But in the absence of such tools, well-placed PRINT statements can reveal a wealth of information to you.

Protecting Data

One of the greatest disasters that can befall a SQL programmer is the accidental loss of data. Such loss can come through a simple moment of inattention. You are in a hurry. The boss wants a test database created, and that means that you have to copy a live database and scramble the social security numbers. You use the database manager to create the copy. Then you fire up the query tool and write a quick routine to replace the social security numbers. You run the routine, and then you notice that you were attached to the live database instead of the test database.

The only way to save face in such situations is to realize that you have to be careful in the first place and that you will make such mistakes in the second place. Redundancy is the only way to protect data. You can recover if and only if you have copies of the data and you have not trashed all copies. Therefore, the guiding principle of working with production databases is to be sure to have good backup copies. Every database goes through some sort of backup routine on a regular basis. Nevertheless, it is always wise to make backup copies of data, even if only on a temporary basis, just before you undertake your work. A SELECT INTO a table created in tempdb, for example, can save you lots of grief. You can always drop the temporary table when you don't need it anymore.

Here are some good habits to get into as you write SQL code to protect against accidental data loss:

▶ Back up the data or create a copy of the data just before you work on it. You are always the first defense against your own failings.

▶ Begin any query session by executing a USE statement to identify which database to use. (Example: USE MyDatabase.) Make sure that this statement heads any query session that you run.

▶ Create all test databases on a separate instance of your database from the production copies. Preferably, this separate instance should be on a different server, so that the potential for conflict between the versions is minimal.

▶ For any operation that might cause data loss, start the query session by executing a BEGIN TRANSACTION statement. If you do not like the developing consequences of your query, you can always execute a ROLLBACK TRANSACTION statement.

Salvation in our example disaster is realizing that the copy you just made has all the data you just trashed. You can carefully copy the data from the copy back to its original location. Providing for such redundancy is always a good programming practice.

Protecting Data Integrity

A cardinal rule of database programming is that you will not put junk into the database. Having made this statement, I have to admit that I have seen many junk-filled databases. I have seen spare currency fields where users have dumped noncurrency codes to identify something about the data stored in that row. I have seen users run out of single-letter record type codes and shift to using upper- and lowercase character codes, even though the database cannot distinguish between upper- and lowercase characters in its sort order. I have seen dates stored in a format that no date function in the database can operate on. All sorts of unfortunate data entry practices abound.

Because junk creeping into your database is almost a certainty, you must be diligent to prevent it from creeping in. If you are writing a program that uses embedded SQL to communicate with a database, you should undertake data validation on the client side before passing data to the database server. Practices like these help to prevent problems down the line:

▶ Use typed variables to hold the data. If you have a date, put it in a date variable. If you have an integer, put it in an integer variable. If you try to assign the wrong type of data to a variable, your compiler will generate a data type mismatch error; you will have trapped the problem and corrected it.

▶ Use type checking functions to make sure that data collected from text boxes can be interpreted as the correct data type. If the data can't be so interpreted, make the user correct the data entry before continuing.

▶ Check all data to make sure that it is within the proper range for the database table it goes into.

▶ Format the data input in the way that the database expects to see it, and in a way that database functions expect to see it. Storing a date as a string in this format is something you can do: MMYYDD (010204, which represents January 4, 2002). However, most date functions will not be able to interpret that string as a date. SELECT DATEPART(m, '010204') will always return the month as 2 (February).

Remember, the only time data verification is overkill is when it makes your client's performance unacceptably slow. Chances are that these basic checks applied at advantageous times during input processing (as when a user changes data entry fields) will not affect performance adversely.

On the SQL side, the most practical advice is to use data types for your columns that represent the data that will be stored in the column. One programmer in my acquaintance uses the numeric data type for all numbers stored in SQL Server, not realizing that numeric is an alias for the decimal data type. Decimal as a data type is a fixed-precision data type (you can set the number of decimal places). It is not a good data type for storing integers, nor is it typically the kind of value you would want in an identity column. If you use data types that are appropriate to the data, you can be reasonably certain that the database engine will generate an error if you try to store invalid data in the column. You also ensure that you are not wasting storage space. A numeric value requires five bytes to store the smallest number in SQL Server. An integer requires four bytes, a small integer just two bytes, and a tiny integer just one byte. If you are storing integers within the range –32767 to 32767, you need only a small integer. In addition, you run no chance that an accidental decimal place will cause surprise round-off errors in calculations. Choose the data type that best optimizes storage for the data and that enforces integrity on the data.

The integer example may seem picky. What's a byte or two, you might say. In a large database, that byte or two could turn into megabytes of wasted space over millions of rows. What is more important, however, is to avoid the truly egregious mistakes. I have seen fields named Email_Address given the data type CHAR(255). I am not sure who out in cyberspace has a 255-character e-mail address, but I am willing to admit that we ought to accommodate that person. I am unwilling to do it with a fixed-width character column that will always contain 255 characters, no matter what the length of the e-mail address. Such columns are what the VARCHAR data type was invented for. It stores only the number of characters necessary.

DESIGN TIP

The bottom line on best practices and coding standards is whether an average entry-level programmer could look at your code and figure out what your coding conventions are in under ten minutes without asking questions. It matters little whether you mark string variables with "str" or "char." What really matters is whether someone else can quickly catch on to your conventions and easily read your code.

Summary

In this chapter, we have focused on programming practices that help you to write good SQL code in two senses. First, when you write a query or a procedure, these practices help you to spot mistakes and weaknesses easily. Second, when you come back to perform maintenance on the code, these practices help you to refamiliarize yourself with the code and what it does so that you don't waste time and money puzzling about what the code actually does. We have looked at a practical definition of best practices, and we have discussed practical ways of implementing best practices.

Preparing Your Troubleshooting Environment

IN THIS CHAPTER:

What to Have Handy

What to Make Ready

What to Set Up

What to Run

How to Run Your Environment

In the previous two chapters, we talked about the types of SQL programming environments you can work in, and we made the choice to demonstrate SQL coding using a little more than the minimalist Notepad, but much less than high-end environments might offer. We also talked about the kinds of practices you should implement to help yourself write good code in the first place, to help yourself review your code (or someone else's) when you have to perform maintenance, and to help yourself spot bugs when they do crop up. Now it's time to talk about how to set up a functional debugging environment so that you can work efficiently.

Efficient programming requires that you have a good set of tools handy. There are a few things you need to keep in easy reach so that you are not wasting time running to a supply closet or setting up a program on an ad hoc basis. These things will be a very personal tool set, and they will depend greatly on the office environment and political structure in which you work. There are also a few things you need to build to make certain that you can undertake common tasks quickly. How you build them depends on what programming languages you prefer and what query tools you like to use. I will offer examples based on my preferences, but you are going to have to translate my examples to your preferences.

In addition, there are some programs that you need to set up. You need to provide yourself some resources, because no matter how good your development environments are, it is always nice to have a crash-and-burn environment completely under your control. Sometimes you cannot effectively troubleshoot a problem on computers owned by someone else, because they won't grant you the permissions necessary to get to the problem. I am going to recommend some free programs in this group. Feel free to use my suggestions, but feel free to imitate my suggestions using other programs.

There are also some programs that you need to have running. Again, I will focus on describing tools that I like or that are freely available. You should feel free to reject my choices in favor of your own. Over time, you will have developed your own personal favorites. (Although, you VI fans in the crowd can forget about winning me over. You have no chance.) When I say you need to have these things running, I mean running in a multitasking environment and ready to use, or at least no more than a double-click on a readily accessible icon away.

What to Have Handy

So here is my list of things to have within easy reach. This list arises from having been a consultant in a variety of settings, and the basic principle I've had drilled home is that you must rely on yourself. No matter what is provided, you have to take care of yourself. So here's the list:

▶ **Printed documentation for your database**   Have this or a good book that covers your database. As a book author, I will freely admit that good books are hard to come by. The best way to find one is to go to the bookstore with at least five questions that have been bugging you in mind. Go through the books on the shelf, and check for answers to your questions in the index to the book. Buy the book whose index can answer your questions. You need to have a printed resource to turn to, because sometimes when you are tight on a deadline, all your networked resources crash on you.

▶ **Formatted floppy disks, virus free**   If your database administrator is like most of the ones I have worked with, you will have to write your own scripts for anything the DBA has to do. This practice saves the DBA time, since you have drafted out your basic needs, and guarantees greater accuracy. The best way to deliver a script is on floppy. The network cannot screw it up, your e-mail server cannot mangle the attachment, and you can always keep a copy in case the DBA loses his copy.

▶ **Access to CD recording**   I have often had to record files on CD to overnight to business partners involved in a SQL development project. You might think that companies ought to be able to handle such transfers of large files across the network, but sometimes this goal is not practical. In my current assignment, the solution used to transfer files from one location to another is to use an external hard drive that connects to one network while files are being generated, and connects to another network while files must be transferred. Prior to the hard drive being installed, we burned the files to a CD and walked them to a machine that could transfer the files. Walking a CD is one time-honored method of transferring data from behind a firewall to Web servers outside the firewall.

▶ **A boot disk**   Preferably two of them. One should be a Windows boot disk (or another operating system, if you use one) for the version of Windows you run. The other should be an MS-DOS boot disk. When your system is in crisis, an old-style DOS boot disk can be a precious commodity. On almost every development project I have been engaged in, I have managed to toast a system. I like to have a salvation disk nearby. If you run Windows NT, a Linux boot disk is a useful commodity. And you want to surf the Web to find all the free Linux utilities you can find for doing things like resetting passwords on Windows NT. If you are heavily dependent on Windows NT, you should spend some money on utilities that allow you to read and write using the NTFS file system from a boot disk. They are very helpful in times of crisis.

▶ **A toolkit**   I have managed to toast modems, SCSI adapters, drives, and a host of other hardware items during projects. I once lost a project because, while I was on the road and teaching at Fort Dix, a tree fell on a transformer, sending a power surge, the result of the transformer exploding, throughout the post. My laptop did not weather this storm well. In fact, every solder joint onboard overheated, and the connections broke. Okay, so most of us cannot repair laptops on our own. But we can work on standard systems, and being able to do so in a timely fashion is better than not being able to do so.

▶ **Installation CDs for all of your software**   As a consultant who works with mainly Microsoft products, I carry my Microsoft Developer Network universal subscription with me. If I need an operating system, if I need a database, if I need a development environment, I reach in my bag and pull out the CD. In some shops, I have been the CD source, because no one on permanent staff could liberate the software from a company source when there was a critical need.

▶ **CDs for the software you like to use**   This should be regardless of who is purchasing your time. As a consultant, I like to be able to diagram things. I have my own copy of Visio that I use for that purpose. If a client does not provide software with similar functionality, I can at least create and print diagrams on my own.

▶ **Internet access**   You need to have access to the Internet with download privileges and mail privileges in a nonrestrictive environment. I have worked for companies whose e-mail restrictions made e-mailing a critical file attachment an all-day process. Whatever you can do to guarantee that you can send files via e-mail and access vendor knowledge bases, do it. If that means investing in CD copies of knowledge bases because firewall restrictions are tight, make the investment. You need access to the information and to the free exchange of information.

▶ **Access to a printer**   I know this sounds like a no-brainer, but I have worked for clients who could not give me access to a printer from the company system. A parallel cable and my HP Deskjet 340, which has seen more air miles than is good for any printer, have been very useful in many situations.

▶ **A paper filing system**   Sometimes all of the electronic world lets you down. So print and file critical documents. Sometimes something that you cannot find electronically you can find by sorting through your filing cabinet.

What to Make Ready

Some things you need to build for yourself, because having them available is invaluable. In this category of items for your debugging environment are programs and tools that you create yourself using your favorite programming language. Some of these tools are operating system–level objects that you need to have available as failsafe tools. Others are just commonsense backup options. Here is my preferred list:

▶ **Two ODBC connections to your database**   One of these should be a system DSN (data source name), so that you can connect from your system to your database using the ODBC standard. The other should be a file DSN that you can transport to any system that might have to access the database. You should not, as a developer, rely on user DSNs. A great consternation while troubleshooting is a DSN that is dependent on how you are logged in. You want either to connect or not to connect. User DSNs are appropriate for computers shared by multiple users. They are not appropriate for development systems. Why do I recommend having ODBC connections? ODBC is an older, more mature database connection technology. Because it has a longer history, it has fewer bugs than any new connection technology. When you are having trouble, you want to fall back onto known, stable entities. I have run into situations where ADO has been considerably confusing, and consultants in my acquaintance have run into them as well. In one case, my boss used the Execute method on the Recordset object to open a database connection using ADO 2.0. One of the queries he attempted to execute, a simple SELECT, would not run, returning an error from the Recordset object that made it seem as though the database was unavailable. We were able to use an ODBC connection to prove that the database actually was available, and we found that connecting to the database using other ADO methods in fact worked.

A critical question in debugging the problem is whether the issue is related to the connection technology, or whether it is related to your query. Falling back on your ODBC connections can help to answer this question.

▶ **A program that connects to your database via these ODBC clients and can issue a single query and receive a single result**   Write this program in your favorite programming language. You will use this program to test embedded SQL queries via ODBC. You want to test this program under a variety of conditions, because you want to know that when you pass the query over to the database, it runs under predictable circumstances.

▶ **A program that connects to your database using your preferred connection technology and can issue a single query and receive a single result**   Write this program using your favorite programming language.

You will use this program to test embedded SQL queries via your preferred connection technology. You want to test this program under a variety of conditions, because you want to know that when you pass the query over to the database, it runs under predictable circumstances.

What to Set Up

You need a private set of tools that are in a crash-and-burn environment. Why do I say this? Precisely because I have worked in situations where the network gurus could not keep a functional environment of any kind up and running to meet a reasonable development schedule. When you need a development client up and running on a 24 × 7 basis, and to service that client you need some kind of a server up and running on a 24 × 7 basis, you need to take matters into your own hands.

The managers will provide the environments that you have to pass through to get your system into a production environment, but your first line of development needs to be an environment where you can do anything you want to do. Here is what you need:

▶ **A database server that can run a simulation (at least) of your database**
You can try queries out without having to rely on the production database, or on a database under the control of DBAs who do not share the philosophy behind your project.

▶ **A client environment where you can issue queries against the database with impunity**   Even if these queries are rogue queries that consume hours of CPU time, you have a place to discover these facts. You want test tools on your desktop, and you don't want to have to argue with anyone about how they function, and you don't want them to be able to damage more formal development, quality assurance, or production environments.

▶ **Some database product that offers you the chance to run queries against a database engine and receive results that are typical of running the queries against your production database**   Borland provides Interbase, and Microsoft offers the Microsoft Data Engine. You can always move from a free tool to a development tool to a QA tool to a production tool. The migration can only reveal the strengths and weaknesses of your intended product. If your initial development takes place in a freeware environment and survives the transition to the production environment, then you are likely to have written SQL code that will perform well across platforms, across different connectors, and across different development tools.

▶ **A simulation of the client environment**   If your program will concatenate images into a file and build a text file that instructs an imaging database how to load the images from the concatenated file, you need to have all of the source directories, all of the output directories, and all of the transport technologies available on computers under your control so that you can simulate the production environment. In many of my consulting situations, I have had to create this environment on a laptop that I brought into the client setting. You want this simulation completely under your control. If you are simulating network connections over a parallel cable, so be it. Your initial pilot will teach you much about what will happen when you move into the more formal environments.

You have to keep in mind that the larger the IS shop, and the more organized the IS shop, the greater the chance that you will not have permissions on the network or the servers or the clients to determine whether your code does what in fact it needs to do. You need to create an environment in which you can develop using components and computers completely under your control. After you have proved your concept in this environment, you are ready to move it into the next level of the controlled environment. Once your concept is proved here, you can move to the next level. How your program works in the environment completely under your control is invaluable information when you try to understand what happens in other environments. Without this information, you are crippled when you try to troubleshoot SQL. A very common problem with queries is not having the permissions to execute to completion. Providing an environment in which to verify that permissions are indeed the problem is important.

What to Run

So what software will you run to manage your development effort? Here is a suggested list:

▶ **A database management environment**   You need a tool that will describe the tables to you, tell you about the stored procedures, tell you about the views, and tell you about any of the other database objects that you have to deal with.

Microsoft calls this tool the Enterprise Manager. Borland provides a similar tool with Interbase, as does any other database vendor.

▶ **A query tool** Microsoft calls this tool the Query Analyzer when it ships with SQL Server. However, you will find the osql command line utility available for command line submission of queries with any Microsoft SQL product. Other vendors provide similar functionality. The more graphical your query tool, the better. You want as much feedback from the tools as possible. SQL error reporting is notoriously bad. Often all you get is an error type near a keyword. You cannot tell where the error is in relation to the keyword AS if you have several AS keywords in the query. The more accurate your query tool is at returning line numbers where the error lies, as well as other information about the location and nature of the error, the better off you are.

▶ **A solid development environment** If you are writing programs that use embedded SQL, you want your favorite programming language, a solid debugger, and the ability to step into any kind of routine from any context. When you are writing SQL code, this goal is unattainable. I know of no language environment that supports debugging SQL routines as a part of the debugging environment. You want, however, to come as close to this possibility as you possibly can. The more debugging information you have available to you, the better off you are.

▶ **A software development environment in which you make every effort possible to provide information about what is happening** To use Visual Basic as an example, when a program runs in the development environment, you have an immediate window that can show you program output as the program is running. However, you will see nothing in this window unless you use Debug.Print statements to provide the output. As you are preparing embedded SQL, a good practice is to use Debug.Print to display the SQL statement you are about to execute. After the SQL statement executes, you want to include Debug.Print statements that force the display of error result codes, return values, output parameters, and any other information that returns from the query. If you are using ADO, for example, the values of Recordset.BOF and Recordset.EOF are very useful, because they reveal whether records were returned to the recordset.

If you are using a graphical query tool, you can use the SQL PRINT statement to force the display of information in the results pane of the tool. Again, you want to display input parameters before the query executes, output parameters after the query executes, and any other information that is available pre- and post-execution that can reveal the status of the query and what it accomplished. You may prefer to store this information in a temporary table so that it does not disappear when the query tool closes, and so that you can refer to it on successive attempts at running the query. A useful structure for the temporary table is an identity column that provides uniqueness for each record in the table, a VARCHAR column that can hold the query you attempted or a description of a value that you are recording, and a VARCHAR column that can hold a value that represents whatever you want to record at the moment. Using this flexible structure, you can insert the query to be attempted (and nothing in the value column) before you attempt the query. You can insert the names of input parameters and their values. You can insert the names of output parameters and their values. And you can insert the name of any fact or value and the resulting associated value at any point during the execution of your query. You wind up with a sequential list of whatever you wish to record about the execution of your query. Essentially, using these three columns, you can track what you want to, and provide yourself with a record of events that can help you to interpret problems.

In Chapter 1, I suggested that you have to fall back on ancient debugging technologies to debug SQL. You do because you cannot rely on common debugging tools to step into your SQL routines to reveal what is going on. Your ability to debug SQL code directly depends on the richness of the low-level resources that you provide for yourself. Your goal in building this environment is to provide as many hooks that you can attach to the events surrounding your query as you can. You will not be able to debug directly, so you must debug by indirection. If you can tell that your query attempted X and returned result Y, you have a starting place for understanding what might have gone wrong. If you can record that Parameter 1 had this value, and Parameter 2 had this value, and that the output parameter had that value, you are describing to yourself facts that can help you to divine the process that actually took place, as opposed to the process that you intended to take place. You can provide yourself an environment that can compensate greatly for the limitations of the SQL debugging environment. And only your creativity limits the quality of this environment.

How to Run Your Environment

Once you have assembled all your tools, you need to plan a way to run your environment effectively. Here is a list of desirables to help you work on SQL code comfortably:

▶ **Enough screen real estate to allow you to view all the relevant tasks at once** My strong bifocals don't allow me to use a resolution much higher than 1024 × 768. When I need lots of screen space, I add a second monitor. Most operating systems allow this capability, but it can be tricky to set up. Once you have it working, though, it is fairly nice.

▶ **All of your tools set up on one machine** This wish is, of course, a fantasy, but try to get as much as you can under your immediate control. It is a pain to have to move files to the machine that has the CD recorder attached, or to have to wait in line to use critical equipment or software.

▶ **An organized desktop** Create a pattern of icons on your desktop, or a set of menus on the Start button, or a set of folders in your Explorer, that allows you to find and launch the tools you need easily. Hunting around for the link that launches your stuff wastes your time and adds to frustration when you are working on a tough problem. SQL problems are maddening to resolve because you don't have the features of an integrated debugger. You want to provide yourself as easy a path as possible to working with your tools.

Summary

This chapter has focused on helping you to assemble the right tools to help you debug SQL code. We've mentioned several tools that you will want to have around and ready to use on demand. Working in an environment that does not provide lots of debugging support means that your level of frustration will be high, and you can easily become confused. You want to organize you tools so that you can work your debugging environment without adding to your frustration.

Having gotten this far, we have laid out our plans, our techniques, and our tools. It's time to move on to some real problems.

PART II

Analyzing Problems

OBJECTIVES

▶ Learn how to troubleshoot setup problems

▶ Explore how to define user relationships to the database

▶ Examine the appropriate use of data types

▶ Create tables using normal forms

▶ Examine how SELECT statements can yield unexpected results

▶ Examine how to insert data into tables

▶ Understand transactional integrity and how to avoid deadlocks

▶ Explore the basic DELETE statement and how it can fail

▶ Explore common aggregate functions and the use of GROUP BY

▶ Master the basic subquery

▶ Learn how to define a view

▶ Practice with federated databases

4

Creating Databases

IN THIS CHAPTER:

Troubleshooting Setup Problems

Database Objects and User Relationships

Protecting Response Time

Securing the Data

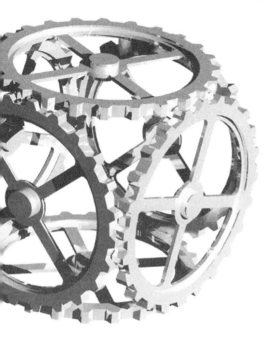

U sually the topic of creating databases does not come up when you discuss debugging code. However, because SQL describes database creation as well as data manipulation, creating databases needs to take its rightful place among the debugging topics. There is a straightforward reason. Many of the headaches that you have when you work with databases arise from the way the database was built in the first place. So before we plunge into what might go wrong with a SELECT statement, we ought to pause to consider how to design the database correctly in the first place.

The SQL standard defines the CREATE DATABASE statement as the means by which SQL creates databases. How CREATE DATABASE is implemented, and the details of the implementation, are vendor specific. In addition, critical characteristics of the database implementation are vendor specific, so debugging your SQL problems sometimes begins at setup time.

NOTE

In this chapter, we will primarily use Microsoft's SQL Server as the example database. Remember that other databases may require the use of a semicolon to terminate SQL statements. Keep in mind that the statements associated with creating databases can be vendor specific.

Troubleshooting Setup Problems

As you plan your database, therefore, if you have not installed your server, you need to read through the planning documentation thoroughly before you run setup. If you ran setup and accepted all the defaults, you need to read your planning documentation now, because you might need to rerun setup. If you have already implemented lots of databases, you could run into a problem that could be solved by dumping all your databases to tape, reinstalling the database server, and then restoring all your databases from tape. This option is, of course, highly risky for the data.

Here is an example of why you need to plan carefully at all phases of implementation. Assume that you have a group of clients who have been using single-character, alphabetic codes to classify documents, the data for which is stored in a SQL Server 7.0 database. When the data services you are providing your clients started, you purchased SQL Server 7.0, installed it on a Windows NT Server, and built the databases. The clients asked you to build a set of tables that contained the data for a variety of document types. The value of document type is often used to join tables together. That is, the users need to issue queries like the following:

```
SELECT Master.Header1,
       Master.Header2,
       Details.DetailLine1,
```

```
        Details.DetailLine2
FROM Master
   INNER JOIN Details
   ON Master.DocType = Details.DocType
```

So far, there is nothing disastrous about this scenario. You create indexes on the DocType columns in order to facilitate the join, and users retrieve the information they need.

Your users at this point only have 23 document types, and they use uppercase alphabetic letters. Next week they are going to add seven new document types, and they decide that they will use lowercase letters for some of them. Their queries will now not perform correctly. Nothing has changed about your implementation of the database. Your users have simply stressed a default characteristic of a SQL Server 7.0 implementation to the breaking point.

Somewhere in the setup for SQL Server 7.0 is the choice for the database sort order. The default value is dictionary sort order, since most people want their data to return in the order it would be listed alphabetically in a dictionary. You might stare at Webster's or American Heritage or Random House for a while before you catch on to the problem. Dictionaries do not distinguish between upper- and lowercase characters in determining the alphabetic sort order. The character "A" is the same as the character "a" in determining the sort. And, in SQL Server 7.0, the sort order is used when you join two tables to determine which values are equal in the JOIN clause. Suddenly where users expect to get two header fields and two detail fields, they get four, and they cannot distinguish between the two documents that have been blended together.

You have three solutions for this problem. One is to back up the databases, reinstall the SQL Server 7.0 product, and make a different choice for sort order during installation. Keep in mind that your choice affects every database. Once installation is complete, restore all your databases. The second is to upgrade to SQL Server 2000 and to set a different sort order on the column that is affected. SQL Server 2000 can set sort order on a per-column basis. The third is to educate your users to use some other type of coding schema that will work properly.

The first solution is dangerous and may be impractical because of the amount of down time involved. The second option may be prohibitively expensive. The third option may be impossible. You might get a response like "The court requires this coding scheme. We have no choice." As a result, you might have to implement a set of procedures that effectively hides the implementation of the document code. The actual code will be one that you can use with the join, and it will map through another table that reports the code that the user wants to see. You get one more join in each query to implement this solution. If your users are the ones who have to write their own queries, they may find even this option unacceptable.

DESIGN TIP

Troubleshooting may take you directly back to installation issues. Don't let this possibility blindside you. Start by being proactive about installation plans.

Another factor that can trip you up is what authority the software has as it runs. To use SQL Server 7.0 as an example again, you need to think about what user account is used by the three services that compose SQL Server 7.0. The default account is a server local account, and this is a very strange beast in Windows NT. The local account has privileges on the server where it is defined. It can be granted membership in any security group on the server. But it will never, ever be available in a Windows NT domain for use on another computer.

Now consider this scenario. You would like to import data entered in one SQL Server database on Server1 to a SQL Server database located on Server2. You use the Data Transformation Services (DTS) to perform the copy, and you use the wizard to make creating the job easier. When you run the package from the Enterprise Manager, the copy job works just fine. When you schedule it to run late at night, it fails.

The reason for the failure may take some time to trace. (Searching the Microsoft Knowledge Base using the search string "DTS near error" reveals a great article on this subject, "INF: How to Run a DTS Package as a Scheduled Job" (ID Q269074), that discusses several other problems that can occur with DTS packages.) The problem occurs when the DTS job attaches to the remote server. It runs under the account used to start the SQL Server Agent service, which schedules and starts the job. If this account is a server local account, it has no privileges on the remote machine. The copy job fails because of an authentication failure.

The solution is to provide Windows NT accounts for the SQL Server services to use that have the security profiles necessary to perform the tasks you want to schedule on your SQL Server. The three services are SQL Server, SQL Server Agent, and SQL Mail. You need accounts that not only have the required file system security profile but also have membership in the right SQL Server security roles, and that have access to the required databases. The SQL Mail account needs to have a valid mail profile installed on the machine where SQL Mail runs.

DEBUGGING TIP

Other issues can arise when database tasks are scheduled. Typically, no user session is associated with a scheduled task. Because of the lack of a user session, mapped drives are not available, for example. No object or characteristic will be available that depends on a user login. As a result, scheduled tasks need not be dependent on such objects and characteristics.

How do you plan your installation so that you can avoid all such setup-related problems? In all truth, you probably cannot plan your way around all of the possible problems that setup choices may create for you. The most important point, however, is that if you want a rock-solid SQL database installation, you have to plan what you are doing from the start. A few hours of reading now may save some difficult workarounds down the line. So definitely review your intentions for the implementation and plan for what you can foresee. If you know, for instance, that you have a dictionary sort order, you can require users to implement a coding scheme that can be recognized by the sort order. Knowing how your system is set up to work can allow you to proactively handle questions when they arise.

For every ten bugs you head off, however, there is always one that will sneak up on you unexpectedly. For these, you still need to take a proactive stance. You need to weigh your alternatives, and pursue the best course of action to handle the situation. The worst position to be in is having users implementing field-level fixes that you know nothing about. The best way to prevent this posture is to proactively manage how users interact with the database.

Database Objects and User Relationships

In general, users interact with specific objects in your database. You control those objects within your database. Or you should control those objects. Perhaps the biggest mistake in planning your database is not to exert control over the database objects that users use. The average database user interacts with tables more often than any other object in the database. If you are a data consumer, you need to collect the data you intend to consume. Data is stored in tables.

The next most likely object that users will interact with is a view, a virtual table. Next down in the list of likely interactions is a stored procedure, but the most likely interaction that users will have with a stored procedure will be mediated by a program that provides database access.

The primary control that you want to have over database objects is security control. Users must have permissions to carry out access, and you want to make sure that you grant users only the permission that they need for any given database object. We will cover defining users and roles later in this chapter. For now, we want to focus on practical rules for controlling access to a database object.

The most practical principle is never to give away more than you need to give away. The average user needs permission to select from a table. Grant nothing more unless there is a compelling reason to do so. Field-level redefinitions of column values cannot happen when users can only select from the table. Defining a class of users that can only select is your first line of defense against surprises caused by user interaction with the database.

Whose Experience Defines "Most Likely"

Your experience with the most frequently used objects may be different from mine. Many organizations cause users to interact most with stored procedures, then views, then tables. The frequency with which objects are accessed has to do with the style of design and programming in your organization. You need to be prepared to deal with the approach that you find in place where you are working. Some SQL programmers feel that direct access to tables implies the use of embedded SQL, a practice in which programs contain SQL statements that access data. Using embedded SQL means that to maintain the database access, you must often revise, recompile, and redistribute the executable for the program. If possible, you want to avoid this approach, because it is hard to maintain. However, the stored procedures you might invoke from a program access views and tables. While the queries you may issue from a program might invoke stored procedures, the procedures are likely to access tables directly. In some respects, the frequency of access to database objects is a matter of perspective. Don't let issues of perspective confuse the way you choose to apply security. No matter what your perspective, you don't want to give away more access than is necessary.

DEBUGGING TIP

I have a client whose users chose to stuff a date value into a currency field that is "unused." Interpreting the value as a date was very nearly impossible. Stripping the decimal point out was the first problem to solve. However, once that problem was solved, guessing whether the user had stored the date year first or year last was the next problem. Inspection of the data revealed that different operators made different choices. The appropriate response to such a user innovation is to say, "Putting date values in a currency field is not supported, and we have just added a date field to your table so you can store the date properly." One method of heading off problems is to practice proactive customer support rather than reactive repair of bad data.

Other principles arise as you grant more permissions to users. Users who can insert or update data should be working with client programs that manage the inserts and updates for them. As a part of this management, data that will be placed in the database needs to undergo extensive validation. The programs should make certain that the data going in is correct in every detail. If it is a date, it should be within range and have the correct number of digits for the year. It should also have appropriate delimiters. If the value is a currency value, it should have the correct number of decimal places, and it should have a sanity check performed for acceptable values. If orders rarely exceed $1,000, then orders larger than this amount ought to be verified. The basic principle ought to be that junk does not go into the database.

Users who can delete data ought to have to answer at least once that they intend to delete this data.

You ought to provide as much detail about the intended delete operation as you can before the user confirms the delete. You might want to condition the queries back to the user according to the severity of making a mistake. If you are about to delete 1,000 lines, I ought to question your intentions more insistently than I do if you are deleting one line. And deletions, on average, should never be real deletions. Most tables should include a column that marks an item for deletion.

Users should update this column when they think they are in fact deleting data, and some administrative routine can later delete such records as a routine maintenance function. If you never throw anything away, you can always recover from a mistaken delete operation. If you throw something away assuming that a user's intention was correct, you will always find a reason to regret having thrown the data away.

DESIGN TIP

Another option for protecting data against accidental deletion is a history table. Before data is deleted, copy it to the history table. You can use this technique in conjunction with a delete flag column. The column is updated when the delete takes place. Later, an administrative stored procedure moves the rows marked for deletion to the history table. The advantage you gain by using a history table is that you keep the primary table smaller in size. As a result, you improve the performance of queries issued against the primary table.

Protect Your Data

Famous last words is a phrase that describes any statement that the user programs will guard data integrity, so the database does not have to. User programs always find a way to fail. The failures are not intentional. Given graphical user interfaces, the number of pathways through the code multiplies rapidly, and there is always one more way through the code than quality assurance testing found. That path, which may be invoked on every thousandth run of the program, may be the one that fails to do proper checks before doing an UPDATE or an INSERT, or that does not present the right sequence of dialog boxes before a DELETE. Protecting data must involve cooperation between the programmers and the database. Any other plan fails to guarantee the consistency of the data.

Users who have higher levels of permission need to be monitored carefully. You need to build in routines that record who did what to whom, whether that is a field that describes who made the last modification to this row, or whether it is a separate table that just logs actions. As I describe how to organize your tables, I will suggest techniques for accomplishing these tasks.

Organizing Tables

The next chapter will discuss normalizing tables. When I say "organizing tables," I mean setting up the details of a table implementation to help you keep track of your data and keep track of your users. Tables are gatherings of entities into meaningful relationships. Entities are data elements that represent facts, opinions, or some meaningful statement about the world. Relationships among these elements bind them into tables. Typically, a single table expresses one relationship among entities. Once you have selected the entities and the relationship and built your table, you need to take care of some details.

Using Data Types

Data types are an often overlooked tool. I can't begin to tell you how many database problems I have had to solve that had, at their root cause, storing everything as strings. Some people feel that all you need to store a date is an eight-character string. And this statement is somewhat true.

However, the moment you wish to perform date math, you have to convert that string to a date. You incur a conversion penalty when you do so, and you incur a conversion penalty when you make the date into a formatted string again in order to store it back into a table as a string. Some people feel that an eight-character string is faster to store and use than a date value. While you might, in a database-specific situation, shave some clock cycles off total processing time by using a string instead of a date, what you surrender by doing so is significant.

First, you surrender validation. Any user can stuff any eight characters into an eight-character string. The value does not have to be a date. And you will find a user who, given the opportunity, will find a way to do so. Second, you surrender data integrity. Chances are users can find a way to store a date as an eight-character string in a way that you cannot interpret as a date when it is absolutely critical that you do so. Third, you place the burden of guaranteeing the quality of data onto programmers, whose programs may fail in some critical way when you least expect them to. Data integrity requires a chain of confidence. Programmers are only a link in that chain. The database needs to provide some enforcement of data types to help the programmers out. By using data types appropriate to the data, you will not lose significantly in terms of performance. You will gain significantly in terms of guaranteeing that the data is valid and proper.

One caveat has to be raised. Don't be foolish about data types. In Microsoft's SQL Server, there is a numeric data type. It is an alias for the decimal data type. This is a fixed-format decimal data type. If you use numeric, the system assumes that you want X number of decimal places, a value that you can supply. Even if you want no decimal places whatsoever, this data type will reserve nine bytes of storage for your number. (The database reserves more bytes if you add more decimal places.) If all you want is a unique integer to identify lines, you have chosen unwisely by selecting the numeric data type. The integer data type, which gives you roughly the same range as numeric, takes only four bytes of storage. If you are seriously concerned about performance, table size does influence performance. Four bytes as compared to nine bytes over a million rows is a significant difference. Choose your data types to fit your data properly.

You set a data type using either the CREATE TABLE or the ALTER TABLE statement in SQL. The general form for these statements is as follows:

```
CREATE TABLE Employee (Employee_ID INT)

ALTER TABLE Employee ALTER COLUMN Employee_ID NVARCHAR(20)
```

In the CREATE TABLE statement, a comma-separated list of columns follows the table name. The data type follows the column name. As you probably know, many other parameters may follow the data type. In the ALTER TABLE statement, you use ALTER COLUMN to identify the column to change. The new data type for the column follows the name of the column.

Referential Integrity

Referential integrity refers to a set of rules that apply to all rows in a table. The rules are specified by column. They describe relationships among data elements, and they guarantee that data elements are unique, or at least that a value in one column in one table is equal to the value of another column in another table.

According to Joe Celko, a noted SQL author and a member of the SQL standards committee, referential integrity constraints are the least applied feature of SQL. I have to agree with him, given my experience with clients. I can find no evidence that using such constraints carefully impacts performance. I can find any number of programmers who believe otherwise, but I believe firmly in using referential integrity.

Constraints of this type fall into the following categories:

▶ **Primary key constraints**   This constraint states that this value will be unique
to this table. When you set up a primary key, you also create an index on the key
that provides fast access to values that are primary keys. Typically, this index
will be a clustered index, which affects the storage order of the table. Data will
be stored in the order defined by the key value. You can change whether primary
key indexes are clustered, but you typically define a primary key as a value that
defines the critical nature of the data. You usually want access to this value using
a clustered index, since the value is central to the relationship defined by the table.

▶ **Foreign key constraints**   These constraints state that a value in this column
must first appear as a primary key in another table, or as a unique value in another
column, either within the same table or another table. If the value is not first
present in the other column, it cannot appear in this column. These constraints
are useful in making sure that unique identifiers of critical data propagate across
tables so that you cannot insert an item into the details table when it does not
first have an entry in the master table.

▶ **Uniqueness constraints**   This type of constraint requires that columns governed
by the constraint must have unique values. Duplicates will not be allowed.

▶ **Check constraints**   These constraints verify that the value of a column matches
a particular pattern, such as the proper format for a phone number or a social
security number.

DESIGN TIP

*Check constraints applied on every column will have an impact on the speed of data insertion,
because to insert into each column you must check the data against the pattern. Use check constraints
judiciously. A good rule of thumb is to use the constraint only when misformatting the data might
cause an error in a program that uses the data. However, the use of primary keys, foreign keys,
and uniqueness constraints does not add appreciable overhead. First, they affect a relatively small
percentage of the columns in the database. Second, they are often associated with indexes that
improve the speed of data access. In most cases, the small overhead of the constraint will be offset
by other factors. Primary keys, for example, are typically indexed by default to improve the speed
of scanning for a preexisting key value.*

What you gain by having constraints in place is data integrity. Primary keys guarantee
the uniqueness of rows in a table. Even if you insert rows containing the same data,
you have a way to distinguish the duplicates so that deletion of a duplicate is possible.

In addition, you are guaranteed by the constraint that inserting a duplicate key value is impossible. The database engine prevents you from doing so. To set a primary key, use statements of this form:

```
CREATE TABLE MyTable (MyTable_ID INT PRIMARY KEY CLUSTERED)

ALTER TABLE MyTable ADD MyTable_ID INT CONSTRAINT PK_MyTable
   PRIMARY KEY NONCLUSTERED

ALTER TABLE MyTable ADD CONSTRAINT
   PK_MyTable PRIMARY KEY NONCLUSTERED
CREATE TABLE MyTable (MyTable_Value VARCHAR(10))
ALTER TABLE MyTable
   ADD MyTable_ID INT DEFAULT 0
                  CONSTRAINT PK_MyTable PRIMARY KEY NONCLUSTERED

CREATE TABLE MyTable (MyTable_ID INT NOT NULL)
ALTER TABLE MyTable
   ADD CONSTRAINT PK_MyTable
   PRIMARY KEY NONCLUSTERED (MyTable_ID)
```

Note that we include the keyword CLUSTERED or NONCLUSTERED with the constraint information. We do this because primary keys are automatically indexed, and we need to tell the database what kind of index to build. Clustered indexes cause a reordering of the rows so that the rows are stored sorted according to the index sort order. Sorting the rows in storage improves performance when you are selecting rows by the value so indexed. However, you can have only one clustered index per table, because a table can be stored in only one physical sort order. You therefore want to choose carefully which column gets the clustered index. Using a clustered index on a meaningless column like Row_Number provides you little inherent performance advantage. Using a clustered index on a column that appears frequently in WHERE clauses, like Last_Name, does provide a performance advantage.

DESIGN TIP

Use a clustered index on the most frequently searched column in a table.

Foreign key relationships guarantee that values defined as duplicates in separate tables are defined in one table location as a primary key and are referenced in all other table locations using the primary key value as a reference benchmark. Foreign key values are often used in joins. Because of this fact, you want to be certain that the DocType in the Master table means exactly the same thing as the DocType in the Details table. If the values of the two columns mean different things, then a join would not be possible. You would always match the master record with the detail records incorrectly, since "A" in the Master table refers to a financial statement, and "A" in the Details table refers to a personal letter. Such a database probably has a DocTypes table where the DocType code is paired with a description. DocType is defined as a primary key in this table, and it guarantees the uniqueness of the DocTypes rows. The Master and Details tables contain a column named DocType, and this column references DocTypes.DocType as a foreign key. This constraint states that for a value to appear in Master.DocTypes or in Details.DocTypes, the value must already exist in DocTypes.DocType. If the value is not already in the DocTypes table, the database engine generates an error.

NOTE

Keep in mind that we could have used a unique index rather than a primary key when creating the foreign key in this example.

You create a foreign key constraint using statements like the following:

```
CREATE TABLE MyTable (Table_ID INT REFERENCES YourTable(TableID))

CREATE TABLE MyTable (Table_ID INT CONSTRAINT
    FK_MyTable_YourTable_TableID REFERENCES YourTable(TableID))

ALTER TABLE MyTable ADD Table_ID INT CONSTRAINT
    FK_MyTable_YourTable_TableID REFERENCES YourTable(TableID)

ALTER TABLE MyTable ADD CONSTRAINT FK_MyTable_YourTable_TableID
    FOREIGN KEY (TableID) REFERENCES YourTable(TableID)
```

DESIGN TIP

Using primary and foreign keys can help to prevent sort order problems of the type I have described in this chapter from affecting your database. They won't completely eliminate all possibilities, but they help to limit the possibilities.

If you do not provide a constraint name, as in the first of the preceding statements, the system generates one for you. You are better off naming your constraints with names that are meaningful to you so that your code is self-documenting. You will also see this syntax, which explicitly names the constraint as a foreign key constraint, in use:

```
ALTER TABLE MyTable

   ADD CONSTRAINT FK_MyTable_YourTable_TableID
       FOREIGN KEY (TableID) REFERENCES YourTable(TableID)
```

You must use this form of the constraint definition with ALTER TABLE to add only a constraint to the table, as in the last query we demonstrated.

Uniqueness constraints are useful when you have already defined a primary key in a table and want to guarantee uniqueness in another column, or when you don't want to use a key but want to make sure that duplicates cannot enter a table. Assume that you have a Documents table and an Authors table. Here you can potentially have a symmetrical one-to-many relationship. One author can write many documents, while one document can have many authors. To relate documents and authors, you need another table, which we will call Document_Author. This table contains rows of two columns, one containing the document identifier and the other containing the author identifier. To select a list of documents by a given author, therefore, you issue a query like the following:

```
SELECT * FROM Documents INNER JOIN Document_Author

   WHERE Author = 'some identifier'
```

This query works well as long as you don't have duplicate entries in the Document_Author table. If you do, you will return duplicate rows in your result set. In other words, you will select the same document more than once. A uniqueness constraint that governs the pairing of the columns solves this problem. Constraints can govern more than one column at once, and a uniqueness constraint of this sort guarantees that each two-column row is unique. That is, there will be only one entry in the table for any given pairing of author and document.

DESIGN TIP

You could also use a multicolumn primary key on this table.

The syntax for uniqueness constraints looks like the following:

```
CREATE TABLE Document_Author
    (Author_ID   INT,
     Document_ID INT,
     CONSTRAINT U_Document_Author UNIQUE NONCLUSTERED
        (Author_ID,
         Document_ID))
```

```
CREATE TABLE Document_Author
    (Author_ID   INT,
     Document_ID INT)
ALTER TABLE Document_Author
   ADD CONSTRAINT U_Document_Author
  UNIQUE NONCLUSTERED (Author_ID, Document_ID)
```

Note again that you must specify whether the unique constraint takes a clustered or a nonclustered index. Unique constraints are indexed by default to improve the speed of the check against the table as you attempt an INSERT.

Check constraints check something when an action takes place against a column. Check constraints can prevent you from allowing out-of-range values into a column. They can check for proper format of data. They can check values in other tables, if you so desire. Generally, these constraints can be used on the database side to validate data. Within a client/server architecture, server-side data validation is usually inefficient. Normally, the client program collects the data to be sent to the database. This program undertakes validation prior to sending the data to the server. Under most circumstances, therefore, check constraints will be something that you won't often use.

However, there are contexts where using check constraints makes sense. If you are working with users who directly access the database using a tool like Microsoft's Enterprise Manager, which allows you to directly open a table in a grid and to make changes directly in the grid, check constraints make a great deal of sense. Whenever the normal mode of data access is a direct connection to the database with interactive editing, you have to assume that typographical errors are as likely as when users interact with the database using a client program. You need to undertake validation under these circumstances to prevent bad data from getting into the database.

To give an example, one database that I created for a client was originally written in Microsoft Access. The client decided to keep data entry in Access, but to copy the

Good Case for a Uniqueness Constraint

Whenever you work with tables that serve to bridge between one table and another, as in our documents and authors example, a uniqueness constraint is wise. In such a table, you often have foreign keys making up most of the columns. However, foreign key constraints will not guarantee the uniqueness of pairings in a bridge table. The foreign key constraint only guarantees that the key value must appear in another table. The uniqueness constraint protects your bridging table from duplicates that affect the results of your SQL queries.

data over to a SQL Server database on a regular basis. A curious fact about Access and SQL Server date processing caused a significant problem in the copying process. Access accepts the first valid year as 100. SQL Server accepts the first valid year as 1753. The data entry operator, who was working in Access, often failed to correctly enter the final digit of a four-digit year. Access looked at the year and decided that the year was within range, and so it happily entered the year into the table. The year was 199. When the DTS package copied the data, it errored out when trying to insert 199 into the date column, because 199 is not a valid year. This was a situation that would be easily resolved using a check constraint on the database. The data entry operator would have to respond to an invalid year at data entry time, and only correct values would go into the database. A statement that shows how to add such a constraint is the following:

```
ALTER TABLE MyTable ADD CONSTRAINT Check_Date
    CHECK (DATEPART(y, Date_Input) > 1950)
```

DESIGN TIP

For check constraints, the practical rule of thumb is to use them under two circumstances: when you allow direct editing of database tables and when users make errors that somehow slip past ordinary data validation. The best policy is to require data validation by a client program so that the database is not burdened with the role of validation. Check constraints are best seen as a reactive response to a problem that cannot be resolved another way.

Triggers

As you design your database, you may be tempted to use triggers. Triggers, like check constraints, should be used sparingly. Triggers are SQL procedures that run when a table experiences an INSERT, UPDATE, or DELETE. In fact, you can define a different procedure to run for each of these three actions. There is no limit on the size of a trigger procedure, nor is there a limit on its complexity. Because of these facts, triggers have the potential to rob you of performance.

Triggers won't cause you to wait for your intended action to take place before returning your data. Foreground performance of a query typically will be responsive. Triggers add, however, to the background processing that goes on in your database. Lots and lots of triggers on each and every table combined with heavy usage will raise the total load on your database server and can affect response time. If you find that your processors are dragging a heavy load and database performance is suffering, you want to look for ways to reduce the amount of background processing your server undertakes. Or you want to add processors, memory, and drive space to your server to handle the load.

Triggers, despite the possible pitfalls, are extremely useful in many situations. SQL Server 2000 allows you to define two types of triggers:

▶ **AFTER triggers** These procedures execute after the named action. Actually, they are the last events to take place in the processing of the table actions. All constraints, data actions, and the triggering action complete, and then the trigger runs. You can have multiple AFTER triggers per action. So an INSERT could trigger 20 actions if you so desire. You can specify which trigger takes the first position and which takes the last position.

▶ **INSTEAD OF triggers** These procedures run instead of the action named in the trigger definition. They run first, before any other action takes place, and you may have only one of these triggers per action.

DESIGN TIP

Not all databases support INSTEAD OF triggers. Check your documentation to see if you can use this feature. If your database does not support this feature, you can use a standard trigger to examine the results of a query using the inserted and deleted tables. You can take action according to what is in those tables.

Often you hear that triggers are used to enforce business rules. This statement has always impressed me as being vacuous, because almost any action that you take in relation to a database enforces some type of a business rule. Table design reflects the entity structure of your business process, for example. I think the best way to understand what triggers can do well for you is to look at a list of possible solutions that triggers can supply. Here is my list:

▶ **Computing columns** Often you compute a column's value because it is some mathematical combination of other columns. If you undertake an INSERT or an UPDATE against a table that contains such a computed column, an AFTER trigger can automatically recalculate the value of the computed column. In this way, SQL database tables make up for not having spreadsheet capabilities.

▶ **Previewing INSERTS, UPDATES, and DELETES** Triggers are passed two special tables, inserted and deleted. For AFTER triggers, these tables contain what was inserted and what was deleted from the table. Triggers can review what is in these tables and take action depending on what has been inserted and what deleted. For example, if you want to guard against data loss, your trigger could place all the lines in the deleted table into an archive table. If you ever need to recover deleted data, you have it somewhere within the database to recover from.

If you want to log inserts or deletes, you could use the trigger to collect the count of records from these tables and insert this information into the log table.

▶ **Replacing INSERT, UPDATE, and DELETE actions** INSTEAD OF triggers can replace one of these three actions. Remember that triggers can be defined on both views and tables. Suppose you don't want to give users direct access to the tables, so you provide them a view. If they attempt to insert data into a view based on multiple tables, the view will not be updatable. An INSTEAD OF INSERT trigger can read the data from the table inserted and update the appropriate tables behind the view. An INSTEAD OF DELETE trigger can convert any delete into the setting of the Deleted column in the table, rather than the actual deletion of the data.

▶ **Cascading actions taken with one table to related tables** In our Authors and Documents example, you can easily imagine a useful trigger. Suppose you delete an author from the Authors table. You also want to delete the entries in the Authors_Documents table for that author. You can often do so by setting deletes to cascade along the lines defined by referential integrity constraints, but you may not wish to do so. You may have foreign key constraints with several tables using the Author_ID, and you may not want all the information related to that author to be deleted. You may instead prefer to set Author_ID to NULL for many of those records, so that authorship could be reassigned. If you use triggers, you can delete the relevant lines from Author_Documents and you can set the Author_ID field of other records to NULL.

▶ **Performing data validation that check constraints cannot undertake**
Check constraints are fairly limited in the kinds of validation they allow you to do. They cannot, for example, look up values in another table to make sure they are present. Triggers, however, are ordinary SQL procedures. They can do anything that a SQL procedure can perform. So you can check to see whether a value being inserted already exists in a table of allowable values. If the value is not present, you can set the field to NULL. For example, if you have a catalog of items, and you want to make sure that the description field of an order refers to a valid description in the table of products, you can do the lookup to verify the value using a trigger.

The basic code template for building a trigger looks like this:

```
CREATE TRIGGER AfterTriggerName
ON TableName
FOR INSERT, UPDATE, DELETE
```

```
AS
    Place SQL statements here
```

The template for INSTEAD OF triggers looks like this:

```
CREATE TRIGGER InsteadTriggerName
ON TableName
INSTEAD OF INSERT
AS
    Place SQL statements here
```

Note that triggers are, like stored procedures, just sets of SQL statements. Also note that you must specify the action for which the trigger is active. For AFTER triggers, you can specify multiple actions. INSTEAD OF triggers replace a single action. Here is a trigger that logs information about deleted records:

```
CREATE TRIGGER AfterTriggerName
ON TableName
FOR DELETE
AS
    INSERT INTO DeleteLogTable SELECT * FROM deleted
```

This trigger just dumps the deleted records into a delete log table. It requires that the DeleteLogTable have the identical structure as the table from which the deletion took place. With a little more planning, you could construct a log table that could serve a more general purpose. You would need to know, for example, the names of all the columns that might be deleted and logged. You would then name the columns in your insert statement and your select statement, so that the columns and values in the log table would have a one-to-one correspondence.

Putting the Database on Disk

All databases reside on disk as files. When you create the database, you have the option of placing the files where you would like to place them. In SQL Server 2000, you use the following form of the CREATE DATABASE statement to specify where the files should go:

```
CREATE DATABASE Sales
ON
( NAME = Publication_Sales,
    FILENAME = 'c:\data\publication_sales.mdf',
    SIZE = 10,
    MAXSIZE = 50,
```

```
      FILEGROWTH = 5 )
LOG ON
( NAME = 'Publication_Sales_log',
    FILENAME = 'c:\data\publication_sales_log.ldf',
    SIZE = 5MB,
    MAXSIZE = 25MB,
    FILEGROWTH = 5MB )
```

Note that you have the option of saying where the data files go and where the transaction log file goes. You also have the option of specifying multiple file locations, as in the following statement:

```
CREATE DATABASE Sales_Archive
ON
PRIMARY ( NAME = Sales_Archive1,
      FILENAME = 'c:\data\Sales_Archive1.mdf',
      SIZE = 100MB,
      MAXSIZE = 200,
      FILEGROWTH = 20),
( NAME = Sales_Archive2,
    FILENAME = 'c:\data\Sales_Archive2.ndf',
    SIZE = 100MB,
    MAXSIZE = 200,
    FILEGROWTH = 20),
( NAME = Sales_Archive3,
    FILENAME = 'c:\data\ Sales_Archive3.ndf',
    SIZE = 100MB,
    MAXSIZE = 200,
    FILEGROWTH = 20)
LOG ON
( NAME = log1,
    FILENAME = 'c:\data\Sales_Archive_Log1.ldf',
    SIZE = 100MB,
    MAXSIZE = 200,
    FILEGROWTH = 20),
( NAME = log2,
    FILENAME = 'c:\data\Sales_Archive_Log2.ldf',
    SIZE = 100MB,
    MAXSIZE = 200,
    FILEGROWTH = 20)
```

Where you place the files affects how your database performs and how easily your database recovers. So there are some basic considerations we need to review.

Locating the Files

The critical factors in choosing database locations are disk spindles, disk loads, and parallel writing. Writing to a single disk spindle creates a bottleneck for performance. The more data you need to get on the disk, the more you fill the bandwidth through which you write to the disk. When the bandwidth is consumed, reads and writes queue up to wait their turn. Any time that you can write to disks in parallel, you ease the load at the disk bottleneck. RAID arrays allow you to write data to several disks at one time. The array consists of multiple disk spindles, and the data is split into chunks that are each assigned to a disk in the array. The writes to the disks go in parallel, so five megabytes going to a five-disk array is actually five writes of one megabyte. Theoretically, it takes only 20 percent of the time to write the file on the array.

You are wise, therefore, to locate your data files on a RAID array for performance reasons. (You are also wise to locate them there to protect yourself from disk failure, so long as you are using RAID 5 or better.) However, there is another file that should benefit from parallel writes of another kind, and that is your database transaction log. The transaction log records all the actions taken against the database since the last backup. If for some reason the database fails, you restore your last backup, and then you apply your transaction log to bring the data current to the time of failure.

You should install a separate disk to hold the transaction log. You can keep it on your RAID array along with the data files (or on the same disk as your data files, if you are not using an array), but doing so puts your data at risk. The most typical reason that you lose your data files is disk failure. If the disk or array with your data files fails, chances are the transaction log is gone too. If you lose your transaction log, recovering to the point of failure is impossible. Keeping your transaction log on a physically separate disk allows you to write to the transaction log in parallel with writes to the data files. Keeping your transaction log separate also improves your ability to recover from a disaster.

One other set of files often gets overlooked, and those are backup files. Most databases allow you to make backups to a disk or a tape device. These backups have properties not associated with your average tape backup of a drive. With SQL Server 2000, for example, these backups work in tandem with the transaction log backups to allow you to recover a damaged database. You can do a full backup of your database, creating a large file that represents the state of the database at a point in time. You can also do transaction log backups, which reduce the size of the log and improve its performance. These happen independently of full backups. When a failure occurs, the recovery process follows these steps:

1. Restore from the last full database backup.

2. Apply each transaction log backup, in sequence, since the last full backup.

3. Apply the current transaction log.

In comparison to the typical drive backup, you gain the chance to recover your data up to the point of the failure. For a typical drive restore, you restore all the files on the drive. Your database will be current as of the point in time when the drive backed up.

To take advantage of these database-specific backups, you need a place to store the backup files. The same drive where the data resides is not a wise choice. If you lose the data, chances are you lost that drive, and you won't have access to your backups. The same drive where you store the transaction log is a better choice. When the backups take place, you are not writing to the same drive as the data, so you are not consuming the bandwidth that gives you access to the database. In addition, you are placing all your recovery information in a single place. When you need it, you know where it is.

Using Raw Partitions

Some databases allow you to install your database on a raw drive partition. SQL Server 2000 offers this approach. That is, you partition the drive, but you do not format the drive. You pass the partition to the database engine in a CREATE DATABASE statement like this one:

```
CREATE DATABASE Products
ON
( NAME = Products_Data,
    FILENAME = 'd:',
    SIZE = 10,
    MAXSIZE = 50,
    FILEGROWTH = 5 )
LOG ON
( NAME = 'Products_log',
    FILENAME = 'e:',
    SIZE = 5MB,
    MAXSIZE = 25MB,
    FILEGROWTH = 5MB )
```

The database builds its own internally optimized file system in the partition and stores the data and log information using this format. The advantage is that you get better performance from this arrangement than you do by using an operating system file system. The risk is that the only software that can read the partition is the database. If you have a problem with the partition, you hope you have good backups and that you experience no trouble during the restore. The disadvantages are that you cannot use this approach with devices like RAID 5 arrays that expect to use a file system associated with the operating system. You also cannot just back the drive up to tape, as you can with a drive managed by the operating system. You must use the database engine's backup facilities. If you need the utmost speed out of your database, weigh the risks and disadvantages carefully.

Protecting Response Time

Everyone wants to communicate with their database at high speeds. When we issue queries, we want them to return in milliseconds, not minutes. Five minutes is an eternity when a user sits at a screen waiting for a Web page to populate with data. To protect this type of response time, we need to make certain that we have done everything possible. Protecting response time is largely a process of building indexes and undertaking appropriate maintenance on the database.

Creating Indexes

The most critical factor in protecting performance is to index your tables. Most database administrators create indexes that are simple in form, and for good reason. If you want to see whether adjusting index parameters affects performance, you have to be measuring performance. In many cases, administrators don't have valid measures of performance to evaluate indexes. However, when you experience slow performance, you automatically have a metric thrust upon you. You have a query that takes forever to complete. You can time it using simple tools like the query analyzer. And you can adjust indexes to try to improve the query performance.

However, as you start tuning, you need to keep in mind that tuning to resolve one problem may create other problems. You have to keep a watch on all your routine database activities, and you need to make sure that you have a balanced plan for reviewing database performance. The query with the problem is definitely the one that needs to be addressed. However, you should choose a set of procedures that you routinely run to monitor as well when you address the problem. You should select a balanced profile of long and short procedures so that you are not inherently skewing your view of performance away from average activity. Poor man's index tuning requires that you have your suite of average activities, and you have to run all the elements of this suite to make certain that each one retains appropriate performance.

DESIGN TIP

Many databases offer automated performance tuning tools. SQL Server has done so since version 7.0. To use such tools, you have to log performance over a period of time. The more performance data you have, the better the recommendations for adjusting database parameters to improve performance. The tool reads the logs and calculates optimal performance using proprietary algorithms.

To simplify your performance evaluations, you can build a single procedure that runs all the others. In between the procedures, include this line:

```
PRINT GETDATE()
```

When you run the procedure from your query analyzer, the procedure boundaries will be marked by a line that has the current date-time stamp in the messages returned from your SQL session. These outputs can be saved to files or printed. You can calculate the intervals and determine what effect your adjustments have had on each procedure. As an alternative, you can write this information to a table, and write a procedure that reads the table and calculates the time intervals using SQL. As we work through additional chapters, we will build such a procedure as an example.

How do you tune using indexes? First, create indexes for any column that is used to join tables or is frequently used in a WHERE clause. Start with simple indexes created in the default way, using a CREATE INDEX statement like this:

```
CREATE INDEX Products_ind ON Products (Product_id)
```

Evaluate the impact of your changes by running your suite of procedures. If you have achieved acceptable performance, you are done.

If you have not achieved acceptable performance, you have two choices. You can create more indexes, or you can adjust the parameters of the indexes you have defined. You should create more indexes only if you can identify candidate columns. Randomly applying indexes to columns is usually not a productive strategy. You invest lots of time in creating indexes and testing, and repeating this process iteratively. You will save time if you study the queries using your columns to pick out columns that are getting used extensively. Trying indexes on these columns maximizes your opportunity for success.

What you can do in addition depends on the database you are using. When index performance seems to take a downturn, you can rebuild the index. How you do so is a database-specific issue. In SQL Server, running database consistency checks defragments indexes and updates their statistics. You can also drop an index and re-create it, although DROP INDEX usually does not apply to primary and foreign key constraints. These you must drop using ALTER TABLE. If you are using Interbase, you get an ALTER INDEX statement that allows you to make the index inactive, and then active again. If you use SQL Server 2000, you can adjust the fill factor and padding parameters used to provide open space on index pages. When an index page gets full, the database engine must split it so that additional lines can be added. Splitting the page is a high-cost activity. When you adjust these two parameters, you control when the page has to be split. However, SQL Server respects your advice only when it creates the index. After that, it uses its own internal algorithms to make the decision.

The impact of your changes is limited to the first page split that has to occur. Then the database takes over.

Advanced index tuning really reduces to running appropriate maintenance routines in a proactive fashion. It also involves realizing that trying to tweak an index excessively is probably a counterproductive activity. Put indexes on the columns that need them, run your suite of procedures to verify that overall performance is maintained, and run your maintenance procedures, which we will describe in a later section, on a regular basis.

Archiving Data

Data history is a fine thing, but as tables grow, response time suffers. One strategy you can apply to protect performance is to move data from the primary table into a historical table when the data is no longer likely to be used actively. If you need to run historical reports, you can always use a UNION query to return data from both tables. Such a union query would look like the following:

```
SELECT First_Name, Last_Name FROM Employee
UNION
SELECT First_Name, Last_Name FROM Employee_Archive
```

If you need to perform manipulations on the full data set, you can use one of two strategies, depending on what your database allows. SQL Server 2000 allows you to build a view using a UNION query. You can always run your data manipulations against the view. When you don't have a view that you can use, you can always create a temporary table and insert the full data set into it, using the following approach:

```
INSERT INTO #temptable
SELECT First_Name, Last_Name FROM Employee
UNION
SELECT First_Name, Last_Name FROM Employee_Archive
```

You can perform additional work against the temporary table, and destroy the table when you are finished with it.

There is a caveat about pulling a UNION into a temporary table, however. You may be dealing with very large amounts of data. Population time for the temporary table may be an issue. You may need to schedule the procedure at an off-peak time to avoid drawing down database performance during peak hours. With a view, you have to remember that the view must materialize before it can be used. SQL databases do apply sophisticated strategies to limit the impact of view materialization and to provide the data you need from the view in a timely fashion. However, if you select everything from the view, you may wait a time for your data to arrive.

Managing Logs and Files

Transaction logs and data files also have an impact on database performance. You need proactively to manage the logs and files so that you do not run into difficulties.

The first issue that you need to consider is whether you have fixed file length limits in place. Some SQL databases require that you specify the maximum size for the data file and for the transaction log file. When the database hits these limits, work stops. Your role in managing such a database is to make sure that you never bump up against those file limits.

Other databases allow you to allocate space to files dynamically, specifying a growth factor that is applied when the file runs out of space. When you are working with dynamically sized files, you need to worry less about running out of room and more about running out of disk space entirely. Your goal is to keep files as small as possible so that the database provides optimal performance.

To provide an example of the impact of file growth, in SQL Server 7.0, as your transaction log grows, performance suffers. In a database that one of my clients uses simply to track logins, 500MB was a magic size. As the transaction log approached this size, inserts became slow enough that the query could time out before the user was successfully logged. Failure to log the user caused the login to fail, so the problem was immediately called to an administrator's attention. The solution to this problem was to truncate the transaction log by backing it up.

There are many factors that you need to manage when you try to keep files in an optimal state. Unfortunately, the commands for performing these tasks are database specific. As a consequence, we will work through setting up a maintenance plan using the graphical interface of the SQL Server 2000 Enterprise manager to give you a sense of what should be in your routine maintenance schedule. In SQL Server 2000, most of the commands used to perform these tasks are options on the database consistency checks command, DBCC. As we look at each graphical option, we will point out the DBCC options that are invoked. For other databases, you need to locate the options available for performing these optimizations in the documentation.

To start the Database Maintenance Plan Wizard, navigate in the tree view to the server you want to work on. Open the Management tree, and right-click Database Maintenance Plans. Select New Maintenance Plan from the context menu, and click Next when the wizard appears. You should see the screen shown in Figure 4-1.

In this page of the wizard, you define which databases you want to operate on. Clicking Next takes you to the first set of operations. You can choose between two ways of dealing with indexes. You can reorganize the data and index pages in order to improve their ability to accept new records without having to split pages, or you can sample the database records and use the information returned to update the statistics fed into the query optimizer when it decides the best way to execute a query against a table. You can also shrink the size of database files. Choosing

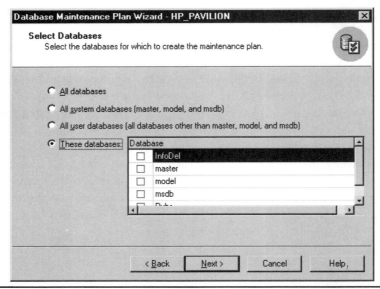

Figure 4-1 *The Database Maintenance Plan Wizard screen, which steps you through the maintenance planning process*

options on this page of the wizard (see Figure 4-2) invokes DBCC SHRINKFILE, DBCC REINDEX or DBCC INDEXDEFRAG (whichever rebuilds the index more efficiently), DBCC NEWALLOC, and DBCC CLEANTABLE.

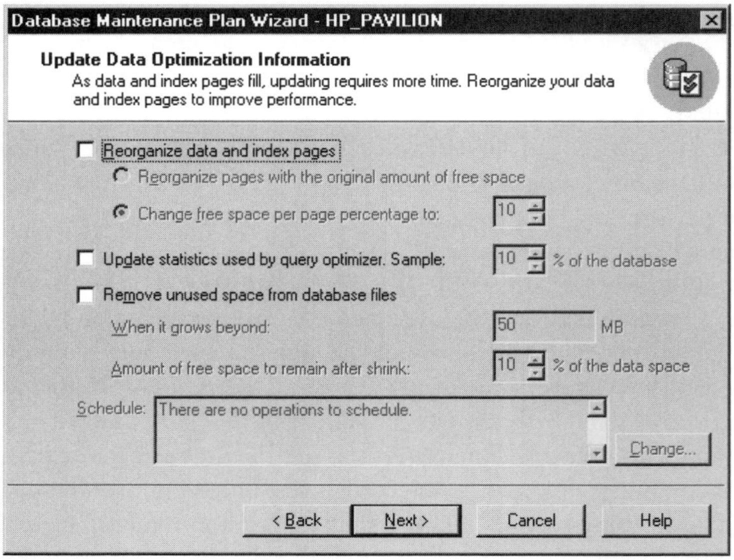

Figure 4-2 *The wizard allows you to define DBCC options.*

The next page of the wizard (see Figure 4-3) allows you to invoke a DBCC procedure called CHECKDB, which checks the integrity of the database objects and repairs problems identified. The option buttons you see in the dialog box invoke switches on the command. Excluding indexes from this operation speeds the database check. However, including the indexes allows you to make certain that your indexes are in their optimal state.

The next four pages of the wizard allow you to set up backups of the database and the transaction log using database engine services (see Figure 4-4). These pages allow you to set the options that create BACKUP DATABASE statements and BACKUP LOG statements that are scheduled to make sure that your data is safe. Backing up your database using database services has surprisingly low impact on database activity. In a manufacturing setting, I once ran a database backup every four hours and a transaction log backup every hour with no change in database performance. The transaction load on the server was approximately one every six seconds, not a high load at all. However, the consequences of a slowdown at the database were fairly high. Boxes on a conveyer belt would missort, alarms would go off, and a production line would have to shut down.

In a quite different setting, where the transaction level on the server was much higher, backups also had no perceptible impact on database performance. While users do not experience much impact, there is an impact, because background activity on the database increases. It is wise to run backups, as always, during off-peak times.

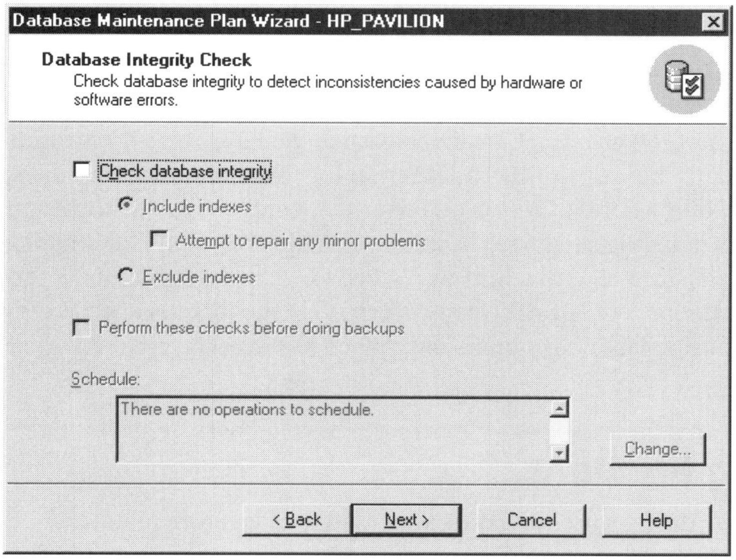

Figure 4-3   *The wizard allows you to set up CHECKDB options.*

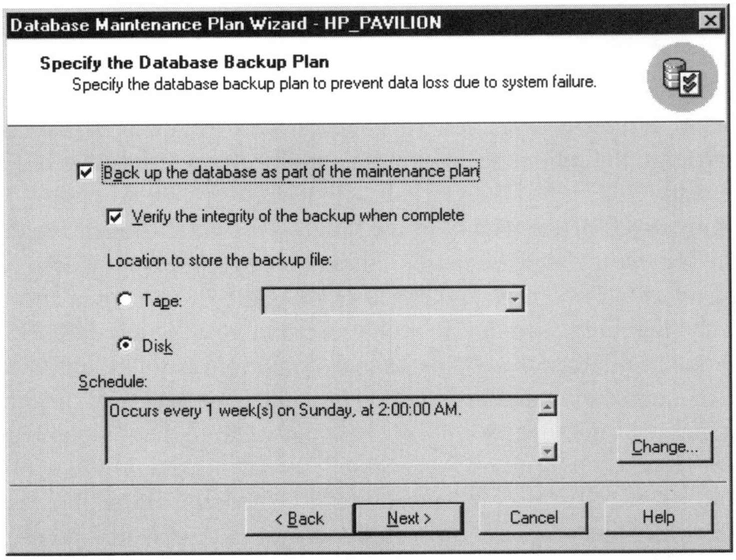

Figure 4-4   *You can set up database backups using the wizard.*

However, you need to balance impact on the database with the need to have backups that will return you to a working state as close to the point of failure as possible.

I have described the general maintenance process. The next question is, how often do you need to perform such checks and backups on your database? An easy answer is once per week, which is a good rule of thumb to keep your queries working effectively. You can't have a solid database if you can't interact with it effectively. However, experience demonstrates that some maintenance tasks require more frequent attention. In the context of the user tracking database that we have recently mentioned, we had to move to daily backups of the transaction log. Within about four days, it would grow to the point where it limited performance. Queries would stop running, and the Web site this database supported became unusable. Practical planning is to start with weekly maintenance, and to adjust that schedule as necessary to meet the demands of your installation. A cardinal rule is to schedule the maintenance at off-peak times, allowing intrusions into busy hours only when absolutely required.

Securing the Data

Keeping your data secure is first of all a matter of running maintenance routines, especially backups, on a regular basis. It makes no difference how you choose to perform backups. You do need to run the verification routine provided by the backup software after every backup. And you need periodically to attempt a restore from your backup media. The safest way is to create a script to build a database with the same structure, and restore to that database. If ever a restore fails, get your backup hardware checked, and replace your backup media. Backups are too important to do otherwise.

In addition to having good backups, you need to set appropriate file system security. Appropriate security may surprise you. Your database needs to be able to read, write, execute, and delete within the file system. Under Windows NT with SQL Server, the default settings are to grant these permissions to the group Everyone. Anyone logged onto the system can therefore do anything to any file, and this security profile may give you pause. Until you realize that you have to log into the system to exercise these permissions. Database users usually do not log into the system.

Your database server sits on the network. It may or may not be a member of a security domain. Database clients attach to the database server, but they do not attach through the file system. They attach through the TCP/IP protocol, through the named pipes service, through some other interprocess communication protocol, or through another networking protocol. The sessions users have when attached to the database do not provide them access to the database server's file system. Such privileges are normally reserved for interactive logins from the server's keyboard.

The only way that users can have access to the database server's file system is if you grant such access by exposing a share or by exposing another service, such as a telnet server, that grants a command line session on the server. Keep in mind that the file and printer sharing service for Windows opens the file system for access, so long as another user knows the IP address of the machine. For the greatest security, do not bind file sharing to any network protocol that allows access to the Internet. You may not wish to allow file sharing on your network in general, if you fear curious or malicious activity from within your own network. For the most part, you need not panic about file system security. Follow the database manufacturer's guidelines for setting permissions and setting up accounts for the database services to use. Then secure keyboard access, and you should be reasonably safe from the file system point of view.

Securing network access is another issue. You need to pay attention to these issues:

1. You want to stay abreast of all the security releases for your operating system and its networking software. The recent panic over weaknesses in BIND (a system for matching domain names to network addresses), for example, has reinforced the need for vigilance. If you postpone implementing security fixes, you are risking software and data.

2. You want to review the services and protocols you are running. Remove all nonessential services and protocols from your database server. If you are not using them, you need not worry about how someone might exploit them.

3. Choose how your clients will communicate with your database server, and implement only the methods you intend to use. SQL Server, for example, allows TCP/IP, Named Pipes, and Shared Memory as communication methods. If you are using TCP/IP as the communication protocol, do not configure Named Pipes or Shared Memory. What is not there to exploit cannot be exploited.

4. Install and run a good firewall. Use a router to connect to the Internet, and use nonroutable addresses behind the router. (Such addresses include 10.XXX.XXX.XXX, the so-called ten network, and the IP addresses that begin 192.168.43.XXX.) Let your router and firewall perform network address translation from the Internet address on the router to the internal addresses on your network.

5. Disable or password the guest accounts on your network. Leaving them open often leads to unexpected connection behavior between systems.

6. Research the issues surrounding your hardware, your operating system, and your database. Take a course on security relating to your platform. Improving security beyond these recommendations requires careful research into the suite of products you are using.

Defining Users

A major layer of security for your database is the database user. No one without a user ID on the database can access the database. You need to plan user accounts so that users can access the database in appropriate ways and not access the database in inappropriate ways. Choosing the right access scheme often takes some forethought.

DESIGN TIP

Some databases allow you to borrow operating system users as the database logins. You are wise to use operating system users whenever you allow interactive access to the database, because these users must first be authenticated as operating system users when they log into a workstation before they are authenticated as database users.

In general, you want to avoid allowing interactive access to the database, except for very qualified users. As interactive users become less qualified, you want to limit them to read-only access. You and I can probably trade stories about an interactive user who accidentally deleted records. I once witnessed two months of financial data purged from an accounting system by accident, for example. One always wants to test the integrity of the backup schema, but not under these circumstances.

For the most part, you want to have users access data through a client program. You want to provide the applications that access the data with a login that is embedded in the application, and you want the application to control what the user can do with the data carefully. You also want to make sure that embedded accounts aren't easily guessable or memorable. Because they are fixed features of your database, and because their passwords are not likely to change in a regular rotation, the names should be meaningless, the names should include numbers and nonalphabetic characters, and the passwords should be long and complex.

DESIGN TIP

If you are writing programs that access a database, be sure to make the username and password an accessible setting so that these items can be changed easily.

The means of adding a user to a database varies with the database. We will use SQL Server 2000 as an example. You will need to locate the specific tools that you use with your database. The process of adding a user involves multiple steps that are common to every database. First, you create the user account. Second, you define the database to which the user has access. Finally, you grant the users specific permissions to use the database.

To add a user to SQL Server 2000, follow these steps:

1. In the tree view, navigate to the Security node for your database server. Right-click Logins, and select New Login (see Figure 4-5).

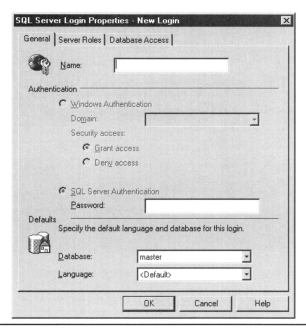

Figure 4-5   *Creating a new login*

2. Fill in the name for the user. If you are allowing a Windows NT account to access the database, select Windows Authentication and enter the domain name for the user.

3. Enter a password for the user. (This option is not enabled when you use Windows authentication.)

4. Select the user's default database, the one to which the user attaches at login time. This database is typically the one the user uses most frequently.

5. Select the Database Access tab.

6. Check the databases the user should have access to, as shown in Figure 4-6.

7. For each database, select the access role the user is permitted to have (see Figure 4-7). (Roles will be discussed in more detail in the next section.) Role membership defines basic permissions for the user.

8. Click OK to create the user.

CAUTION

Most databases ship with a default administrative user. In SQL Server, this user is named SA, and by default has no password. Be sure to change the passwords for the default administrative user so that someone could not connect using the defaults and gain administrative control over your data.

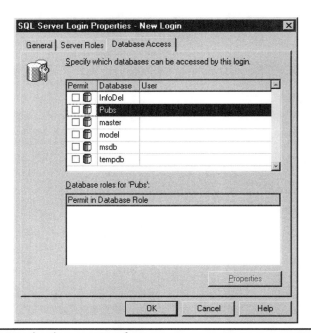

Figure 4-6   *Selecting database access for a new user*

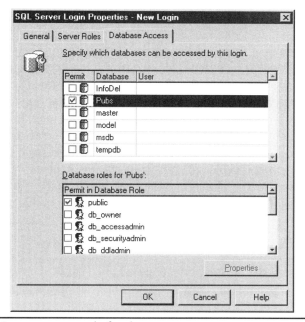

Figure 4-7   *Selecting an access role for the new user*

If you prefer to create users using SQL commands, SQL Server 2000 provides four stored procedures that accomplish the same steps that we just used the graphical interface to undertake. These are sp_adduser, sp_grantdbaccess, spaddrolemember, and sp_defaultdb. Here is a code fragment that demonstrates adding a user to a database named Pubs. The user is named test, and the password is "password." The user is added in the public role by sp_adduser, and the db_datareader by sp_addrolemember:

```
USE Pubs
--Necessary because sp_grantdbaccess works on the current database
EXEC sp_adduser 'test', 'user', 'public'
EXEC sp_defaultdb 'test', 'Pubs'
EXEC sp_grantdbaccess 'test', 'test'
EXEC sp_addrolemember 'db_datareader', 'test'
```

DESIGN TIP

If you are using a Windows NT account, use sp_grantlogin instead of sp_adduser.

Defining Roles

Roles are the method by which users are granted most permissions in a database. Roles are collections of users, much like *groups* in operating system security. When you add users to a role, they inherit all the permissions granted to the role. Adding users to roles is simpler than granting each individual user the same set of permissions. Controlling permissions on roles is easier, because you have one object on which you set the permissions, not one object for every user. In a typical database, you may need only four or five roles to control user access for all your users.

Databases include default roles that are built into the database for your use. For example, SQL Server 2000 includes a public role into which every user logged into the database belongs. It also includes db_datareader for users that need only to read data and db_datawriter for users who must update the database. In addition, you have the following administrative roles:

▶ **db_owner**   Has the permissions assigned to all built-in database roles.

▶ **db_accessadmin**   Has the correct permissions to grant access to Windows NT users.

▶ **db_ddladmin**   Has the correct permissions to modify and delete database objects (like tables).

▶ **db_securityadmin**   Has the correct permissions to manage roles and permissions.

▶ **db_backupoperator**   Has the correct permissions to back the database up.

▶ **db_denydatareader**   Denies select permissions so that members cannot read data.

▶ **db_denydatawriter**   Denies update permissions so that members cannot change the database.

DESIGN TIP

These roles are defined in the database itself. SQL Server 2000 also provides server roles that are defined on the server and have permissions across all databases.

Obviously, you can get quite far using just the standard roles. For most client programs, db_datareader and db_datawriter are all you need. However, if you do find that you need to create a role, you can easily do so using the Enterprise Manager. Follow these steps:

1. Navigate to a database in the tree view and right-click Roles, as shown in Figure 4-8.

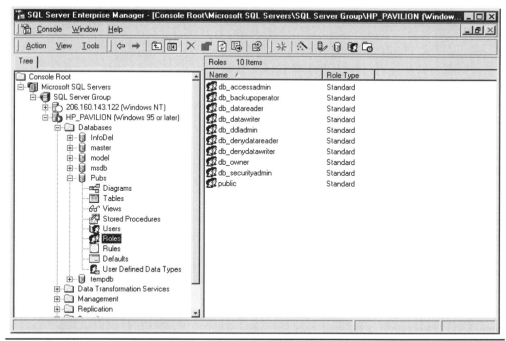

Figure 4-8   *Choosing the Roles option*

2. Select New Database Role from the context menu (see Figure 4-9).

3. Select Standard Role and enter a name for the role.

4. Click Add to select users to be members of the role (see Figure 4-10).

5. Click OK to add the role to the database.

If you want, you can create a role using sp_addrole and grant permissions to the role using the GRANT statement. Here is a sample script for undertaking such a task:

```
EXEC sp_addrole 'newuserrole', 'db_owner'
GRANT SELECT ON Authors TO newuserrole
```

DESIGN TIP

Application roles are special roles that contain no members. Only an application attaching to the SQL Server can activate an application role using the password you provide. When the application activates a role, normal database security is suspended on the assumption that the application authenticates the users. If you choose to use application roles, be very careful to make certain that the application performs the authentication. This feature is specific to SQL Server.

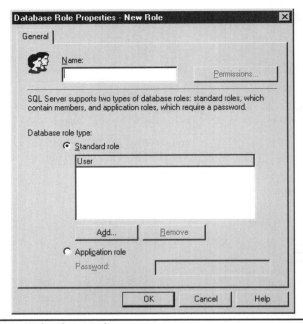

Figure 4-9   *Selecting a database role*

Figure 4-10   *Adding select users*

GRANT has some interesting quirks in SQL Server 2000. First, finding a complete list of permissions is difficult. The basic ones are SELECT, INSERT, UPDATE, DELETE, and EXECUTE. However, statements can also have permissions attached to them. The average user cannot execute CREATE TABLE without getting permission to do so. The permission for executing a statement is the name of the statement. So to allow a user to execute CREATE TABLE, you grant the CREATE TABLE permission.

Second, GRANT does not allow a user who is a member of a role to grant a permission inherited from the role. You may have CREATE TABLE permission because it is assigned to your role. However, you cannot grant that permission to another user. You must grant the permission as the role, using syntax like this:

```
GRANT SELECT ON Authors TO henry AS newuserrole
```

This seeming circumlocution invokes the role name as the granting agency. Just remember, if you can't seem to grant a permission you probably need an AS phrase in your GRANT statement.

Summary

This chapter has focused on issues that apply to databases and database servers that can have an impact on the SQL statements that you write. Sometimes when you encounter a problem, the problem is not a bug in your statement. Some problems are direct consequences of how you installed the database server and how you created the database and the users of the database. This chapter has reviewed problems of this sort and focused on recommendations for preventing problems down the line. It has also focused on making you aware of some of these issues so that you can recognize them when you encounter them.

Normalizing Tables

IN THIS CHAPTER:

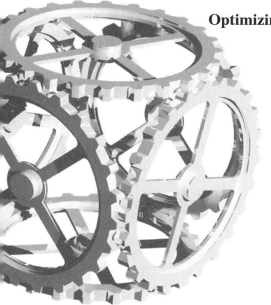

Normalization is often described as the process of designing tables. In a sense this statement is true, but normalization also has a mystique surrounding it that few SQL users understand. Dr. E.F. Codd first defined the relational model in 1970. In the relational model, formal mappings between and among sets are called *relations*. Relations participate in a predicate calculus that defines the mapping of the characteristics of one set onto another set. A simple example of a mapping of set characteristics is the statement "You are my reader." In this statement, there are at least three sets: *you, readers,* and *readers that belong to me.* The mapping expressed by "my reader" claims that among the set of general people who read books, there is a set of readers who read my books. That is, "reader" is a noun that serves as a subject, and "my" maps the attribute of "belongs to the set who read my books" onto that particular reader. Having established this set mapping, "You are my reader" maps the membership of "belongs to the set who reads my books" onto the set with one and only one member represented by "you."

If we wanted to develop a more formal way of representing these representations using mathematical notation, we could do so. In fact, a branch of mathematics known as *relations* has done so. The mathematicians who developed the theory noticed that they could represent the same relationship using a variety of alternative notations. Because of these alternative notational forms, they developed the notion of *normal forms* for relations. Normal forms express the relation in a notational form that has the most desirable characteristics both for expressing the relationship and for performing calculations on the relationship.

Given these preliminary concepts, you can see why the process of defining tables can be called normalization. Tables express relationships by gathering groups of facts together in a way that describes a case. The columns classify the facts into different categories. Gathering the classifications represented by the columns into a table that describes an entity of some type expresses the mappings of the attributes represented by a column onto the entity represented by the table. Individual rows in the table represent cases, or particular instances, of the entity represented by the table.

If you study elementary logic, you inevitably come across the following syllogism:

> All men are mortal.
> Socrates is a man.
> Therefore, Socrates is mortal.

This syllogism discusses the entity *man.* It introduces two attributes associated with instances of *man,* names and mortality. A table that represented this relationship within a database would represent the entity *man.* The table would have two columns, *name* and *mortal.* It would have one row, and the entries for the columns would be "Socrates" and "yes."

DESIGN TIP

You may have already spotted a flaw in this table design. If all men are mortal, we do not need a column to express mortality. Having the column implies that there might be nonmortal men. It is unwise to include columns in a table that can express nonsensical relationships.

Thirteen Rules

So far, we have been trying to use a table to visualize a set of relationships. The basic ground rules for this visualization are that first, a table represents a set of relations (or mappings of attributes) that describe a single entity. Because the columns are gathered together in a table, they represent some sort of an entity, rather than an unrelated collection of facts. Because a table describes something, we can think of many different ways to describe that something. Variations could range from something as simple as whether we will split the zip code off from the rest of the address to whether we will include names of grandparents in a table that describes a set of individuals who are treated by a doctor. A central question is what are the most relevant gatherings of the facts represented by columns in our table. Which is to say that we can describe entities in tables in several alternative ways. And because of this fact, we can devise normal forms for describing the entities in our tables. The normal forms are the best optimized for performing operations on the tables within the database.

The original relational model described 13 rules for visualizing the relationships represented by a table, 9 structural features for tables, and 18 manipulative features for tables. The second version of the model extended the 13 rules to 333 rules. We will not exhaust ourselves with a discussion of all these rules, but if you are going to design tables in order to have a well-optimized database and to prevent bugs in SQL code later on, you need to have at least some appreciation for the factors that go into formally expressing the relationships described by tables. To further this appreciation, we will walk through the 13 rules, and then describe several normal forms that allow you to express relationships captured by tables.

The first rule is Rule 0, and it will seem like a tautology to you. It states that relational databases use only their relational facilities to manage data. For you as a table designer, this rule has little meaning. For the database engine, however, this rule has great meaning. The database engine must satisfy this requirement in managing data. What this rule means is that the database engine must not manage data using a procedural methodology. When you write a program in most computer languages, you define a procedure that has steps. You start at step one and end at the last step. By contrast, in a relational database, you don't define procedures (although many implementations of SQL allow procedural actions such as loops). Instead, you declare what the database should do, as in "Give me all the rows in table C that have the value 2 in the last column." The database engine has to translate this definition of a new relation within the data into a way to return the information to you. That is, the database must define a relational method that performs this task. Because computers are calculation engines, eventually each relational facility reduces to a set of procedures the computer can perform. But the database engine must start with a declaration of a relation and return the resultset that the relation defines.

Rule 1 states that items of information in the database should be represented in a single way. In a relational database, this single way is to locate data in a row in a table. The table contains columns, and the row-column position forms a container for a data element. The basic data structure for the database, therefore, is the table. Ad hoc data structures are not allowed. For you as a table designer, this rule is fundamental. It means that if you want to define data storage for any type of data, you must do so using a table.

Rule 2 states that access to each value in the database must be guaranteed. Each value in the database must have an address path made up of the containing table name, the containing column name, and the value of the primary key in the containing row. As you know, most SQL databases will allow you to create tables that do not have primary keys. This rule suggests that such a practice is not wise. For you as a table designer, it suggests a basic practice: use primary keys.

DESIGN TIP

Even in tables for which you don't wish to use data elements as a key, you should use a primary key. Set up an identity column, if nothing else. I have run into situations where a database refused to perform a DELETE because the row could not be uniquely identified. Without unique identification, more rows than anticipated might get deleted. A primary key guarantees that each row can be uniquely identified.

Rule 3 states that a relational database should have a representation of missing data and inapplicable information that is separate from the representation of data. That is, missing and inapplicable information should not be represented as a data type. SQL uses NULL as this representation for both cases. You should be aware as a database programmer that a NULL returned from the database means that there is no data present at that row-column intersection, or that your requested database operation produced inapplicable results. Practically, as a table designer, you need to decide how to handle NULL values. Will you allow them? What will you do with missing data in a record if you don't allow nulls? That is, you will never be able to enter a partial record if you completely disallow NULL values. You need to determine whether you can afford not to record partial values when you design a table.

DESIGN TIP

You need to determine how to handle NULLs returned to a program in a recordset. In many languages, assignment of a NULL to a variable produces an error.

Rule 4 requires that the database maintain an online catalog that is accessible via its relational features. That is, any information required to structure the database should be stored in database tables and accessed via the query language. In any SQL database, you will find a set of system tables that describe the structure of the database. You can read the data in these tables using a SELECT statement, and you can change the data using an INSERT statement (so long as you have the privileges). Keep in mind that the implementation of these tables is database specific. You cannot count on identical table structures across vendors. But you can read information about system structures relating to any database from these tables. For example, you can get a list of indexes for a table if you need one.

Rule 5 states that there must be a data sublanguage in the relational database. This sublanguage is required to have linear syntax, to allow both programmatic and interactive access to the database, to allow you to define data structures, to allow you to manipulate data, to support security, to support data integrity, and to support transaction management. This requirement demands a lot of the database, but it provides you a lot as a table designer. First, you get the data definition language (DDL) component of SQL that allows you to define a table. You get the data manipulation component of SQL that allows you to put data into tables and retrieve it. You get the osql utility, which allows command line interactive access to your database. You usually get an isql utility that provides a graphical editor that interacts with the database. These are the primary SQL tools you use to define tables and store data.

Rule 6 states that views (or virtual tables) should be updatable. The most important point to note about this rule is that most databases don't adhere to it. Some views are updatable, but most are not. You need to remember that, if you are using a view and need to update the data in it, you structure the view so that it can be updated. The rules for doing so are vendor specific.

The next few rules are self-explanatory in many respects. While they help you to understand more about visualizing tables in SQL, they offer few practical hints or helps to table designers. Rule 7 states that the database must provide INSERT, UPDATE, and DELETE operators for tables. Rule 8 states that the data should not be structured in a way that is physically dependent on a device. That is, tables should not have their structure defined as fitting onto an IDE drive that uses the FAT16 file system. Data should be structured independently of the device. Rule 9 states that data should be logically independent. This rule basically states that whatever is stored at a row-column intersection should not be dependent on the nature of the storage container or any other element of data. These rules give you the ability to store your data in tables and take action on the data. They are important precursors to your work in designing tables, but they do not directly affect what you do.

Rule 10 states that integrity constraints should be separate from the data and be separate from programs that access the data. You can therefore specify integrity constraints separately from designing data storage, and these constraints should be stored in the database catalog, where any program (including the database engine itself) can reference them. This rule prevents, for the most part, programs from failing because integrity constraints have changed. However, it also places a requirement on you as a table designer. If you want data integrity, you have to declare the constraints yourself, and you typically have to do so in a separate step from creating the table. (Most implementations of SQL do allow you to place constraints in a CREATE TABLE statement, however.) The main point is that you have to remember to create the constraints. You can easily overlook this step while working on tables.

Two additional rules, numbers 11 and 12, work behind the scenes to protect your tables. Rule 11 states that a new release of the database should not break applications already in existence. This principle is called *distribution independence*. Rule 12 states that there shall be no low-level back door to your tables that allows you to skirt the rules applied by SQL when you design the table. This principle is called *nonsubversion*. Together these rules guarantee that you can trust the tables you create to remain functional and not to suffer damage because someone accessed them using a low-level language that subverts security, integrity, or similar issues.

As these rules indicate, tables serve as the physical containers to hold data that satisfies the formal expression of a relation. The table is a standard container. It is not dependent on the storage device that contains it or the data that is in it. It maintains a practical interface, and you are guaranteed that there are no back doors to the table through which data could be corrupted. The trick in designing tables is expressing the relation that defines the table clearly and properly. The normal forms of the relations that define tables allow you to express such relations in optimal clear and proper ways.

First Normal Form

To begin designing tables, you must first gather together all the data objects that you want to put in your database, and you must name them using generic names. While you usually cannot physically put all the data elements on a table and start sorting them into piles, the metaphor is fairly accurate. You have to know what you want to store before you can design storage, and you have to classify the individual data elements so that you can tell what classes will represent columns in your table. Many of your data elements may have physical existence, like the horses in your stable. Many data elements may not have physical existence, like the projected earnings for a race horse. Whatever the data intended for storage, assembling the list of data items is always the starting place for creating tables.

The next step is to block data elements into the groups that will make up the tables. Normalization is the process of defining these groups so that they express a clear and proper relation. The normal forms of such relations allow you to determine milestones in defining the tables. When you have achieved a particular normal form, you know both that you have removed a particular problem from the table design and that you have designed the table in a way that the database engine can understand and use. Remember, SQL databases receive declarative language statements and must determine the best procedure for implementing the state of affairs represented by the declarative statement. Normal forms of tables place tables in a state that allows the database engine to apply declarative SQL statements in an optimal fashion.

As you sort the data categories into tables, you might find yourself classifying all the elements of a building into a table. You might have a set of elements like the following:

```
House
Living room
Dining room
Bedroom 1
Bedroom 2
Bedroom 3
```

While this list of elements does make up what a house is, the database engine will have trouble with it. The list contains a repeated group, bedrooms. This group becomes problematic, because houses vary in the number of bedrooms they have. For a table that describes houses to adequately represent any house, you would have to include enough bedroom columns to satisfy the requirements of any builder. You would have to accommodate even eccentric home owners, like Sarah Winchester, who kept her house under constant construction, adding rooms constantly.

First normal form (1NF) for a table sets the following requirement: remove repeated groups to another table. It can be stated as a practical principle: repeating groups of data define their own table. In terms of our example, we will have a Houses table and a Bedroom table. House contains all the data elements that are unique to a house. Bedroom contains the list of bedrooms.

As your tables approach 1NF, you can readily notice a couple of factors about tables as expressions of relations. First, tables like House and Bedroom cannot be completely independent of one another. You must have a way to relate the bedrooms to the house they belong to. Because of this need, you have to share a value between the House record and the Bedroom records that relate to it. This value must uniquely identify the House record, or else the Bedroom records could refer to more than one house. As you place tables in 1NF, therefore, you will find it useful to define primary keys for each table, so that each record is uniquely identifiable. The primary key constraint so defined guarantees that primary key values are unique. You should also define foreign keys, which are instances of primary keys in one table referenced in another table. Foreign key constraints guarantee that the foreign key value must first already be a primary key or unique value in another table before it is inserted as a foreign key.

In our example, we need a primary key for the House table and a primary key for the Bedroom table. We can call these columns by the names House_ID and Bedroom_ID. We also need to include House_ID as a foreign key in the Bedroom table. The SQL statements to create such tables and constraints would look something like these:

```
CREATE TABLE House (House_ID INT,
    Living_Room VARCHAR(25),
    Other_Columns VARCHAR(10),
    PRIMARY KEY (House_ID));
CREATE TABLE Bedroom (Bedroom_ID INT,
    House_ID INT,
    Bedroom_Name VARCHAR(25),
    Other_Columns VARCHAR(25),
    PRIMARY KEY (Bedroom_ID),
    FOREIGN KEY (House_ID) REFERENCES House(House_ID));
```

You have probably noticed additional facts in considering gathering elements into tables. One is that columns need to represent atomic values. Longinus originally defined the atom as an element that cannot be further subdivided. Classical chemistry treats elements as such atoms. Data items stored in columns should be atomic in this sense: You should not perceive the need for further subdivision of the data element.

This dictum will not preclude your changing your mind later. For example, you can store a street address in any number of ways. You can write it all into a single column, in which case you see the entire address as atomic, which is one possible view. However, as in chemistry, you may begin to see subatomic structures on which you would like to search, like the state or the zip code. Searching on subatomic structures is difficult, because you have to parse the data element retrieved from the column to find the subatomic structure. Because of this fact, addresses are commonly stored in multiple columns. As you place tables into 1NF, you want to look for possible subatomic structures actively, and break them out into their own columns.

Another fact is that tables should represent a single entity. Repeated groups are a strong hint that you have merged more than one entity into a single table. If you use the principle of relevance, you can also spot elements that deserve to be in a separate table. Each table has an entity, and its purpose is to describe that entity. No information irrelevant to the entity should appear in the table. Bowling_Scores_Of_Occupants is a column you could place in the House table, for example. However, you have to raise the question of how this data element is relevant to describing a house. Bowling scores really do not describe a house, and they may or may not describe the occupants of a house. (Whether they do depends on whether the occupants bowl.) Items that stretch the principle of relevance probably deserve to be in a different table.

Yet another fact is that tables gather together into hierarchies. It may take several related tables to describe a house. We have already noted two that are useful. Full description of an entity often requires several tables, and these tables relate along the lines of foreign key constraints. The typical foreign key captures a one-to-many relationship. For each instance of the primary or unique key, there are many instances of the foreign key. That is, we relate one house record to many bedroom records. Entities described in a database are often complex objects with many parts. Each complex component may require its own table for adequate description, and entities may be made up of multiple, identical components. The components themselves may subdivide into hierarchies of tables, too.

In addition to one-to-many relationships among the components of an entity, you may find that many-to-many relationships also occur. In the kitchen of the house, for example, you have cabinets, and cabinets contain cooking utensils. Any number of cooking utensils can be stored in a cabinet, and more than one cabinet can contain cooking utensils. You have a set of cabinets that maps to a set of cooking utensils. A simple foreign key relationship cannot capture this relationship. You need a way of mapping many cabinets to many utensils, and you have to preserve the flexibility to reassign a utensil from one cabinet to another. The best way to accomplish this mapping is to use a table to bridge between the cabinet entity and the utensils entity. This table would have two columns, one for the cabinet identifier, and one for the utensil identifier. A row in the table links a cabinet to a utensil. Not having a row in the table means that a cabinet or a utensil is unassigned. Having multiple rows in a table means either that the utensil is stored in multiple cabinets, as can happen when you have multiple copies of the same utensil, or that a cabinet contains multiple utensils. Such tables are said to bridge many-to-many relationships. The SQL to create such a table looks like this:

```
CREATE TABLE Cabinet_Utensils (Cabinet_ID INT,
    Utensil_ID INT);
```

As you bring tables into 1NF, therefore, you resolve many issues about the data relationships that you are working with. You also make your basic data categories, and map out the first approximation of the table structures needed to contain the data. You do not, however, put the data into optimal form. Other normal forms of the relation you are expressing in your tables, however, help you to do so.

DESIGN TIP

Among the data, you will also notice one-to-one relationships. Many data elements have a one-to-none relationship, which is to say that they are unrelated.

Further Normal Forms

Additional normal forms of relations help you to optimize your tables. In understanding these forms, you have to understand the notion of *dependency*. Column A depends on Column B if by knowing the value of Column A you can determine the value of Column B. To illustrate this notion, we are going to imagine a database that stores information about students at an elementary school. If you have a table that stores Student_ID and Teacher_ID, knowing the Student_ID allows you to determine the value of Teacher_ID, because students can have only one teacher at this school. You might have to look for the student's name on every class list to find the teacher, but you can do it.

If you have a table that stores the Student_ID, the Teacher_ID, and the Room_ID, you have an additional dependency in the table. If you know the Student_ID and the Teacher_ID, you can easily determine the Room_ID. Students have only one teacher, and teachers have only one room in which they teach. You might have to search through records one by one to find it, but you can find the Room_ID. In this case, we have a pairing of columns that depends on another column.

You can also have *multivalued dependencies.* In this case, knowing one column value allows you to determine the possible multiple values of another column. If I know Student_ID, for example, I can determine the valid values of People_Allowed_To_Remove_From_School_Grounds (the list of responsible adults who may take the student off school premises). Assume for now that these two columns are in the same table.

To describe a dependency, you normally state that Column A determines Column B, for single-valued dependencies. A notation for expressing this relationship is A → B, which is read "A determines B." For multivalued dependencies, you state that Column A determines many values of Column B. The notation for this relationship is A →→ B, which is read "A determines many Bs."

What about dependencies is bad? Nothing inherently is evil about a dependency. You will probably find tables that have dependencies in them that no one has bothered to remove. However, dependencies often point to difficulties in the table design. If we were truly to design a single table that recorded all the information about a student, including people allowed to remove the child from the school premises, we would be forced to have a set of columns to hold these names in the table. We would either have to add a column as necessary to accommodate the maximum number of desired names, or we would have to set a limit on the number of names so that we could make our table structure predictable. A better solution is to have a table to hold these names with Student_ID as a foreign key, so that any number of names can be entered for a student. Multivalued dependencies point to this solution.

Other types of dependencies point to similar solutions. There are normal forms to help you find these solutions for your tables.

Second Normal Form

Dependencies among keys and columns are not inherently bad. In fact, your ideal circumstance is to have a primary key X for a table such that each column Y that is not a key has the following relationship with X: X → Y. X can be a single column, or it can be a multipart key. When X is a multipart key, you need to be very careful about dependencies.

When some part of a multipart key determines another column in the table, you have a situation that points to using a table structure like that used to resolve multivalued dependencies. The dependency itself is called a partial key dependency.

It indicates that some column in the table is more intimately associated with just part of the key than with the entire key itself. If some part of a key determines a column in the table, but not the rest of the columns in the table, then the key data in the determined column has a special relationship with the key. Data in the determined column is more predictable than data in the other columns. As a result, the data is likely to represent a separate entity with which the entity identified by the key part has a relationship. Information about such entities is best placed in a lookup table, a table that contains the possible values for the column and that is linked to the original table using a foreign key. Or you should consider choosing different key values, so that the key determines all columns equally.

For example, in our elementary school, the Students table contains the column Student_ID, which is the primary key. It also contains the Teacher column. We have noted that, if you know the value of Student_ID, you can easily determine the value of Teacher. The key is dependent on Teacher. The school employs a limited number of teachers. We need to track data about them anyway, and the Student_ID value is not the best way to uniquely identify teachers in the database. Because of these facts, you are better off having a Teachers table that contains information about teachers. In the Students table, simply include the Teacher_ID as a foreign key in a column so that you can easily look up which teacher is associated with a student.

Removing Partial Key Dependencies From Tables Places Them In Second Normal form (2NF). A partial key dependence arises when you have a multipart key, and the dependency exists for only one of the columns that make up the key. Dependencies relating to parts of keys point to the need to move the column on which the key depends to another table.

Third Normal Form

Another type of dependency that can interfere with table design is a *transitive dependency*. If Column A determines Column B, and Column B determines Column C, then Column A determines Column C. The determination of Column C by Column A is called a transitive dependency. It is indirect, and it is mediated by another column.

Transitive dependencies usually interfere with the unique identification of rows in tables. You want each row to be uniquely identified by the key, and nothing but the key. Transitive dependencies can lead to additional columns being involved in the unique identification of rows. If such a situation occurs, you will find yourself violating a primary key constraint when you attempt to manipulate data.

Removing transitive dependencies places a table in third normal form (3NF). The trick to achieving 3NF is recognizing the transitive dependencies in the first place.

The only sure way of doing so is to iterate through your columns in order to verify which pairs of columns are dependent. You need to make a list of these pairs. It might look like this:

```
Student determines Teacher
Student determines Parent
Class determines Room
Teacher determines Class
```

After you have your list, you then need to look for links in the list where the right term of the dependency in one item depends on the left term in another item. In our contrived example, you see a transitive dependency between Teacher and Class. Class should be moved into another table, which leaves a foreign key in the teacher table to link the teacher to classes.

Boyce-Codd Normal Form

Removing transitive dependencies does not resolve all table problems. Keys can still limit the way you interact with your data. Consider a table that tracks student awards in the annual school fundraising sale. It might have the following columns:

```
Sales
Points
Award
```

Note that in this arrangement, we have these dependencies:

```
(Sales, Points) → Award
Points → Award
```

That is, if we know how much you sold and how many points you have, we can tell what your award might be. If we know how many points you have, we also can tell what your award might be. Assume that the data looks something like that in Table 5-1. You can assume that either Sales or Points is the key (or both, if you want).

Sale	Points	Award
$10	20	Stickers
$20	40	Pen and Pencil
$30	60	Box of Candy

Table 5-1   *Sample Data for the School Sale Example*

This table is in 3NF, and it will work just fine, so long as you add all three items in a row at once. However, what if you want to change the association of an award with a point value? Then you must also include a sales figure in the INSERT. What if you want to change the association of a point value with a sales figure? Then you must also include an award in the INSERT. You are doing more work than you need to in order to update the data.

Another normal form, Boyce-Codd normal form (BCNF) gets you out of this dilemma. BCNF requires that for all dependencies such that $X \rightarrow Y$, X must be a *superkey* for the table schema. A superkey is a set of columns that uniquely identifies rows in a table, but from which you can remove a column without affecting the functioning of the key. In other words, if you pull a column, you are still uniquely identifying rows. It is a key that has extra values in it, just for good measure. It guarantees that the relationship between the key and other columns is always one of $X \rightarrow Y$.

In our award example, we would split the table into two tables, one containing Points and Award, the other containing Sales and Points. Points then functions as a foreign key in the second table. You make the key for each table a multipart key including both columns, which effectively creates the superkey. And you are then in BCNF.

DESIGN TIP

It is common practice to remove the extra values from a superkey once you have finished normalizing your tables.

Fourth Normal Form

Fourth normal form (4NF) is very straightforward. Examine your tables for multivalue dependencies. Reduce the number of these dependencies to only one per table. You are then in 4NF.

As you allow more than one multivalued dependency in your table, you create a situation where you must add multiple rows to add a single value to a column. Assume that teachers in our elementary school can team-teach. This places a multivalued dependency in the Students table. We can have a situation where the following are valid rows in the table:

```
Johnny      Mrs. Smith
Johnny      Mr. Munson
```

If we now wish to add an entry for Johnny in the table, we must add at least two rows because Johnny has two teachers. If we add another column that represent a multivalued dependency determined by Johnny, and the column can take two values, we would have to add four rows to the table just to add a student to the table. You would prefer to insert a student with one INSERT, not many. Move multivalued dependencies to separate tables. In this example, have a Teachers table, and build a Students_Teachers table that pairs Student_ID with Teacher_ID. You can have multiple rows in the Students_Teachers table for either a student or a teacher. You can always look up who are which students' teachers by using a join among the Students, Teachers, and Students_Teachers tables. And you can update any table with a single INSERT statement. You do need to remember that, when you add a student, you need to add a line or lines to Students_Teachers to link the student to a teacher. You must perform a similar action when you add a teacher. But this solution allows you better control over the information and the relationships that obtain among the entities than if you kept all the multivalued dependencies in the same table.

Fifth Normal Form and Beyond

Additional normal forms do exist. Fifth normal form states that your tables should not create bogus rows in a join. For example, if you have a Teacher_Principal table, a Teacher_Aide table, and an Aide_Principal table, a three-way join on these tables will produce bogus rows. Such a phenomenon is known as a *join anomaly*. Tables 5-2, 5-3, and 5-4 provide sample data.

Teacher	Aide
Mrs. Martin	Susan
Mr. Munson	Tom
Mrs. Martin	Sally

Table 5-2   *A Sample Teacher_Aide Table*

Aide	Principal
Susan	Mr. Henley
Tom	Mrs. Johnson
Sally	Mr. Henley

Table 5-3   *A Sample Aide_Principal Table*

The following SELECT will produce rows that do not exist in the constituent tables:

```
SELECT TA.Teacher, AP.Aide, TP.Principal
   FROM Teacher_Aide AS TA,
      Aide_Principal AS AP,
      Teacher_Principal AS TP
   WHERE TA.Teacher = TP.Teacher
      AND AP.Aide = TA.Aide
      AND AP.Principal = TP.Principal
```

You will get a row from this query, for example, that contains the following items:

```
Mr. Frankenstein
Mrs. Johnson
Tom
```

In the tables, however, Mr. Frankenstein is assigned no Aide.

Unfortunately, there is no algorithm that will successfully detect when you have created such a situation. You need to test your table structures with practice data and multiple joins to see whether you have avoided a join anomaly. You also need to watch for circular references among three or more tables, the condition that produces the join anomaly in the first place.

There are additional normal forms beyond the fifth, but they are highly specialized and relate mainly to recognizing table problems from the point of view of a computer

Teacher	Principal
Mrs. Martin	Mr. Henley
Mr. Munson	Mrs. Johnson
Mr. Frankenstein	Mrs. Johnson

Table 5-4   *A Sample Teacher_Principal Table*

aided software engineering (CASE) tool that attempts to detect table problems automatically from a table schema that you create. As with 5NF, the algorithms for applying the forms are not complete. For practical work, therefore, 5NF is the limit.

As you can see, various normal forms help you to express the relation that describes your data in more and more refined ways, and help you to resolve issues about how to access your data. A critical question remains, however: Have you optimized the tables for best performance?

Optimizing Tables

When you start talking about the optimal form of a table, you enter the territory of strongly held opinions. The fervor behind the discussions becomes almost religious in its intensity. You can find lots of opinions, and asking whether your tables are optimized is the rough equivalent of raising the question whether you have chosen the correct operating system to underlie your database. Everyone will have a benchmark to discuss, and someone else will claim that the benchmark is tainted. We want to avoid the complexities that these overloaded opinions can raise, and get to practical issues that provide results. And really, there are very practical guidelines to follow.

Normalizing to Optimize

Usually, normalizing your tables leads to the best performance. In general, you want to apply these principles in normalizing in order to optimize:

► You want your tables to achieve at least third normal form. When tables are in this form, you have removed dependencies and anomalies that create difficulties.

► You want to apply additional normal forms when they simplify the data structure in some tangible way.

► You want to limit the number of bridging tables that mediate many-to-many relationships. That is, if further normalizing introduces a many-to-many relationship that requires an additional bridging table, don't apply that normalization unless you see some clear performance advantage in adding the many-to-many relationships.

► You want to avoid circular references among the bridging tables. They lead to join anomalies.

If you adhere to these principals, in general, you are optimizing your database by normalizing your tables.

Considering Denormalization

Now we come to a statement that is guaranteed to cause arguments. You can overnormalize your tables. You can easily tell when you have reached this point. If you have to create a five-way join just to select complete student information from the elementary school database, you are approaching the practical limit of normalizing tables. Joins have a cost. You can reach a point where the value of normalized tables is outweighed by the overhead of the joins required to extract the data.

Where this cost line gets drawn depends on your database, your hardware, and the environment in which you use the database. Any database server can return the results of one SELECT a minute when the SELECT is run on a quad-processor server with four gigabytes of RAM. As the transaction load increases, as hardware resources become scarce, and as your database engine exhausts its capabilities, you can experience the overhead of joins getting in the way. Under these circumstances, you might want to denormalize the data for some purposes.

How might you do so? First, you can create special tables to hold the denormalized data. You can use INSERT with a SELECT to pull data from the normalized tables back into the denormalized table. Save this query as a stored procedure, add a command that truncates the denormalized table ahead of the SELECT in the procedure, and schedule the procedure to run at off-peak hours. When speed is of the essence, you can hit the denormalized table. When you absolutely need the latest changes to the data, you can run the query with the joins.

Summary

This chapter has focused on normalizing tables. We've looked at the process of normalization and tried to demystify it. We've looked at what a relation is, what a normal form of a relation is, and what many of the most useful normal forms are. We've also suggested ways to optimize data access both by normalizing tables and denormalizing tables.

CHAPTER 6

Using Data Types

IN THIS CHAPTER:

Using Data Types

Converting Data Types from
One Database to Another

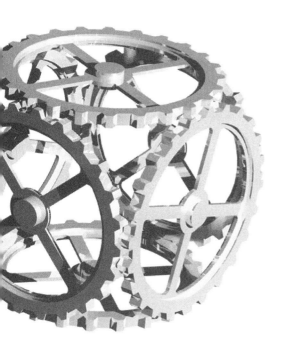

SQL databases offer you a variety of data types to work with. The goal in using a data type is, of course, to best express the data. In a database, you can always use a single data type to store all the data. Almost any type of data can be represented as a string of characters. If you wish, you can express all data in this fashion, and store it in your tables.

However, expressing all data as a single type leads to inefficiencies. One inefficiency is easily demonstrated with integers. Take for example the integers that can be represented as ranging from 0 to 256. These numeric values can all be stored in a single byte if you store them as numbers. When you store them as characters, though, most of these numbers require two or three bytes of storage, because you must store two or three characters.

Dates illustrate a different type of inefficiency. A date stored as a string will always be properly formatted as a date and will require very little processing for you to display in a program. Performing math on the date, a common operation in database programming, becomes very difficult with dates stored as strings. You must convert the string into some sort of a data type that can represent a sequence, do the math, and then return the date to string format.

A one-type-fits-all approach to storing data leads to difficulties. It is true that you can optimize a storage system to store data as strings with blinding speed, and you can find data products on the market that do so. Basis is an example. However, you purchase this speed at the cost of having to work harder to manipulate data once you have retrieved it from the storage system. You also purchase the speed at the cost of having no low-level enforcement of data integrity via the data type. If you are storing a date as a string, the only validation applied against the date is whether it is a proper string. If you store a date as a datetime value, the date must be a proper date within the range of the database datetime type, or the database engine throws an error.

So there are advantages to using SQL data types. However, there are some tricks as well. In this chapter, we are going to focus on the tricks so that you don't run into problems with data types as you work.

Using Data Types

As we have noted, all SQL databases provide you with data types to work with. However, not all SQL databases provide the same data types, and expectations that various data types raise can be confusing. If you have ever stored a number like 40,000 in a variable and then wondered why the value kept truncating to 32,767, you have one of the more interesting data type experiences, an implicit conversion.

Your variable was declared to be an integer, and the default limit on an integer was 32,767. The implementation of SQL that you used accepted your declaration of the variable as an integer, accepted your attempt to store 40,000 in the integer variable, and converted your value to a valid integer when you assigned 40,000 to your variable. Of course, it did not produce an error because the default action was to convert the data to the type of the variable.

DEBUGGING TIP

If you experience changes in the value of a variable or column that are unexpected, check for a type conversion that you did not expect to occur.

Fortunately, most SQL databases are more sophisticated in the way that they handle data types. Nevertheless, data types are not completely standardized. Some are, but vendors typically offer extensions of the data types that are standardized. To use integers for comparison again, Borland's Interbase offers you one integer data type. Its range is –2,147,483,648 to 2,147,483,647. By contrast, Microsoft's SQL Server offers you BIGINT, INT, SMALLINT, and TINYINT. All four of these data types store integers. They just have different limits, as shown in Table 6-1.

The additional data types offered by SQL Server allow you to optimize your storage needs a little more effectively. The INT data type in both Interbase and SQL Server requires four bytes of storage. The BIGINT type offered by SQL Server requires eight bytes, the SMALLINT two bytes, and the TINYINT just a single byte. If you know that your numbers will always fit within a certain range, you can save storage space by using SMALLINT or TINYINT. You need to use BIGINT only when you know you are using very large numbers.

DESIGN TIP

In general, you should use a storage type that conserves storage space. While disk space is cheap, you want to squeeze as much potential out of the disk space you have. Data always grows faster than you think it will.

Data Type	Range
BIGINT	–9,223,372,036,854,775,808 to 9,223,372,036,854,775,807
INT	–2,147,483,648 to 2,147,483,647
SMALLINT	–32,768 to 32,767
TINYINT	0 to 255

Table 6-1   *Ranges of Microsoft's Integer Data Types*

Rather than simply compare and contrast data types across databases, we want to look at some generic issues that surround the use of data types in SQL databases. Having some factors standardized and some factors extended by individual vendors leads to some interesting possibilities for bugs, especially if you have to work on two or more different databases. For example, identifying variables for a stored procedure is different depending on the vendor. Microsoft does it this way:

```
DECLARE intCounter INT
```

Borland does it this way:

```
BEGIN DECLARE SECTION;
          BASED ON EMPLOYEE.SALARY salary;
END DECLARE SECTION;
```

Borland requires the formal markers to indicate where variables are being declared. It also expects that you will be basing the variable on the data type of a column in a table. As a result, you name the table and column after BASED ON and follow the name of the column with the variable name.

Numeric Data Types

SQL implementations offer a variety of numeric data types. In general, you will find INTEGER, DECIMAL, NUMERIC, FLOAT, and REAL data types, as these are all defined within the SQL standard. However, their exact implementation is not defined within the SQL standard. As a result, on SQL Server, NUMERIC and DECIMAL are the exact same thing. On other databases, they are different. In the standard, NUMERIC data has a *precision,* which is a number that states how many significant digits you can have in the base of the number. It also has a *scale,* which is a number that tells you how many decimal places the number may have. DECIMAL data has a scale required by the standard, but the precision is defined by the implementation. Because of this difference, you may find subtle differences in calculations when you use the two data types. Small machine databases often fail to implement these two data types because of the overhead the differences require in the math libraries. Just be aware that what you can calculate with a NUMERIC data type may lead to slightly different results using the DECIMAL data type.

DEBUGGING TIP

If you are performing calculations on numbers, you are wise to convert the two numbers to the same data type for the calculation, and then to convert the result to the proper data type explicitly.

SQL offers exact and approximate numeric data types. The exact types have a known precision and scale. They are INTEGER, NUMERIC, and DECIMAL. Among the exact types, NUMERIC and DECIMAL can vary in their implementation, as we have noted. SQL also offers approximate data types, which are numbers represented using a mantissa and an exponent, such as 2^{32}. The approximate data types are DOUBLEPRECISION, FLOAT, and REAL. DOUBLEPRECISION is basically an integer that is twice as wide as the integer type. It can hold larger numbers and is similar to Microsoft's BIGINT. FLOAT stores floating point numbers, and it allows you to specify its precision. The SQL standard requires that FLOAT numbers have a binary precision. REAL numbers, however, are left up to the implementation to define. As a result, you can expect varying behavior across databases, and some slight expectation violations until you are comfortable with what your database actually does.

Doing Math

When you do math in SQL with numeric data types, you need to be aware that SQL does not define a lot of rules about how math is done. Multiplication and division operators have the same precedence. Addition and subtraction have the same precedence. Multiplication and division are performed before addition and subtraction. Perform the following calculation the way you would have done it in algebra class:

```
3 + 4 * 2 - 6 / 2
```

You were probably taught to do multiplication first, so the calculation reduces to the following:

```
3 + 8 - 6 / 2
```

Next you perform division, making the calculation have this form:

```
3 + 8 - 3
```

Next comes addition, making the calculation have this form:

```
11 - 3
```

Finally, you do subtraction, and you get this result:

```
8
```

   SQL does not do math that way. Instead, you do the multiplication and division from right to left, because they have the same precedence. Your calculation looks like this after this step:

```
3 + 8 - 3
```

Next you do addition and subtraction from left to right, giving you this result:

```
8
```

We should congratulate ourselves, because we got the same answer both times. Try this expression, however:

```
2 / 2 * 6 * 4
```

   Algebra class would yield the result 0.041666666666666666666666666666667, because you do all the multiplication before the division. SQL rules give you the result 24. That is, when working as in algebra class, the expression looks like this after your first pass through the operator precedence, doing all multiplication first:

```
2 / 48
```

If you take the SQL approach, after the first operation the expression looks like this:

```
1 * 2 * 6 * 4
```

   This critical difference arises from placing division at the same level of precedence as multiplication. The division operation therefore takes place at the same time as the multiplication. You therefore divide 2 by 2, yielding the result 1, and then continue with the multiplication operations in the same pass through the expression.

DESIGN TIP

Do not rely on operator precedence when doing math with numeric data. Explicitly order your calculations using parentheses.

The variation in operator precedence can lead to rounding errors and overflow errors, especially if you are working with numbers that are near the boundaries of their data types. If you encounter rounding and overflow errors when performing math in SQL statements, suspect an operator precedence problem.

Rounding is not a simple problem when you work with databases. Some users prefer the scientific rounding method that we were all taught in algebra class. If the last digit is 0, 1, 2, 3, or 4, you drop the digit and leave the digit to the left unchanged. If the last digit is 5, 6, 7, 8, or 9, you drop it and add one to the digit on the left. Scientists prefer this rounding method. In financial settings, however, another rounding method minimizes the impact of rounding error. The difference has to do with the digit 5. If you have a 5, you want to round up about half the time and down about half the time. As a result, some probabilistic decision rule is applied when you round a number whose last digit is 5. If you are always expecting to round up, this method could surprise you.

DEBUGGING TIP

Find out what rounding system is implemented on your implementation of SQL. Some SQL implementations implement a rounding function that lets you control what method is used to round the number. Popular names for these functions are ROUND and TRUNCATE.

Conversion Issues

SQL provides CAST to allow you to convert from one data type to another. Its generic form is the following:

```
CAST  ColumnOrVariableName AS DataTypeName;
```

With numeric data types, you should not expect many problems. However, you need to be aware of two specific possibilities: truncation and rounding. If you cast to a data type that is smaller than the original data type, as in casting from BIGINT to TINYINT, a truncation will happen or an error will occur. In casts that involve a change in precision or scale, rounding will occur. Normally, if you are going to lose data because of the conversion, you will get an error. Rounding will not produce an error. You must remember that most implementations of SQL assume that when you use CAST you do so intentionally. So expect some behind-the-scenes rounding to go on.

Time-Related Data Types

Time is a problem in databases. The reason is that time is a problem in general. Periods of days and years are problematic. We are all taught in school that there are 365.25 days in a year, and that this is the reason that we have leap years every four years. In fact, there are 365.2422 days in a year, and this leads to an additional leap day every four hundred years. Even deciding when the millennium actually begins is not a trivial task. The monk who did the original specification for the Christian calendar made the year 1 the year Christ was born. There was no year zero. So the recent millennium technically begins in 2001, not 2000.

Even time is not quite the same as you thought it might be. GMT is no longer the standard. We now use UTC, universal coordinated time, and it can be fractions of a second off Greenwich Mean Time, because GMT is based on astronomical observations, and UTC is based on an atomic standard. Time zones were originally devised by railroads in order to develop accurate schedules and to avoid collisions on the tracks. However, some countries do not use time zones. They use solar time, where clocks are set to noon each day when the sun is in the correct position. Time in a database is normally determined by the system clock. Databases that must interact over a network need to keep their clocks synchronized so that date and time information can be accurate across the distributed tables.

Each database that you work with will implement its own method of dealing with dates and times. The SQL-92 standard articulated standardized methods for handling date and time data; however, the standard is complex, and no database has completed an implementation of this standard in detail. As a result, you can expect the first valid date to differ across databases. A typical scheme for representing dates is to choose a starting date, and to represent each date forward from the reference date as a number incremented by one. This schema allows you to do date math simply, because you do the math with the underlying date numbers and convert back to a display form for the date when it is time to present the date in human readable form. Similar schemas are used for representing time values.

The critical issue for you is to discover the quirks of your implementation of date and time values. Microsoft SQL Server begins its dates at 1 January 1753 and ends them at 31 December 9999. Borland's Interbase and Microsoft Access use 1 January 100 as the starting date, and 31 December 5941 as the ending date. SQL Server is therefore going to cause you grief if you intend to store records relating to a medieval town that existed between the years 1100 and 1400. Interbase and Access won't have problems with such data.

In addition to knowing whether your SQL implementation can handle the dates you need to store, with databases like Interbase and Access, you need to know something about how calendar anomalies are handled. In Great Britain, for example, 2 September 1752 was followed not by 3 September, but by 14 September. If you need to use date math that occurs at this juncture, you need to have an understanding of how the anomalies are handled. Obviously, by starting at 1 January 1753, Microsoft has sidestepped a thorny date problem.

Because of the number of anomalies that can surround date and time data, you need to take lots of responsibility for managing the particular date anomalies associated with your data. If you are working with the year 1752, for example, you need to know whether you have data that relates to Great Britain in its cultural context, or to some other location. Other locations did not observe the foreshortened September that Britain did.

In general, if you are working with contemporary dates and times, you have far fewer problems. You can still find some cultural contexts where the time observed is not standardized by ISO. However, you can usually work around these problems elegantly, because such cultures will either observe UTC for database purposes or have a regimen by which the system clock is set correctly for the culture.

In general, you can expect to have DATE, TIME, and TIMESTAMP data types available. DATE and TIME are readily apparent, but TIMESTAMP may not be so immediately obvious. TIMESTAMP is a data type that is unique to the database. It combines date and time information with a signature unique to the database. Because of this signature, a timestamp on a row from database A will be different from a timestamp generated at the exact same time in database B. Such differences are useful when the database is managing transactions across multiple machines or time-sensitive updates across tables.

Your implementation will provide functions for doing date math and time math, for creating dates and times from numbers, for converting other data types to dates and times, and for converting dates and times to other data types. At this time, you cannot expect these functions to have been standardized.

With all this seeming chaos relating to dates and times, you need to focus on a few simple principles to avoid making errors with date and time data types. Here is a practical list:

▶ Know your cultural context. You need to be aware of holidays, resettings of the calendar, changes of calendar, and time synchronization customs. For the most part, you will have to develop your own methodologies for handling these curiosities. Chances are the database engine itself has ignored these issues or sidestepped these issues.

▶ For date or time gaps, such as the adjustment of the calendar in 1752, create a table that lists each date in the gap. You can check to see whether a date needs adjustment using a clause like WHERE SuspectDate IN (SELECT Date FROM DateAdjustmentTable). You can also store adjustment instructions or formulae in a column as well. Once you have identified a suspect date, you can quickly determine what to do with it.

▶ If you need to keep track of first and last days of the month, calculate the first day using a function like MAKEDATE. You can always tell what the first day of the month is because its day number is 1. For last days, build a table of last days that has a column for the month and a column for the last date. Look up the last day from this table when you need it.

▶ To handle leap years, create a table that lists all of the leap years for the foreseeable future. You can then test for leap years using the IN keyword and a subquery.

DESIGN TIP

You could also take the approach used by many financial databases, which is to keep a list of financial periods in a table. Each entry for a month has the appropriate number of days for the month. Each year has 12 entries in the table. Every fourth entry for February contains 29 days.

▶ When you store dates, use four-digit years and use the emerging standard of YYYYMMDD. Doing so makes date calculations more efficient.

▶ When you store times, use a twenty-four hour clock. You can easily convert to any other format, and doing time math with a twenty-four hour clock is more efficient. You don't have to convert to twenty-four hour format before calculating, or else figure the wraparounds between morning and afternoon.

▶ If you need to track starting and stopping dates or times, select the starting point and stopping points into a view or temporary table. There is no easy rule to apply in finding beginning and ending points. These relate to business rules that are context specific. Chances are, however, you will use the MIN function to find an early date or time, and the MAX function to find a later date or time. You will probably set limits on these functions using WHERE clauses.

▶ Once you know time interval boundaries, you can easily calculate the length of the interval, and check for contiguity of intervals. Length is simple date or time math done using the DATEADD function. Checking boundaries does not inherently require the use of cursors, but often using two cursors, one to hold the early interval and one to hold the late interval, simplifies the task of comparing the end of one boundary to the beginning of the other.

▶ Be flexible in using subqueries to pull out different date elements from the same table, or from different tables, in order to meet your needs.

Character Data Types

SQL offers a variety of string data types. You have at least CHAR for fixed-length strings and VARCHAR for variable-length strings. If you use a Unicode-aware database, you will have data types like NCHAR or NVARCHAR that represent Unicode characters instead of just ASCII characters.

CHAR stands for character, and you declare such a data type using CHAR(n), where n is the number of characters in the string. Such strings always have n number of characters. The string is padded with blanks to fill out the string. NCHAR stands for national character, and you declare the data type in the same way as CHAR. The critical difference is that NCHAR uses more bytes to store each character, so as to accommodate the various alphabets used in the world.

VARCHAR stands for variable character. You declare such values as VARCHAR(n), where n is the maximum number of characters the column or variable can hold. If the length of the string falls short of n, no padding takes place. Only the number of

Why Fixed-Width Strings So Often Appear

Databases of varying types have used fixed-width strings to store data. The normal procedure for using data stored in such fields is to retrieve the value, pass it through RTRIM, and then pass it through LTRIM. You would then have the data element you sought to retrieve. Data stored in such fields was always stored as character data of fixed width. The reason was that some systems used a fixed column width as a storage optimization strategy. Once you had the data, you had a string. If it represented some other type, you had to undertake an explicit conversion from string to the desired type. If automatic type conversion did not convert the desired type back to a string at storage time, you had to undertake that conversion yourself as well.

Obviously, the variable character data type helps to reduce the need for this strategy, as have improvements in database engine optimization strategies. However, you should not be surprised to find yourself working on such a database. Once fixed-width columns for data are implemented, retreating from the strategy is not easy. Either you must convert all of the active historical data to variable-length storage types, or you must have two different strategies for selecting and manipulating the data, one for the data prior to the conversion date, one for the data after the conversion date. You will be very lucky to have a single approach manipulate preconversion and postconversion data successfully.

The moral of this story is quite simple: make careful choices about data types at design time. Changes after the database is set up and functioning often come at great cost. Conversions are difficult to plan, and they are fraught with ad hoc decisions about unexpected conversion failures. Sometimes data elements refuse to convert properly, and you have to create a workaround. The workarounds can be as aggravating as the formats that you wish to abandon.

characters necessary is stored. NVARCHAR stands for national variable character, and it is declared in the same way as VARCHAR. The difference, of course, is that NVARCHAR uses enough bytes to store the Unicode characters that represent alphabets for all national languages.

If you are used to strings in programming languages, you are used to strings represented as arrays or as objects. C, for example, represents strings as an array. C#, Microsoft's new language offering, represents strings as objects. Each language compiler makes a choice about how to represent strings internally, and all string functions make use of this format to process strings efficiently.

You cannot expect this behavior from SQL. SQL sees strings as a set of characters that appear between single quotation marks, as in 'THIS IS A STRING.' Two single quotes represents a single quote within a string. While SQL does provide a series of string functions that can manage string data types, such as LEFT, RIGHT, and LEN, these functions are not using a standard method of representing strings. As a result, you can expect that each implementation of the SQL language has its own method of representing strings internally. The standard does not define what this representation should be.

Because the handling of strings is not standardized and relies on such a minimal specification of what a string is, you run into a variety of problems. For example, how should string equality be defined? In SQL, because the definition of a string is minimal, the answer relies on comparing length, and if length is equal, the characters position by position in the string. However, is 'and' equal to 'AND'? One argument would be that they are equal, since they represent the same word. Another argument would be that they are not equal, because they do not have the same characters in identical positions.

Databases handle these problems by implementing collation sequences. A typical solution, for example, is to choose dictionary sort order, in which upper- and lowercase characters don't count. This sort order defines 'and' as equal to 'AND.' However, you can use other collations, in which these two would not be defined as equal. Collation sequences have been defined for all national languages, and typically you can choose between case sensitivity and case insensitivity for your language. The sequence you choose not only affects string equality but also affects join behavior. If you join WHERE table1.column1 = table2.column2, your collation sequence will affect how the join behaves. Is table1.column1='and' and table2.column2='AND'? If you are case insensitive, the row will be included in the join. If you are case sensitive, the row will not be included. The moral of the story is to know what collation you are using.

In addition, the choice of CHAR or VARCHAR types will affect the way strings are ordered. A value that is CHAR(50) will always have 50 characters. As a result, the first rule for determining string equality for any two instances of data in such a column is always satisfied. Equality is always determined, therefore, by comparing the character positions in each string for equality. If you mix in data that is VARCHAR(50) and expect to compare for equality, CHAR(50) will always be unequal to VARCHAR(50), unless both strings have 50 characters and have the same characters in the same positions.

This equality factor will always affect how strings are ordered. VARCHAR(50) strings are likely to be ordered before CHAR(50) strings when you perform a GROUP BY or ORDER BY. And collation sequence will affect the ordering in both cases. You will have VARCHAR and CHAR having equal participation in ordering only when they have equal length. And then they will have to be ordered according to case-sensitive or case-insensitive collation.

NOTE

Collation sequences are available for most national languages and for many common sorting sequences within each national language.

With strings, you need to be aware of the nature of the values you are comparing, and the exact comparison methods. With databases like SQL Server 2000, where collation can be set by column, the exact rules for handling strings can change on a column-by-column basis. Because of these facts, if you are having problems with strings, suspect two sorts of issues. First, you might have a conflict between fixed- and variable-length strings. Second, you might have a collation issue.

Converting Data Types from One Database to Another

Imagine that your company has decided to move from SQL Server to Oracle, or from Oracle to MySQL, or from MySQL to Interbase. This does not seem, on the face of it, to be a major problem. You simply script the database, run the script to create the tables, and copy the data. That's what it seems. The reality is a bit more daunting.

Data types will cause you a problem. They are not standard, so what you call a CLOB in Oracle will not have that name in another database. Just as the name is not inherently standard, the length of the data type will not be standard. A CLOB in Oracle is a large object of character data. It may be up to 4GB in size. SQL Server has a data type for storing large objects of character data called the TEXT data type. It holds up to 2GB of data. For many projects, you just heave a sigh of relief because you don't store any single data element that even approaches the lower size limit. However, many organizations do. Part of the decision to change database engines has to be, therefore, a consideration of what data types you have in use and whether you are pushing the limits on data size.

In addition to the types of data, the ANSI code page on which the types are based can cause you significant problems. ANSI code pages have numbers that they were assigned prior to the time when the IBM PC first entered the market. Each code page represents a way of displaying characters. On the US code page (437), the hexadecimal value of 0xA5 represents the character N. On another code page, however, it might represent an entirely different character, say the yen sign. If you move data to a computer that runs another code page, you need to think about how you are going to translate from one page to another. ODBC drivers often translate between code pages for you. However, you cannot always expect this translation to be perfect. You need to examine this issue before you make the conversion, because errors will be both costly and time-consuming to correct once the data is moved.

NOTE

Moving data from Unicode to ANSI will also create translation problems.

Collation sequences will also affect how you plan to move data from one database engine to another. If you use the same collation sequences both before and after the move, you should have no trouble. You may wish, however, to take this opportunity to change the collation sequence, as in the case where a case-sensitive sort order would solve client problems. Not all collation sequences yield the same results when applied to the same data. If you shift from the US English sequence to the French sequence, for example, alphabetization rules will not be the same. The occasional character with an accent mark in the formerly US English data will be interpreted differently in the French collation sequence, because accent marks are not oddities in French. They are instead functional spellings, and they affect pronunciation. Since collation affects joins, you may find that data that joined correctly before the conversion no longer does.

Migrating data from one system to another requires careful planning and testing. You need to check subsets of each of your tables to see what is currently in use. Compare the data types in hand with the data types that will be in place after the migration, and look for the differences that will apply. You need especially to watch for overruns of the type sizes. If you are changing code pages, you need to migrate a small sample of your data that includes representative usage from the current code page. First, you need to examine the data to see if any characters have changed. Then, you need to try the routine procedures you use on the data to see if they all yield the expected results. Finally, if you are changing collation, you need to move a subset of your tables over, and you need to try all your standard queries out to see if the results are as expected. Once you have signed off on the results of all the tests, you are ready to migrate. On the way to this state of readiness, expect to put in place several data-scrubbing routines that correct for the surprises you encounter as you test migrating the data.

Summary

The emerging SQL standards create interesting issues relating to data types. You may run into conflicts in the way numbers are defined, especially relating to type conversions and calculation precedence. You can experience all sorts of conflicts with dates and times because dates and times are handled so many different ways in different cultures. You can run into difficulties with strings because of the loose definition of what a string is, and because of conflicts based on the collation sequence defined for the database.

Selecting Data

IN THIS CHAPTER:

The most natural action to take once data is stored in a database is to retrieve the data. Data retrieval is the domain of the SELECT statement. However, rarely do we wish to retrieve all the data at once. We usually prefer to retrieve a subset of the data that meets our needs at the current time. And we often prefer to have this subset summarized conveniently, showing us totals and averages. SQL allows you to perform each of these tasks using the SELECT statement.

The features you can employ to craft a SELECT, however, often lead to unexpected results. In fact, a SELECT statement can lead to one of two possible outcomes: either you receive the data you expected, or you are surprised by the data you receive. When you receive the second outcome, you of course have to trace your way through the SELECT declaration in order to find out why you have been surprised. Usually you find that your surprise is based on the database engine doing exactly what you asked it to do. The problem with computers is that they are very, very literal in their interpretation of statements. The problem with data engines is that they often contain features of which you are not aware. Both the literalness of interpretation and combinations of hidden features can lead to problems for selects.

We have mentioned examples of features that can cause problems for SELECT statements already. Collation order can have unintended effects. Suppose your WHERE clause looks like this:

```
WHERE ThisColumn = 'a'
```

You can expect to have problems if the collation sequence is not as you expected it to be. If your collation is not case sensitive, this clause will recognize both 'a' and 'A' as valid matches. If your collation is case sensitive, only 'a' will match. The difference can dramatically affect the size and character of the rowset returned.

Rounding method is another example. The following WHERE clause will be affected by the rounding procedure in effect:

```
WHERE ROUND(ThisColumn) = 5
```

If you are using scientific rounding, you can always expect that values of 4.5 through 5.4 will round to 5. If you are using a commercial rounding method, 4.5 will round up about half the time and round down the other half. Since an algorithm makes the selection of which to do, your query will return rowsets that are different on subsequent tries of the query. If you have 200 different values that could round, you can expect at least 400 different outcomes (actually, more). The number of possible outcomes is large enough that the results of successive runs of the query may seem random.

Literalness, of course, creates problems when your intentions in writing the query do not match exactly what the query says to do. The computer can understand only what the query says to do. Language processors have yet to develop algorithms for understanding intentions. When you get unexpected results, your first reaction ought to be to check for a mismatch between what you intended and what you said. This is the most likely cause for the problem. After you eliminate this possibility, you need to check for unexpected effects from features like those we have mentioned.

We will approach our review of possible problems and their solutions with SELECT by first examining the basic statement, looking for issues that can cause a conflict between your intentions and what the query literally says. Then we will look at some of the feature issues that can crop up, beyond those that we have just mentioned.

The Basic SELECT Statement

The basic SELECT statement has the following form:

```
SELECT ColumnList FROM ATable;
```

In place of ColumnList, you can use the wildcard *. When you do, you will return all the columns from the table.

The basic form of the SELECT statement causes few problems. If you want to return all columns from a table, use the wildcard. If you want to return a select group of columns from the table, use a column list, as in the following:

```
SELECT Column1, Column2, Column3 FROM MyTable;
```

In this case, you return the values of three columns from the table. You return all the rows from the table. This simple form of the SELECT statement is very straightforward and problem free.

When you start restricting the output of a SELECT statement, you begin to create situations that may not return the results that you expect. In general, you can restrict results by using aggregate functions, by using joins, or by using a WHERE clause.

Aggregates as Complicating Factors

Aggregate functions create complicating factors by introducing groups into your rowset. Groups are not inherently a problem, unless you are trying to summarize your data. That is, the following query does not inherently raise problems:

```
SELECT MAX(Column1) FROM MyTable;
```

While the MAX function introduces a group into the resultset, the group does not interfere with your understanding of the results. That is, you can count on receiving the maximum value stored in Column1 from MyTable. Nothing else will happen. The only group created in the data is the group of all records that returns the maximum value of Column1. For example, selecting the MAX value of lorange in the Pubs database offered by Microsoft as an example with SQL Server requires the following query:

```
SELECT MAX(lorange) FROM roysched
```

This query returns the following resultset:

```
Lorange
40001
```

Introducing other groupings, as in the following statement, usually does not cause problems:

```
SELECT MAX(lorange), MIN(hirange) FROM roysched
```

This query implies that we have grouped by both lorange and hirange. As a result, the data will be grouped by the values in lorange, and then by the values in hirange. The result of this operation will return the maximum value from lorange, which defines a group. From the group of values defined by MAX(lorange), MIN(hirange) will be defined. The value of MIN(hirange) is calculated from the group defined by MAX(lorange). For most cases, you will receive the maximum value of lorange, and the minimum value of hirange, as in the following resultset:

```
lorange     hirange
40001       1000
```

The data is first grouped by the possible maximum values of lorange. Then, from each possible maximum value of lorange, the minimum value of hirange will be returned.

As a result, we receive the minimum value of hirange only when the value of hirange is selected from the same group that the maximum value of lorange was selected from. In actual fact, there is only one solution to this set of groupings. We receive the minimum value of hirange because there is only one group defined by the maximum value of lorange, and it contains all the same data members that allow definition of the minimum value of hirange. This group has only one minimum value for hirange, which is the minimum value for this column.

Aggregate functions introduce groups into your data. The first aggregate function creates a group based on the value of that function. The second aggregate function returns a value based on the group defined by the first aggregate function. If you want the minimum value of Column2 where Column1 is at its maximum value, you have issued the correct query. If you want the maximum value of Column1 and the minimum value of Column2, no matter what groups have been formed, you are not guaranteed this result. To get the true minimum value of Column2, you should use a subquery, and avoid the grouping problem altogether. The query would take this form:

```
SELECT MAX(Column1), (SELECT MIN(Column2) FROM MyTable) FROM MyTable;
```

Under most circumstances, you do not need to worry about these interactions among aggregate groupings. For the most part, they work out correctly. Groupings can cause problems only when you are not aware of them. The most common situations where groupings can introduce unexpected effects is when you are dealing with nonaggregate elements. Such a scenario begins to play out when you have a query of this form:

```
SELECT MAX(Column2), Column3 FROM MyTable;
```

What happens under these circumstances is that you receive an error. You are informed that Column3 must be a part of an aggregate function or that it must be a part of a GROUP BY phrase. When you make Column3 a part of an aggregate function, the same factors come into play as in the previous examples. Chances are, the groupings will not have deleterious effects.

However, suppose you create a query of this form:

```
SELECT MAX(Column2), Column3 FROM MyTable GROUP BY Column3;
```

Here, you change the way that grouping takes place. Now Column3 defines a group, and the action of the aggregate function is changed. Notice the change in the resultset returned by the following query:

```
SELECT MAX(lorange), hirange FROM roysched GROUP BY hirange  .
```

This query returns the following results:

```
lorange                 hirange
0                       1000
1001                    2000
2001                    3000
3001                    4000
3001                    5000
4001                    6000
5001                    7000
6001                    8000
8001                    10000
10001                   12000
12001                   14000
10001                   15000
12001                   16000
16001                   20000
20001                   24000
20001                   25000
24001                   28000
25001                   30000
24001                   32000
30001                   35000
32001                   40000
40001                   50000
```

Notice that we have not received the maximum value of lorange. We have received 19 maximum values of lorange, the one associated with each group defined by the values of hirange. Hirange has 19 values associated with it, and grouping by this column creates 19 groups, each of which pairs with a maximum value of lorange. The roysched table has 86 rows. Within these rows, there are 19 unique values of hirange. The maximum value of lorange associated with each one of these 19 groups is the highest value of lorange associated with a given unique value of hirange that defines the group.

When you work with aggregate functions and groups, therefore, you need to be very aware of the granularity of the groups you define and their effect on the aggregates. A HAVING predicate used with an aggregate function can produce similar effects. Consider the following query, again based on the Pubs database:

```
SELECT COUNT(title_id) FROM sales HAVING SUM(qty) > 30
```

On the face of things, this query appears to return the count of title_id values associated with a sum of the qty values that is greater than 30. However, the result returned, the value 21, does not in fact meet this expectation. The table contains only 21 rows. It contains only 16 unique title_id values. Ten of these title_id values are associated with sales totals of less than 30. Clearly, something unexpected has happened.

What has happened is that the first aggregate function defined a group, the total of countable values of title_id in the database. The count is 21, the total number of values for this column in the database. HAVING seeks to apply to a group, and it applies to the group that the COUNT function defines. From this perspective, HAVING sums the qty column for this group. This sum will always be greater than 30, given the values of qty in the database.

DESIGN TIP

When you create groupings of data, explicitly define your groups using GROUP BY.
This methodology allows you to be more aware of what the groupings will return.

When you use aggregation and grouping, you need to be careful to define groups that are meaningful within the data. You should always use a GROUP BY phrase when you are planning to partition data into groups. You wish to leave nothing about grouping, whether enforced through aggregate functions or the GROUP BY phrase, to chance. Aggregations and groupings can have unintended effects.

Joins as Complicating Factors

Joins can also lead to unintended effects. Really, the only problem a join can create for you is selecting data the wrong way from a table that is party to the join. Join syntax can lead you into subtle delusions about what the join is doing, and you can easily wind up with null values, too few rows, or too many rows that you did not intend.

Join syntax comes in two forms, the first being the so-called old syntax that looks like this:

```
SELECT * FROM Table1, Table2 WHERE Table1.Value = Table2.Value
```

In this query, you are asking for all the rows from both tables where the Value columns are equal. If the Value columns are not equal, that row pairing between the two tables is not returned. This type of join is called an *inner join.* If you need to return all the values from one table, regardless of whether there is a matching row in the other table, you place a plus (+) sign following the table name that needs to return all rows. This type of join is called an *outer join.*

NOTE

Some SQL databases allow only one table to return all rows per query. Under these circumstances, you sometimes have to frame queries wisely to get the results you need, working around this constraint.

The problem with this original join syntax is that it is terse. It is hard to look at the query and immediately perceive what type of join is in force. As a consequence, you can easily create queries that return unexpected rows. The SQL-92 standard addresses this problem by providing a more explicit join syntax, as follows:

```
SELECT * FROM Table1 INNER JOIN Table2 ON Table1.Value = Table2.Value
```

Note that the notion of a join is explicitly mentioned, and the type of join is explicitly mentioned. These facts help to cut down the mental clutter that can confuse you about what relationship the join establishes. Outer joins are of three types, depending on whether you want all the rows from the leftmost table mentioned in the join syntax, all the rows from the rightmost table in the join syntax, or all the rows from both tables, as these three queries demonstrate:

```
SELECT * FROM Table1 LEFT OUTER JOIN Table2
   ON Table1.Value = Table2.Value

SELECT * FROM Table1 RIGHT OUTER JOIN Table2
   ON Table1.Value = Table2.Value

SELECT * FROM Table1 FULL OUTER JOIN Table2

   ON Table1.Value = Table2.Value
```

Even with these enhancements, joins are likely to produce four kinds of unexpected results, each of which has a direct cause and an easy resolution:

▶ You receive null values in a join where you are not expecting them. The cause is that you are undertaking an outer join of some type where you did not intend to undertake one. Change the join to an inner join, and the null values should disappear.

▶ You receive fewer rows than expected. The cause is that you are undertaking an inner join when you intended an outer join. Change the join to an outer join that returns all the rows from the table you expected all the rows to return from.

▶ You receive more rows than expected. You are conducting an outer join when you did not intend to do so. Change the join to an inner join to remove the unwanted rows.

▶ You are receiving rows that do not represent valid data. You have created a join that constructs rows that do not represent valid pairings of data. You have joined on a value that produces the invalid pairings of rows between the tables. Reevaluate the value used in the join, and also verify the integrity of the data in the column.

WHERE Clauses as Complicating Factors

WHERE clauses are the normal means that you use to filter data returned from a table. You don't need a listing of all the rows in a table. You need, for example, only those rows where the Active column contains a value that evaluates to TRUE. WHERE clauses have this syntax:

```
SELECT * FROM Table1 WHERE Value = expression
```

WHERE clauses can only go wrong when the expression does not represent all the rows that you intended to select, or it represents more rows than you intended to select. Unfortunately, perceiving these differences is often difficult. How often do you check the 200,000 rows returned from a financial table to make sure that each row bears a date later than the expressed date, as in this query:

```
SELECT * FROM ClosingDetails WHERE ClosingDate > '2000/03/12'
```

The usual practice is that we take it on faith that we have expressed the query correctly and that it has returned all the right rows. Quality assurance practitioners, however, can show us that oftentimes this assumption is invalid.

Putting every query you write through quality assurance testing is often impractical. However, you can implement practical checks that do not require the visual inspection of each row returned to verify that your expectations are being met. You should construct corroborating queries to verify expectations.

In the preceding query, reverse the inequality sign and note the number of rows returned. Then, use a query like the following to get a count of all the rows:

```
SELECT COUNT(*) FROM ClosingDetails
```

Do the math to verify that the total number of rows minus the number of rows returned by the query in question matches the number of rows returned from the query with the inequality sign reversed. Such an approach does not take much time, and it does help you to trap errors that are typographical, the result of too much coffee, or the result of working on the project under too much pressure. Inattention can arise from many sources. Applying queries to check queries helps to trap the errors that arise from inattention.

NOTE

Quality assurance testing is never inappropriate, especially for queries that support mission-critical reports.

A Look at a Complex Query

Let's examine a complex SELECT statement to see just how complicated selecting data can become. Imagine that you are writing reports for a medical facility in which patients can stay for long periods of time. The weight of a patient is critical information, because changes in weight signal possible health problems. Because of this fact, patients are weighed weekly.

Weight trends are significant over both the short term and the long term. The report needs to show the weight trend over a period of several months. Such health facilities therefore track weight over a period of six months or so to see whether a patient is maintaining a stable weight, or whether weight is gradually increasing or decreasing. They also track weight weekly over the last month, checking for precipitous changes in weight. The goal is for a patient to maintain a stable body weight. Either sudden changes or slowly accumulating changes can indicate problems.

To present a picture of patient weights, you need to select the last month's weekly weights and the last several months' weights in order to present them for comparison in a report. Imagine that you have a centralized database for all your facilities. In this database, you have a Patient table that holds patient information and has PatientID for its primary key, a Facility table that holds facility information and has FacilityNumber as its primary key, and a PatientWeightHistory table that holds weights for patients. PatientID is a foreign key in the PatientWeightHistory table, and FacilityNumber is a foreign key in the Patient table.

The definition of the Patient table looks something like this:

```
CREATE TABLE [dbo].[Patient] (
     [PatientID] [int] NOT NULL ,
     [FirstName] [nvarchar] (20) NULL ,
     [MiddleInitial] [nvarchar] (1) NULL ,
     [LastName] [nvarchar] (35) NULL ,
     [BirthDate] [datetime] NULL ,
     [SSN] [nvarchar] (11) NULL ,
     [Gender] [nvarchar] (1) NULL ,
--Lots of other patient information would appear here
     [MedicaidNum] [nvarchar] (14) NULL ,
     [MedicareNum] [nvarchar] (12) NULL ,
     [AdmitDate] [datetime] NULL ,
     [AdmissionWeight] [int] NULL ,
     [FacilityNumber] [int] ,
     [NursingStation] [nvarchar] (8) NULL ,
     [Bed] [nvarchar] (10) NULL ,
     [MedicalRecordNumber] [nvarchar] (20) NULL
)
```

The definition of the Facility table looks roughly like this:

```
CREATE TABLE [dbo].[Facility] (
     [FacilityNumber] [int] NOT NULL ,
     [FacilityName] [nvarchar] (50) NULL ,
     [AddressLine1] [nvarchar] (30) NULL ,
     [AddressLine2] [nvarchar] (30) NULL ,
     [City] [nvarchar] (50) NULL ,
     [State] [nvarchar] (2) NULL ,
     [Zip] [nvarchar] (10) NULL ,
     [Phone] [nvarchar] (20) NULL ,
     [Fax] [nvarchar] (20) NULL
--Lots of other facility information would appear here
)
```

The PatientWeightHistory table looks like this:

```
CREATE TABLE [dbo].[ PatientWeightHistory] (
     [PatientID] [int] NOT NULL ,
     [MonthAndYear] [datetime] NOT NULL ,
     [Week1Weight] [int] NULL ,
     [Week2Weight] [int] NULL ,
     [Week3Weight] [int] NULL ,
```

```
        [Week4Weight] [int] NULL ,
        [Week5Weight] [int] NULL ,
)
```

An important matter to note is that the PatientWeightHistory table is a list of records in which each record holds one month of data. Each record includes five possible weekly weights, in order to accommodate the four months of the year that include five-week endpoints. The fact that one month can contain five weights while other months can contain only four creates a difficulty in retrieving the data and performing math on the data. Let's assume that in tracking the weekly weights for the last month, doctors want to see differences in pounds from week to week. We need to be able to tell whether we are using Week 5 for the calculation for the current month, and we need to be able to tell whether, in calculating the change for the first week of the month, we are subtracting Week 5 or Week 4 from the previous month from Week 1 of the current month.

The structure of the PatientWeightHistory table also requires that we use either subqueries or self-joins to retrieve the weights for the previous months. We can assume that in tracking weights over several months we will arbitrarily choose one week as the reference week for that month. Since each month has a Week 1, we will use that weight as the reference weight for tracking weights over several months. We cannot retrieve the weight for a previous month in the same table scan that retrieves the Week 1, Week 2, Week 3, Week 4, and Week 5 weights for the current month. The current month's weights are determined using a WHERE clause that matches the most recent PatientWeightHistory record with the result of GETDATE(). Weights for previous months must be retrieved by using DATEADD() to subtract month numbers from the result of GETDATE(). Either we must retrieve the historical information using subqueries, each with an appropriate WHERE clause, or we must join PatientWeightHistory to itself one time for each historical month to be retrieved and set the join conditions so that we retrieve the appropriate historical record.

Either choice has penalties. Joins are usually faster than subqueries. However, each time you join a table to itself, each row on the left side of the join is paired with each valid row on the right side of the join. Typically, this operation results in the pairing of one row on the left with more than one row on the right. You must use multiple join conditions to limit the number of rows returned. Since our query must return six or more months of historical data, the join logic for the operation will be long and complex. Furthermore, telling whether you have made a mistake with your join logic will be difficult. Patients who maintain a stable weight might have the same number for several consecutive weeks and months. How can you tell whether you accidentally pulled July's weight when you meant to pull the June weight? For such situations, subqueries provide more readable logic, and you can test subqueries independently of the main query. Because you can compartmentalize testing in this fashion, you have an easier time telling whether you are retrieving the right data. You can request multiple fields, MonthAndYear and Week1Weight, for example, in the subquery as you test it to verify your results. You can then drop the unneeded fields when you merge the subquery with the main query.

So you have a choice, speed or verifiability? When I was confronted by this possibility in working with a client, I chose verifiability because I found that indexing the tables on their keys improved speed enough to make performance acceptable. Here is the version of the weekly weight query that uses subqueries to retrieve and process historical monthly weights:

```
SELECT Patient.PatientID, Lastname + ', ' + Firstname
   + ' ' + Middleinitial as PatientName, FacilityName
   GETDATE(), AdmissionWeight, Week1Weight, Week2Weight,
   Week3Weight, Week4Weight, Week5Weight,

--These subqueries get previous week 1 weights from the
--7 previous months for each patient.
   (SELECT Week1Weight FROM PatientWeightHistory
      WHERE PatientWeightHistory.MonthAndYear = DATEADD(m, -1, GETDATE())
      AND PatientWeightHistory.PatientID = Patient.PatientID)
      AS PreviousWeight1,
   (SELECT Week1Weight FROM PatientWeightHistory
      WHERE PatientWeightHistory.MonthAndYear = DATEADD(m, -2, GETDATE())
      AND PatientWeightHistory.PatientID = Patient.PatientID)
      AS PreviousWeight2,
   (SELECT Week1Weight FROM PatientWeightHistory
      WHERE PatientWeightHistory.MonthAndYear = DATEADD(m, -3, GETDATE())
      AND PatientWeightHistory.PatientID = Patient.PatientID)
      AS PrevioiusWeight3,
   (SELECT Week1Weight FROM PatientWeightHistory
      WHERE PatientWeightHistory.MonthAndYear = DATEADD(m, -4, GETDATE())
      AND PatientWeightHistory.PatientID = Patient.PatientID)
      AS PreviousWeight4,
   (SELECT Week1Weight FROM PatientWeightHistory
      WHERE PatientWeightHistory.MonthAndYear = DATEADD(m, -5, GETDATE())
      AND PatientWeightHistory.PatientID = Patient.PatientID)
      AS PreviousWeight5,
   (SELECT Week1Weight FROM PatientWeightHistory
      WHERE PatientWeightHistory.MonthAndYear = DATEADD(m, -6, GETDATE())
      AND PatientWeightHistory.PatientID = Patient.PatientID)
      AS PreviousWeight6,
   (SELECT Week1Weight FROM PatientWeightHistory
```

```
      WHERE PatientWeightHistory.MonthAndYear = DATEADD(m, -7, GETDATE())
      AND PatientWeightHistory.PatientID = Patient.PatientID)
      AS PreviousWeight7,

--These lines calculate the difference in weight for
--the last five weeks.
   Week5Weight - Week4Weight AS ChangeInPounds1,
   Week4Weight - Week3Weight AS ChangeInPounds2,
   Week3Weight - Week2Weight AS ChangeInPounds3,
   Week2Weight - Week1Weight AS ChangeInPounds4,
   Week1Weight -  (SELECT CASE
                WHEN Week5Weight > 0 THEN Week5Weight
                ELSE Week4Weight
                END  FROM PatientWeightHistory
                WHERE PatientWeightHistory.MonthAndYear =
                   DATEADD(m, -1, GETDATE())
             AND PatientWeightHistory.PatientID = Patient.PatientID)
             AS ChangeInPounds5


FROM Patient INNER JOIN PatientWeightHistory
   ON Patient.PatientID = PatientWeightHistory.PatientID
   INNER JOIN Facility ON Patient. FacilityNumber = Facility.FacilityNumber

WHERE DATEPART(m, PatientWeightHistory.MonthAndYear) =
   DATEPART(m, GETDATE())
   AND DATEPART(yy, PatientWeightHistory.MonthAndYear) =
   DATEPART(yy, GETDATE())

--Order the data by Lastname
   ORDER BY Patient.Lastname
```

Note that there are a couple of additional issues in this query. First, the CASE predicate was used to condition the calculation of the difference between the Week 1 weight in the current month and the Week 4 or Week 5 weight of the previous month. If there is no Week 5 in a month, the weight for that week will be zero or NULL. Basically, the logic is to use the Week 5 if it has a value; if Week 5 has no value, use Week 4.

Second, note that the use of GETDATE() to determine the current month assumes that you will run the query on the correct day to match the result of GETDATE() with PatientWeightHistory.MonthAndYear under some circumstances. We are also assuming that the MonthAndYear datetime value will have a conventional day associated with it, such as the first day of the month. When we work with DATEADD() in the queries, we are often assuming that the day portion of the date is identical between the

MonthAndYear value and the result of GETDATE(). If we cannot make this assumption, then we have to dissect MonthAndYear and the result of GETDATE() into month and year values as we do in the WHERE clause for the general query in order to match records correctly.

Constructing this SELECT query involves us in making many choices that have potential consequences. Some of these choices are forced upon us by the nature of the data and the business context in which we are working. Others are forced upon us by practicality and the need for optimization of the query. In general, the risks we faced in this select were:

▶   Making a mistake with the date logic, and so selecting the wrong weight value

▶   Making a mistake in difference calculations by using the wrong weight value from the previous month

▶   Making a mistake in query optimization by using subqueries rather than joins

▶   Making a mistake in selecting a weight value by choosing the join option and then setting the join conditions incorrectly

A Few Practical Suggestions

When you work with the SELECT statement, cultivate these habits:

▶   Wherever possible, use column lists. Extract only the data you need to help performance.

▶   If you use aggregate functions, be aware that they create a group. Run other queries that get the same data or a complement to the data to make sure that your aggregate calculations are getting the values you expect.

▶   Never use a HAVING predicate without using a GROUP BY. You want to know what grouping your HAVING predicate attaches to in order to perform its work.

▶   Diagram your joins. Make certain you know which table is on the left and which table is on the right.

▶   Wherever possible, use the SQL-92 join syntax. This syntax causes you to express the type of join you are creating, and forces the name of the left-hand table to be on the left and the name of the right-hand table to be on the right.

▶ Be wary of joining a table to itself. Such joins, while possible, often produce spurious rows in the resultset.

▶ Remember that outer joins often introduce null values into a resultset. Be prepared to handle these values when you work with the results.

▶ Express your WHERE conditions carefully. Check them twice before accepting them as correct.

▶ Run queries that get data complementary to that returned by your WHERE condition in order to verify that your WHERE clause is performing as you expect it to.

In general, working with SELECT is straightforward. Because it is straightforward, however, the types of bugs that appear are fairly insidious. They are the type that, once you see them, you realize how obvious they really are. If you keep to these habits, you will be able to see the obvious with reasonable ease.

Summary

In this chapter, we have focused on troubleshooting SELECT statements, showing you some of the most common problems that may come into play. In general, you need to be careful of the way you work with aggregates and grouping. You need to express joins carefully. And you need to run simple checks to reveal whether your WHERE clauses are in fact behaving as expected. We will return to the issue of working with SELECT later when we discuss joins and subqueries in Chapters 12 and 13, respectively.

Inserting Data

IN THIS CHAPTER:

The only standardized way to add data to a database is the INSERT statement. Vendors typically supply some sort of bulk load program so that large amounts of data can be added, as when you convert from one database to another and need to load hundreds of thousands of rows all at once to a table. These programs, however, are vendor specific. You will usually find a bulk copy program that runs from a command prompt. You may find stored procedures that handle bulk inserts. Or you may find programs that use ODBC drivers to allow movement of data from any ODBC-compliant data source to another. The humble INSERT statement is the only method defined in the SQL standards.

Using INSERT seems as though it would not be terribly dangerous or problematic. You add a row. If you don't like what you have done, you have the information to delete the row. Under most circumstances, these statements accurately describe working with SQL data. However, several factors can conspire to complicate this scenario.

Consider, for example, what happens if duplicate rows creep into the database. Such a scenario is not difficult to encounter. SQL databases do not require the use of primary keys. Everyone agrees that you should use primary keys on your tables. However, as a consultant, I have worked with many tables for which this convention was overlooked. I've also encountered many tables the "key" for which was managed by a program, and it was the program's responsibility to make certain that the key value was unique. On at least one occasion, the program read the maximum key value and failed to increment it properly before storing the new value. Duplicate rows appeared. Using a true primary key managed by the database would have caused a constraint violation error and would have prevented the duplication. But this database resided on a client system, file-based database in its primary form. This data was then copied back to a SQL Server database nightly. To simplify the copy, the primary key constraint was removed.

Duplicate rows can be fiendish. You can encounter situations in which the database will refuse to delete a duplicate because it cannot uniquely identify the row. Normally, DELETE will delete anything that matches its criteria, both single rows and multiple rows. Some implementations and some table structures can produce this problem. Furthermore, you may find deleting exact duplicates to be an unwanted operation. Other tables may depend on the duplicate row for a lookup, and you may not wish to remove the row at all while other users are issuing queries against the database.

On the other hand, duplicate rows in lookup tables can cause subqueries to fail. Often, subqueries must return one and only one value, or the main query fails. In this context, both the presence of duplicate rows and the operations necessary to remove the duplicates can cause problems. If several duplicates have crept in, the maintenance necessary to correct the problem may require that the data be unavailable for an extended period of time. Taking a database down for an hour of maintenance means losing an hour of productivity for someone. Downtime always translates to increased costs somehow.

Using INSERTs properly is therefore important, but even more important is creating a database environment where properly functioning INSERT statements cannot cause problems. Building this kind of environment requires careful planning and database design, as well as good SQL programming habits.

The Basic INSERT Statement

The INSERT statement has two basic forms:

```
INSERT INTO MyTable (Columns) VALUES (Values)
INSERT INTO MyTable (Columns) SELECT Columns FROM AnotherTable
```

In the first form of the statement, *Columns* represents a comma-delimited list of the column names that should receive the values. *Values* represents a comma-delimited list of values. In the second form of the query, *Columns* is the comma-delimited list of target columns. The SELECT statement can be replaced with any valid SELECT statement that you can create.

The INSERT statement knows what value to insert into which column using a very simple algorithm. The first column on the list receives the first value, the second column receives the second value, and so on until you run out of column-value pairings. This algorithm can lead to two common sources of errors.

Especially when inserting a query to return the values, the query may not return as many columns as you expected. Your INSERT fails, therefore, because there are more columns in the list of target columns than there are columns containing values to insert. This error is less likely to occur when you are framing the query, because you will receive the error as you work with the INSERT statement and immediately correct the problem. This error is more likely to cause problems after the query is framed and used as a stored procedure, or embedded in a program. The INSERT will work just fine for months and then suddenly stop working. The source of the error lies not with the query, but the context in which it runs. Someone has changed the structure of the source table, not realizing that a query somewhere depends on it. And suddenly that query breaks.

Typically, you find in SQL implementations that you can omit the column list in the INSERT statement so long as you provide the values in the exact order in which the columns appear in the table. Such abbreviated INSERTs can work just fine for awhile and then suddenly break. Again, the problem lies not with the query, but with the underlying tables. A change to the destination table can break the abbreviated INSERT. Assume that for some reason there is a need for a new column in the destination table. The column is appended to the others, so it is in the last position. SQL does not start with the first column, inserting values in sequence, and then ignore the additional column. It throws an error when it encounters the extra column for which it has no value.

DESIGN TIP

When you have to add columns for an existing table, be sure to specify a default value for the column. If an INSERT has no value for the column, the default value will be placed in the column, and an abbreviated INSERT will not fail.

If all columns in a table have default values, you can create a row with all default values using an INSERT statement of this form:

```
INSERT INTO MyTable DEFAULT VALUES
```

This form of the statement is especially useful where a record starts out with values that start at a threshold level and then change values as time goes on, as in a record that contains the values returned from several instruments that measure temperature and humidity in the rooms of an art gallery. You might have a set of tables that represent hourly observations of temperature and humidity in each room. The table for a given hourly observation would contain columns for date, time, temperature, and humidity. If each receives a default value, the program that manages the instrumentation can update the appropriate columns as necessary with observations. If you detect default values for one of the instrumentation readings, you know that the instrument had failed.

Inserting into Multiple Tables

As much as we might wish to, INSERT does not allow you to add data to multiple tables. While UPDATE allows a FROM clause that enables you to define a complex data set based on multiple tables that can govern what values are updated, INSERT allows only one table as a target. You can select data to insert from multiple tables using this form of the INSERT statement:

```
INSERT INTO MyTable SELECT *
   FROM SomeOtherTable JOIN YetAnotherTable
```

The SELECT statement that defines the values to insert can be any legal SELECT statement. It can involve multiple joins, lots of subqueries, and whatever else you desire. Our main point is that the complexity of this statement follows MyTable. You can only have a single table as the insert target.

When you have to insert data into multiple tables, you must partition the data into the rowsets that belong to individual tables yourself. For example, if you need to add data to a table and to a bridging table that relates to it, you must break down these actions into two INSERT statements. If you consider the Pubs database that Microsoft offers as an example with SQL Server, when you add an author to the database, you do so with the assumption that you have to add contract information about at least one title that the author is working on. Because of this fact, not only must you add the author's information to the author table, but you must also add an entry to the title_author table, and an entry to the titles table. Your client program that governs this data input must collect the required information. The SQL behind this program must have INSERT statements of the following form behind the Insert button (keep in mind that you need to substitute actual values in the VALUES clause to do any real insertions):

```
INSERT INTO authors
(au_id, au_lname, au_fname,
phone, address, city,
state, zip, contract)
VALUES
(authored, authorlname, authorfname,
phone, address, city,
state, zip, contract)

INSERT INTO titles
(title_id, title, type,
pub_id, price, advance,

Royalty, ytd_sales, notes, pub_date)
VALUES
(titleid, title, type,
pubid, price, advance,
royalty, NULL, notes, pub_date)

INSERT INTO title_author
(au_id, titele_id, au_odr, royaltyper)
VALIUES
(auid, titleid, NULL, NULL)
```

Obviously, inserting data is not a trivial issue when it involves multiple tables. If you have followed this example carefully, you have noted a couple of facts. First, there are foreign key constraints involved. That is, the title_author table is expecting to receive only values that have already been added to titles and authors. The specific fields involved are au_id and title_id. The other fields in this table can accept null values, but these fields must already exist in the other tables. Because of this fact, you must order your inserts to meet the demands of this constraint. Data must be inserted into titles and authors first, then into the title_author table.

DESIGN TIP

As the INSERT operation grows in complexity, you must be careful to order the steps in the process to achieve the desired result. If your queries do not achieve the desired results, check the order of your INSERTs carefully.

Common Complicating Factors

The average INSERT statement can encounter complicating factors. Some of these factors relate to the design of the INSERT statement, some relate to the design of the database, some relate to constraints. Other factors that can create problems are the use of null values, missing values, or multiple values. Each of these problems has a solution. Who implements the solution depends on who has the security authority in relation to the database to implement the solution.

Database Design

INSERTS can fail because of inadequate database design. A case that demonstrates this factor is a client who used a non-SQL database at the client site, and a SQL database at their home site to support a Web site. Data was copied from the client database to the SQL database on a daily basis. The copy, of course, required that one INSERT per row copied had to take place. In the non-SQL database, there were no constraints. The clients could enter anything into the database, subject to the rules of validation imposed by the client program. The critical issues that arose in this context related to keys, sort orders, and client innovations.

Keys created a problem because the client database, which optimized the file system for storing data in files, really did not care about keys. The SQL database that supported the Web site had to care about keys. The client database included a USER table, which listed all the users allowed to use the database over the Internet. To access the database via the centralized Web site, you had to have an entry in this table. At the centralized database, the USER table was replicated. Because of the replication, the USER table required a primary key. The difficulty in assigning a primary key lay in the fact that users at the client site had not respected the normal primary key constraint.

At the client site, the database often contained a blank user. This was a user who had no user name, no user password, and no user characteristics. For the client, such a user was a great convenience. When you start your software, you simply press ENTER when a login dialog box appears. You are into the system, you can do what you want, and you don't have to mess with a user login.

At the central database that supports the Web site, the database could not support a blank user. Replication had to be supported. Each user had to have a primary key value. A NULL primary key was not accepted. To allow the client database to import into the Web site database, some sort of primary key had to be created for the USER table. The solution was to provide an identity column for the USER table at the Web site database. As the data was imported from the client site, the USER table was imported as is, with the addition of the identity column, which provided default values. The USER table at the Web site could therefore support unique identification of rows. The users at the client site could continue to support the unknown user. Basically, the Web site database isolated the problem row by giving it an identity value. Imports did not fail because of the violation of a primary key constraint. However, the Web site never used the blank user isolated using this technique. In this way, the two databases could carry out their respective missions. Their designs were incompatible on the face of the facts. However, special mappings allowed the two databases to map columns from one to the other without obstruction.

Database design can create a variety of complicating factors. Cataloging all the possibilities is nearly impossible. The best way to avoid such problems is to think carefully about design at the outset. You can head off most problems if you adopt these design and programming practices:

▶ Use multipart keys based on actual data instead of identity columns wherever possible. Be aware that an identity column can cause an INSERT to fail if you attempt to insert an identity value.

▶ Avoid the use of null values in columns. Improper handling of nulls can also cause an INSERT to fail.

▶ Provide default values for columns wherever possible. Even if a column is not present in an INSERT because you have used no column list, the INSERT will not fail if the column has a default value.

▶ Choose your collation order wisely, and live with the consequences. If you are case insensitive and try to use a case-sensitive key, an INSERT can fail if a lowercase key value has a corresponding uppercase value already in the table (and vice versa).

▶ Limit your use of constraints, or document them thoroughly for everyone who must frame queries. Constraint violations cause INSERT statements to fail. Check constraints are often the most maddening constraints to work around, because you may guess every possible format except the one that the database designer put in place.

▶ Use a SELECT to check whether a row already exists in a table before you attempt an INSERT. This strategy is useful with bridging tables, where all the columns participate in a primary key constraint, a foreign key constraint, or a uniqueness constraint. A multipart INSERT operation of the type discussed earlier in this chapter can fail on the third INSERT statement if the row linking one table to the other already exists in the bridging table. (Remember, you can add rows independently to title, author, and titleauthor. There are no foreign key constraints in place, only the primary key constraint on each table. Someone could add a row to titleauthor without making certain to add related rows in the other two tables.)

▶ Wrap insert operations that insert into multiple tables in a transaction. If you experience a failure, you at least know that the entire operation failed and you are not left with tables that are in an inconsistent state.

▶ Be sure to match the data type of the column to the data type of the value you are trying to insert. Type mismatch errors can and do occur, and they will prevent you from inserting data.

Constraints

Constraints can cause an INSERT statement to fail quite handily. Before anyone has worked with SQL for very long, they have seen the error message "Operation failed because of primary key constraint violation" or "Operation failed because of foreign key constraint violation." You can also see similar errors for check constraints and uniqueness constraints. These errors always translate into one of these conditions:

▶ You tried to insert a value, and you shouldn't have tried.

▶ You tried to insert a value, and it was already there.

▶ You tried to insert a value, and it was not present in another table where it had to be.

▶ You tried to insert a value, but it was in the wrong format.

Trying when you should not have tried usually relates to an identity column, whether used as a key value or simply as a counter. Identity values are usually managed by the database engine. You set the column properties so that the column is an identity column, you provide the seed value at which the column starts its values, and you provide the increment added to the previous value to generate the next value. The column cannot accept null values, and its next value is automatically generated. If you attempt to insert a value into this column, you will receive an error. Quite simply put, if you create an identity column, don't insert to it. You are not allowed to.

DEBUGGING TIP

Most databases provide a property that you can toggle on and off and that will allow you to insert a value into an identity column. This property is useful when you have to merge data from another database that has identity values within it and you wish to preserve those values.

Trying to insert a value when it is already there is a problem that arises when you duplicate the value of a primary key, and an error that you violated a primary key constraint gets returned. (A similar error occurs when you have a uniqueness constraint on a column and the value is already present.) This error will sometimes surprise you. It can relate to issues of case sensitivity and collation, but such errors mainly arise from inattention on your part. Typically, you are inserting into a lookup table or a bridging table, thinking the values were not there, when you already have them present. Another possibility is that your primary key is not correctly formed and does not provide true unique identification of rows. The solution in this case is to add a column to the primary key to guarantee uniqueness. Yet another possibility is that you have been overzealous in applying a uniqueness constraint when you truly should not do so. In this case, the solution is to drop the uniqueness constraint.

Violation of a foreign key constraint is the error that arises when you attempt to insert a value in one table when it is not first present in another table. The usual source of this error is working with inserts to multiple tables. You break down the insert operation into separate INSERT statements, and you follow the order that is most salient to your thinking when you build the statements. The problem is that this order is not always the order the database engine needs for the inserts. You need to reorder the inserts so that the foreign key is inserted in its primary location prior to inserting it into the table where it functions as foreign key. Of course, there is always the possibility that you forgot to frame one of the INSERT statements that you should have framed.

Check constraints will inform you when the value you want to insert is in the wrong format. A common practice is to store telephone numbers in a text column. Because data entry operators will be very creative with the use of dashes, periods, and parentheses—all common delimiters for a telephone number—database administrators put a check constraint on the column to make sure that the telephone number is in the preferred format, whatever the organization decides is the appropriate format. If you are coming to the database without much experience and no documentation, you will probably find out what the preferred format is after you receive an error announcing that you have violated the constraint. The solution, of course, is to find the correct format and use it.

Null Values

Null values can create problems in an insert. The first scenario is a column that cannot take a null value. If you leave this column out of your INSERT statement, two types of events can occur. First, the database attempts to insert a null value for the column because you have supplied no value. It checks the column properties and finds that it cannot insert a null value, but it does find that you have supplied a default value, and so the database engine inserts the default value for the column. In this case, you have no problem. However, another possibility exists. The database attempts to insert a null value in this column, finds that the column properties do not allow it to do so, but finds no default value available. The database therefore returns an error. In this scenario, you must add the column to your INSERT statement and provide an appropriate value for the column.

   This scenario plays itself out very commonly when the source of the offending null value is masked by a subquery that returns the data to be inserted. An INSERT of this form effectively hides the true values of the columns from your view:

```
INSERT INTO MyTable
SELECT Column1, Column2, Column3 FROM AnotherTable
```

Since you are not listing the values themselves in this INSERT, you do not see a NULL appearing in the values list very easily. Nor do you see the column properties in the two tables readily. AnotherTable may allow null columns. MyTable may not. When a NULL returns in the SELECT, it will cause a problem in MyTable if at least one column disallows null values.

   What is most maddening about problem null values is that your queries can run correctly under many, if not most, circumstances, only to break mysteriously one day. What allows this scenario to play out is that normally AnotherTable is populated with data values—not nulls—when INSERT statements take place against it. A moment's inattention in one INSERT can allow a NULL to creep into the table. Eventually, that NULL will be returned by the SELECT, surprising you.

Missing Values

Missing values can cause problems with the INSERT statement in a direct way and an indirect way. The direct way is for you to leave the column list out of an INSERT and to supply too few values to match the number of columns in the table. SQL does not insert the values one by one until it runs out of columns and stops. SQL will attempt to insert the values into the columns one by one until it runs out of columns, and then it will check the properties of the remaining columns. If the columns have default values, the default values will be inserted. If the columns don't have default values, SQL returns an error. This error usually gets you after your INSERT statement has been working properly for some time, and then surprisingly stops working. The reason is that someone has added a column to the table, changing the way your INSERT statement interacts with the table.

Another way that missing values can affect an INSERT statement is when a subquery fails to return a value for use with the insert. In this case, a NULL returns, and you are thrown into one of the NULL value scenarios we have just described.

Multiple Values

Sometimes an INSERT statement will surprise you by inserting more than you expected into a table. This scenario arises when you are using a SELECT to acquire the values to insert, and you are expecting only one record to return. No matter how carefully you thought through the conditions on the select, you suddenly get more than one value. Your INSERT statement will not set limits on the amount to insert from the rowset returned by SELECT. It simply inserts all the values returned.

Normally, you would not experience a problem with the extra data. You probably wanted to insert all the rows returned, even though you were expecting only one. However, getting more rows than expected can push you into a scenario where a NULL value appears and causes problems. If a join in the SELECT statement causes extra rows to appear in the resultset, you may be inserting duplicate rows that you do not want to insert. These extra rows could push you into a constraint violation, because they will be exact duplicates.

Examining a Complex INSERT Statement

To get a sense of how complex an insert statement can be, let's take a look at a complex one to see what kinds of complications we you might need to look for. The following INSERT statement inserts data into a temporary table whose rows will eventually build a report. The temporary table holds the ID of a sales outlet, the sale date, the ID of the source of the data (such as product category, vendor source, or similar information), and the sum of the sales amount associated with this data source:

```
-- Create temporary table which will hold the summary information
CREATE TABLE #BusFactSaleSum
 (outlet_id varchar(10),
 sale_date smalldatetime,
 data_source_ID varchar(30),
 sale_amount float)


-- Populate temporary table with summary information
BEGIN TRAN
 INSERT INTO #BusFactSaleSum
 SELECT ol.outlet_id,
  ISNULL(busfact.sale_date, @report_start_date),
  rptspec.data_source_ID,
  SUM(ISNULL(busfact.sale_amount, 0)) AS 'sale_amount'
 FROM outlet_list ol
  INNER JOIN Report_specification rptspec
   ON rptspec.report_id = @report_name
   AND rptspec.calculation_formula = 'sum_sales'
   INNER JOIN report_specification_detail rptdet
    ON rptdet.parent_category
    = rptspec.base_category
   AND rptdet.base_category_type
   = rptspec.spec_category_type
  INNER JOIN business_fact busfact
   ON busfact.outlet_id = ol.outlet_id
   AND busfact.metric = rptspec.Spec_metric
   AND busfact.source = rptspec.spec_source
   AND busfact.fiscal_period
   = rptspec.spec_fiscal_period
   AND busfact.base_category_type
   = rptspec.spec_category_type
   AND busfact.sale_date >= @report_start_date
   AND busfact.sale_date < @first_of_month_following
   AND busfact.base_category_type
```

```
   = rptdet.base_category_type
   AND busfact.base_category = rptdet.base_category
 GROUP BY ol.outlet_id,
   busfact.sale_date,
   rptspec.data_source_ID

IF @@ERROR = 0 BEGIN
 COMMIT TRANSACTION
END ELSE BEGIN
 ROLLBACK TRANSACTION
END

DROP TABLE #BusFactSaleSum
```

The goal of this insert is to place one record in #temp_data for each data source for which we track sales information. A later SELECT statement will pull these sums and hand them to a reporting system, such as Crystal Reports or PowerBuilder, for rendering as a report. Reporting systems that rely on such data usually roll up the data into a variety of summary statistics, usually offered by sales outlet, manager, district, region, country, and so forth. However, you have to get the basic business facts into a table before you can hand them to the reporting system, and that is the job of this INSERT statement.

Reports generated in this fashion normally define the nature of the report in a report specification table. Here is the rough structure that you might use to specify the kinds of rows you would want in a report:

```
CREATE TABLE [dbo].[report_specification] (
   [row_identity] [int] IDENTITY (1, 1) NOT NULL ,
   [report_ID] [varchar] (30) NOT NULL ,
   [data_source_ID] [varchar] (30) NOT NULL ,
   [report_heading] [varchar] (100) NULL ,
   [report_heading_sort_order] [int] NULL ,
   [report_data_type] [varchar] (10) NULL ,
   [report_row_show] [varchar] (10) NOT NULL ,
   [report_row_new_page] [varchar] (10) NOT NULL ,
   [report_row_color] [varchar] (10) NULL ,
   [calculation_formula] [varchar] (30) NULL ,
   [spec_metric] [varchar] (30) NULL ,
   [spec_source] [varchar] (10) NULL ,
   [spec_fiscal_period] [char] (1) NULL ,
   [spec_category_type] [varchar] (50) NULL ,
   [base_category] [varchar] (50) NULL ,
) ON [PRIMARY]
```

This table's goal is to define the nature of a row in the report. It contains the ID of the report, so we can tell which rows belong to which report in our system. It also contains the data source ID for the products, vendors, and whatever other major categories of data that we wish to track. The data source ID field defines a line for a report. There will be a line for each source of sales that we wish to track. There are fields for information about the header for this row in the report, the data type for the row, whether to show the row, whether to start a new page before or after the row, and the background color to use for the row. There are also fields for the calculation method to use in summing the row, the kind of business metric this row represents, the profit center source for this metric, the fiscal period this metric participates in, the category of sales information that this row represents, and a type for the category. Category types are a way of classifying categories into larger categories. The category might be 'ladies ready to wear,' and the type might be 'clothing.' We can use the pairing to track specific instances of clothing. Using the information in this table, we can generate any row that we want to for a report.

Along with this table, there is a table that would record the basic business facts of sales. Such a table might look like this:

```
CREATE TABLE [dbo].[business_fact] (
    [metric] [varchar] (30) NOT NULL ,
    [outlet_id] [varchar] (10) NOT NULL ,
    [source] [varchar] (10) NOT NULL ,
    [sale_date] [smalldatetime] NOT NULL ,
    [fiscal_period] [char] (1) NOT NULL ,
    [base_category] [varchar] (30) NOT NULL ,
    [base_category_type] [varchar] (30) NOT NULL ,
    [sale_amount] [float] NULL ,
) ON [PRIMARY]
```

This table holds sales information. But it also tracks what metric the sales data participates in, what outlet generated the sale, its profit center source, the date of the sale, the fiscal period over which such sales are reported, the category of this sales information, and the type of the category.

Reporting systems usually have a way of linking additional information to a report specification by adding details to the report specification. The details might be added in a table that looks like this:

```
CREATE TABLE [dbo].[report_specification_detail] (
    [base_category_type] [varchar] (30) NOT NULL ,
    [base_category] [varchar] (30) NOT NULL ,
    [base_category_sort] [int] NULL ,
    [parent_category] [varchar] (30) NULL ,
```

```
    [parent_category_sort] [int] NULL ,
) ON [PRIMARY]
```

The details table shares the base category and base category type with the report specification table. This pairing of columns allows you to join the two tables to create a resultset that contains one row for each detail associated with the report line. The details table adds information like sort orders and a parent category that can also be associated with any given category. Such a parent category is one more way of linking this base category to a larger category. Using joins, you can create an endless means of classifying summary data using base categories, category types, and parent categories.

Of course, you would need a table to identify your sales outlets. It might look like this:

```
CREATE TABLE [dbo].[outlet_list] (
    [outlet_id] [varchar] (10) NOT NULL ,
    [outlet_name] [varchar] (30) NOT NULL ,
    [outlet_category] [varchar] (30) NOT NULL ,
    [outlet_parent_category] [varchar] (30) NULL
) ON [PRIMARY]
```

Now, if all this seems like an unwieldy system, the answer is that it is an unwieldy system, and we are using such a system on purpose to point out some issues. Such tables and queries do exist in the real world. Ours is just a bit contrived to show some issues that you need to plan for.

An interesting exercise is to create the tables, insert just a few lines of made-up data, and then to play with the joins. The INSERT operation is very straightforward. You might notice the lack of a column list. This is a potential problem. However, this is also a temporary table that is part of a larger stored procedure. It is local in scope, and it ceases to exist when the stored procedure stops running. No one can alter the table definition and break your query. It is created within the stored procedure and dropped after the procedure ceases execution.

The more interesting problems with this join are the lack of columns associated with it. Take a close look at the first join:

```
FROM outlet_list ol INNER JOIN report_specification rptspec
        ON rptspec.report_id = @report_name
        AND rptspec.calculation_formula = 'sum_sales'
```

This join links the two tables in an inner join. The values associated with the join in the equalities are not two columns, one in each table, with the same value. Instead, the join syntax uses what is effectively a WHERE clause in the average query. Column names in the report_specification table equal the values of two expressions.

The result of the join is for each row from outlet_list to be paired with each row in report_specification. Each outlet therefore has one report line associated with it for each line in the report.

The next part of the join works more like you might expect a join to:

```
INNER JOIN report_specification_detail rptdet
      ON rptdet.parent_category = rptspec.base_category
      AND rptdet.category_type = rptspec.spec_category_type
```

Essentially, we are joining on common column values. In this case, note that the base category of the report_specification is set equal to a parent category of the report_specification_detail table. This causes summing to be done for the parent category identified by the report specification details, not the base category. Each record in the previous join is now paired with each record in the report_specification_details table that has the parent category identified. This could be one record, but it is more likely multiple records, each with a different base category assigned in the report_specification_detail table's base_category column. Because we are selecting the parent category to sum in the report_specification_detail table, we also sum all of the possible pairings of base_category and parent_category defined in the table. What is a base category for a report row in the report_specification table is used, therefore, to select a parent category and all of its possible detail pairings with base categories in the report_specification_details table. Our aggregate function SUM applies to all the rows generated by this join, so we sum across all the base categories in the report_specification_details table associated with a given parent category in this table. A possible point of confusion is that the base category for the report row is actually a parent category in the report details.

So far the join works. If you isolate just these facts and check the resultset returned, you will get exactly what we have described, one row for each report detail. The problem lies in joining to the business_fact table. If you do it exactly as specified, you have no trouble and get the sums you expect:

```
INNER JOIN  business_fact busfact
      ON busfact.outlet_id = ol.outlet_id
      AND busfact.metric = rptspec.Spec_metric
      AND busfact.source = rptspec.spec_source
      AND busfact.fiscal_period = rptspec.spec_fiscal_period
      AND busfact.category_type = rptspec.spec_category_type
      AND busfact.sale_date >= @report_start_date
      AND busfact.sale_date < @first_of_month_following
      AND busfact.category_type = rptdet.category_type
      AND busfact.base_category = rptdet.base_category
```

However, if you do not use all of these options, you get spurious rows. How do the spurious rows get generated? First, let's isolate items that are not relevant to causing the problem. The checks for dates do not produce the problem. If you leave them out, you get all dates. If you change them to manually specified dates, you get the data for those dates. Changing any other issue leads to problems.

Focus first on this line:

```
AND busfact.base_category = rptdet.base_category
```

This part of the join sets the business fact base category equal to the base_category in the report_specification_details table. In this query, not all instances of base_category are equal. Using the one from report_specification_details allows you to sum all the base_categories associated with the parent category. The parent category was used earlier in the join to get all the rows in the details table that match the parent and pair them with the rows in the report_specification table. The parent category contains multiple base categories, and we are now picking these base categories within the parent category to sum on. We want to have a sum for ladies ready to wear, for example, that is a component of the parent category but does not represent all of the parent category. The reporting system will perform the calculation for rolling all the subcomponents of the parent category into a single sum for the parent category. Right now, we want one sum for each subcategory of the parent, and we will rely on the reporting system to take care of the rest. If you use another instance of base_category associated with the report_specification table in this equality, you will have too few rows returned in your resultset. You will sum only those instances in the report_details table where the base category in this table is the same as the base category for the report row. Remember that, while these two columns share the same name, they have different functions.

Other parts of this join suppress Cartesian-like products. This line in the query does so in particular:

```
      AND busfact.category_type = rptdet.category_type
```

The first five conditions in the join do as well. Altering any of these lines, even just inserting a hard-coded single value, causes the extra lines to appear. The reason is that we have two tables, report_specification and report_specification_details, that when joined to the outlet_list table produce more rows than we need for the calculation. We have a one-to-many pairing of rows in outlet_list with rows in report_specification. Each outlet gets a set of rows that represent all the lines in the report. Rows in report_specification have a one-to-many relationship with the rows in report_specification_details. Each record that represents a line in the report for an outlet has a pairing with all the matching records in report_specification_ details. This join produces an explosion in the number of rows, and we really do not need all of them. When we join each of these rows to the business_fact table, for example, we have multiple instances of each business fact, one for each pairing of a report row and a report row detail. We need to include only one instance of each business fact in our calculation of sales revenue. A sale is a single sale, but we have artificially turned it into a sale for each report row and detail. We use the equalities in the last part of the join logic to limit ourselves back to including only one instance of each sale in the calculation.

To reduce this overabundance of records in our join, we use columns from both the report_specification table and the report_specification_details table to join to the business_fact table. The reason that changing one of these conditions, even by manually specifying a value instead of the column in the other table, causes multiple rows to appear in the join for the same business facts, is that we are altering the way we have reduced the number of rows involved in the join to the business_fact table. Without solid documentation, this query is a minefield for someone taking over this query to perform maintenance. At each step in the join, what looks like a simple equality is actually a delicate balancing act between being able to select the correct business facts without duplicates and being able to specify multiple details about a specified line in a report. The query works, but it is very complex. Making changes to it is very difficult, and with a design like this one, you can easily have difficulty framing new queries to pull exactly the rows you need. Forgetting one of the key conditions places unexpected values in the calculation. The numbers returned may have the appearance of correctness, but they might in fact be wrong. Testing queries under these circumstances against scenarios with known results is absolutely essential.

How might you simplify this query? There are two answers. One is to start with a different table design. Try to fold the information split out into the report_ specification_details into the report specification table. In doing so, you avoid the need to explode the number of rows and then trim them back. The other option is to use subqueries to retrieve the values you need from report_specification_details without joining to the table. There is a performance penalty for using lots of subqueries in a single SELECT statement. However, you may find that you have to wait a long time for the results anyway. Queries behind reports of this type often take, as a total set in a stored procedure, between 20 and 40 minutes to run anyway. If you are waiting this long for results, waiting a little longer may not matter.

DESIGN TIP

MS SQL Server users may also opt to use derived tables. Derived tables, from my experiences, have improved performance more than twofold.

A Few Practical Suggestions

Having examined some of the complications that affect INSERT statements, we want to distill all that we have learned into a few best practices to guide framing such statements. These guidelines focus on writing INSERT statements given the database context you are handed. Here is the suggested list:

▶   Use a column list in every INSERT statement, unless you are working with local temporary tables that are completely under the control of your database session.

▶   Provide an explicit value assignment for each column. Default values are useful, but the database administrator can change them at any time. Be sure you know what value is going into the column.

▶   Check to see whether a row exists before you attempt an INSERT. Use this technique especially when you are not guaranteed that the database is using primary keys on all tables.

▶   Order INSERTs into multiple tables to accommodate the constraints that apply to the tables.

▶   Use transactions with all attempted INSERT statements. If there is an error, you are then guaranteed that the database will be left in a consistent state.

Summary

In this chapter, we have looked at troubleshooting the INSERT statement. We examined the basic statement, and we looked at common complicating factors. We considered how to insert into multiple tables, the effects of missing values, the effects of multiple values, and the effects of NULLs. We also studied a complex insert scenario to understand in detail the compounded effects of a variety of complicating factors.

Updating Data

IN THIS CHAPTER:

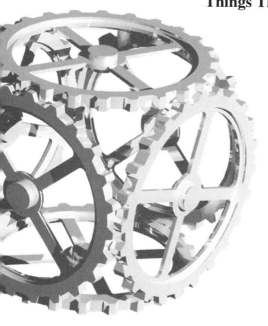

I t's a fact. Things change. In the database world, that means updating data. An update action differs from an insert action because the row(s) already exists in the database; you just want to modify one or more of the columns. Internally, depending on the data types and the SQL product, many updates actually delete the previous data and insert the updated data, followed by a commit transaction.

The basic theory of data modification in a SQL database is transactional integrity. Although select and data modification statements are all wrapped in transactions, the update statement requires transaction theory mastery. Misunderstanding transactions, locks, or isolation levels will cause you troubled times. Therefore, this chapter opens with transaction theory.

Transactional Integrity

Transactional integrity is a critical concept to SQL data modification statements. By design, any modification, or group of modifications, must be an atomic, or stand-alone, transaction. In fact, every SQL statement is an implicit transaction even if the code is not explicitly wrapped with BEGIN TRANS and END TRANS.

A transaction must work, or fail, as a complete unit. If you are updating a million rows and the last row in the data set fails to update because of a unique constraint, then every row must fail the update. Transactions are an all-or-nothing proposition. If the entire transaction is not accepted, then nothing is accepted.

The classic example of a transaction is a general ledger double entry system. Funds can't be spent in one accounts payable account unless there's a balancing entry subtracting the funds from the fund source account. If either entry is missing, the books will not balance. Both entries must be completed or the accounting system is in a state of error.

Another example is a payroll system. Three primary actions—debiting the funds from the payroll account, incrementing the employee amounts, and preparing the file to print the check—must all complete correctly; or the entire set of actions must fail together. As a complete, multistep transaction, all steps must be completed as a set. If some of the steps are written, and then there's an error, the completed steps must be undone, or rolled back.

While desktop databases have some features for transaction handling, as a rule desktop databases do not properly implement transactional integrity. In contrast, server-based SQL database products tend to excel in the area of transactional integrity. Of course, the programmer's proverb applies, "Cheap, easy, or powerful—choose any two."

The ACID Test

Database developers live and die by the principle of consistency. So, it's no surprise that there's a database standard for transactional integrity. It's called the "ACID test."

A – Atomic

C – Consistent

I – Isolated

D – Durable

Of these four attributes, or benchmarks, of transaction quality, each is at least partially dependent on the others.

Atomic Transactions

Transactions are considered *atomic* when each transaction completes or fails as a unit. Partial transitions never write to the disk. SQL databases enforce the atomic nature of transactions extremely well, whether it is implicit, or implied, as in the case of a single statement, or it is explicit, using BEGIN TRANS and COMMIT TRANS. You can be sure when using a server-quality SQL database that the transaction will be atomic.

In some SQL database products, you'll have to code the commit transaction or it will fail. Other SQL database products will commit the transaction unless you code a rollback command. As long as you adhere to your SQL database product's conventions, you will be fine.

Transactions can be atomic in multiple server situations as well. If a transaction spans multiple servers, a distributed transaction manager component handles transaction commitments or rollbacks across multiple servers. Replication scenarios can implement a two-phase commit that can allow each remote server to tentatively commit the transaction locally. Only when each server has confirmed a tentative commitment is the transaction fully committed. Two-phase commits are valuable in the financial sector. This type of commitment prevents two ATM users in separate states to withdraw the same funds from one account.

Consistent Transactions

A SQL database product's transactions are *consistent* if the results of each transaction are predictable and repeatable regardless of what another transaction may be doing. Given a small sample set of data and a SQL statement or batch of SQL commands, you should be able to work the transaction through in your head, or on a whiteboard, and reliably predict the result of the SQL statements. It's not so much a question of a buggy database engine, but of other transactions or users causing questionable results.

Consistent transactions require that the transaction not be affected by other transactions; therefore, they must be separated from the other transactions. The ACID rules are similar to the normal forms, in that the normal forms are interdependent and must all be implemented (at least the first three) to build a good database design. In the same manner, a transaction can't be consistent unless it's also isolated from other transactions.

Isolated Transactions

Each transaction must be *isolated;* that is, it must live and die (or rather must begin and be committed, or rolled back) on its own without influence by any other transaction. This separation between transactions is called the *isolation level.* Think of it as a fence between transactions. Isolation levels can be very complex and are implemented via share locks, update locks, and exclusive locks. The SQL standard defines four levels, or degrees, of isolation between transactions. Microsoft employs all four levels; Oracle offers two isolation levels and thus improves performance with the simplified locking scheme.

The four isolation levels are defined by how they deal with three types of transaction isolation violations: dirty reads, nonrepeatable reads, and phantom reads. These transaction isolation violations are described as follows:

▶ **Dirty read**   Seeing other transactions' noncommitted changes

▶ **Nonrepeatable read**   Seeing other transactions' committed changes

▶ **Phantom read**   Seeing rows selected by a WHERE clause change as the result of other transaction

Each of the isolation levels progressively presents a higher degree of isolation between transactions, as shown in Table 9-1. Read Uncommitted, the loosest level

Isolation Level	Dirty Read	Nonrepeatable Read	Phantom Read
Read Uncommitted	possible	possible	possible
Read Committed	prevented	possible	possible
Repeatable Read	prevented	prevented	possible
Serializable	prevented	prevented	prevented

Table 9-1   *Isolation Levels and Transaction Violations*

of isolation, permits all three transaction violations. Serializable, the tightest transaction isolation level, prevents all three possible isolation problems.

A dirty read error is when the first transaction writes some data, but before it commits the transaction, a second transaction reads from those rows and sees the first transaction's changes. If the first transaction's update is rolled back, the second transaction has seen erroneous data. The Read-Only Committed Data isolation level solves this first problem.

The nonrepeatable read error occurs when the two transactions read from a row and the first transaction then writes and commits the data to the row. If the second transaction then reads the row again, it should see the same data as it did at the beginning of its transaction. If it sees the first transaction's update to the row, the transaction anomaly is called a nonrepeatable read. The Force Repeatable Reads isolation level corrects this problem.

Both dirty read and nonrepeatable read errors involve updates to existing rows. Phantom errors involve the isolation of the selection of rows between transactions.

A phantom read is when a set of rows is selected by one transaction, and another transaction updates the underlying data, adds rows, or deletes rows, such that the rows returned by the first transaction's SELECT and WHERE statements are changed. If the first transaction reselects the same criteria and sees a different set of rows, the new rows are referred to as phantom reads. Phantoms are the hardest to prevent because prevention involves locking not only the row but also the selection path by which the row was selected. The tightest isolation level, serialized, prevents phantom reads.

You can select the isolation level within each connection by setting a global variable. Be aware that a tighter isolation level will hurt performance, so use only what you need. For most applications, the database default of read committed will provide sufficient isolation between transactions. Read-only applications, such as OLAP, analysis, or reporting applications, require only the loosest isolation level, so lower the isolation level and increase performance. Financial applications tend to require serialized isolation for the absolute transaction integrity.

Durable Transactions

A transaction is *durable* if it's fully recoverable in case of system failure. Or, if the transaction cannot be completed, then in case of failure, the transaction must be rolled back. A database transaction log meets this requirement, which explains why you can never simply turn off the transaction log in a SQL database. Most desktop databases do not meet this requirement.

The transaction log records every write before it is written to the data file. Once the transaction is committed and written to the data file, then the transaction log records that the transaction is complete. If the server goes down, it can tell by looking at the transaction log (when it comes back up) if any transactions need to be rolled back, or written to the disk if they were committed but not written to the data file. In both cases, the transaction log provides durability to the transaction.

Log shipping and cluster servers boost the scalability and availability in high-end applications. Log shipping is essentially sharing the log with another server, so that if the primary server goes down, a warm fail-over server can take over. Client applications need only connect to the backup server. If you can program the client application to automatically switch, this option can save considerable funds compared to server clustering.

Several servers, clustered together, can share the same drives using very sophisticated fiber optic hard drive controllers. If the primary server/CPU goes down, the backup server instantly takes over. In a clustered scenario, the front-end application connects to a virtual server and is unaware of which actual server is processing the requests. Any fail-over switching or sharing of the processing load is completely transparent to the front-end connection. It works great, but costs a fortune.

The good news is that, while the high-end SQL database products support clustering and warm fail-over servers, with a good backup plan for the data file and the transaction log, a transaction is durable even without a rack full of servers.

Types of Locks

The SQL standard works with two primary types or locks: share locks and exclusive locks. In actual practice, however, the types of locks within a SQL database product are much more complex and involve up to a few dozen types of intent locks and latches, or minilocks. In addition, the granularity of the lock, from row to table, further complicates the locking scheme.

The first type of lock is the *share lock,* sometimes called a *read lock.* It indicates that a connection is currently looking at the data—nothing more. An unlimited number of connections can hold a share lock. But, the isolation requirement for transactional integrity can keep another transaction from writing to the data while any share lock is holding on to the data.

An *exclusive lock,* also called a *write lock,* means the transaction is the only transaction looking at, or working with, the data. A transaction can't get an exclusive lock if there are any other locks. And if a transaction has an exclusive lock, then no other transaction can acquire any other lock. Many desktop databases only work with this type of lock.

There's also often some type of intermediate lock claiming to be next in line for an exclusive lock. MS SQL Server calls theirs an Update lock, even though it's really just an "I want to update" lock. It's easy to confuse an Update lock with an update operation. The Update lock in SQL Server is only the intent to update. The exclusive lock is the actual update operation.

Table 9-2 illustrates how a lock affects other transaction's attempt to gain a lock.

The main problem here is that if your application tends to grab and hold on to share locks when the application reads data, then update operations (which require exclusive locks) will tend to wait and time out.

Lock Granularity

The other big question about locks concerns the number, and size, of the locks. The SQL database product will have to balance the number of locks being requested with the size of each lock. For example, if you want to grab a share lock on 1000 rows, is it better to lock 1000 rows, lock 20 data pages, or lock the table? It might be fastest to lock the table, since only one lock is involved; however, such a bulky action might increase the likelihood of other transactions timing out as they wait to acquire their locks. Within MS SQL Server, the granularity options available are: row, data page, extent (eight pages), table, and key (a special type of lock involving indexes).

The SQL database product's lock manager allocation will dynamically handle this portion of the lock problem well enough automatically, but I do want to pass on a couple tips.

Clustered indexes keep the data in the same physical order as the index. If the application tends to read, or update, in a specific order or a specific set of rows, then clustered indexes help reduce the number of data pages being locked. An excellent candidate for this technique is a foreign key. Order detail rows tend to be read and updated together. A clustered index on OrderDetail.OrderID will improve performance and reduce the number of locks.

Transaction One Has A:	Transaction Two Tries to Acquire A:		
	Share Lock	Update Lock	Exclusive Lock
Share Lock	OK	OK	Wait
Update Lock	OK	Wait	Wait
Exclusive Lock	Wait	Wait	Wait

Table 9-2   *Gaining an Exclusive Lock*

Use locking hints in your SQL statements to reduce the number of locks. A quick read to populate a combo box probably doesn't need any locks. While several table locking hints are offered by each SQL database product, the most common lock hints are (nolock) and (rowlock).

Return only the rows required. Although it's a standard tip offered in every list of tips for client/server development, reducing network traffic is the primary reason given. However, reducing locks is even more important, and selecting only what you need with a careful WHERE clause will reduce locks.

Optimistic and Pessimistic Locking

Atomic locking within a single update statement, or transaction, is important, but a lock during an update is often just a split second. A more difficult issue facing database developers is locking the data during user reads and updates. Here's the problem: Joe opens a customer record to review the record, and Sue opens the same customer record to edit the customer's address. While reviewing the record, Joe edits the credit limit. Sue saves her changes, and then Joe presses his Save button. What's going to happen? Will Joe's update overwrite Sue's address change? Will anyone receive notification of the potential problem? Will Sue's update prevent Joe's update? It all depends on your code.

There are two general approaches to this problem: optimistic and pessimistic. The optimist says: "Hey, I don't think there will be a problem, so I'm not going to lock any records. Whoever writes last, writes best—no problem here." The pessimist assumes that Murphy was right, "If I give those users a chance to foul up my data, they will. So I'm going to lock that row as soon as they look at it and keep it locked until they finish with it. I'm not taking any chances."

Pessimistic locking, in the form of long-term locks, will not ensure happy users. If Joe opens a large set of records before a long lunch, others will soon complain to you. Locking on reads is a big mistake. With a little extra work, the optimist's plan will make everyone happy.

Making Optimistic Locking Work

Optimistic locking is on the right track, but updates must handle any concurrency issues. Drawing on the previous example with Joe and Sue, here are two techniques that will make this optimistic locking scheme work.

The first technique is to update only columns that have actually been edited by the user. Sue's UPDATE statement should read as:

```
UPDATE Customer SET Address = '123 S. Main St.' WHERE CustomerID = 77
```

When Joe updates the credit limit for the same customer, his UPDATE statement also updates only the affected column:

```
UPDATE Customer SET CreditLimit  = 5000 WHERE CustomerID = 77
```

Updating only the affected columns reduces network traffic and database engine work, and the chance that a user will overwrite another user's updates is significantly limited. Using column-level updating is a "very close solution" and all but guarantees you won't have a problem. I've used this solution in several projects without any headaches.

A second technique is to use a timestamp column as an update check. The timestamp will automatically refresh with a new, meaningless value with every update. By reading the timestamp when the row is retrieved, you can compare that timestamp value with the one found when you update. If the timestamps are not identical, then you know that someone else has updated the row since you read the row. The key is that you know the row has been touched.

In this iteration of the example, Joe and Sue both read the same row. The timestamp's original value is 12548652:

```
(Timestamp = 12548652)
from Sue:
SELECT * FROM Customer WHERE CustomerID = 77
from Joe:
SELECT * FROM Customer WHERE CustomerID = 77
```

After both reads, the timestamp is still 12548652. Now, Sue updates the address:

```
UPDATE Customer
SET Address = '123 S. Main St.'
WHERE CustomerID = 77
AND Timestamp = 12548652
The WHERE clause is based on both the CustomerID and the timestamp.
```

Because the row has not been updated, the timestamp is the same as it was during the read, so the update occurs without error and the timestamp is automatically updated by the database engine, indicating the row had been altered:

```
(Timestamp = 94523792)
```

When Joe updates the credit limit for the same customer, his UPDATE statement also updates the row by ID and timestamp:

```
UPDATE Customer
SET CreditLimit  = 5000
WHERE CustomerID = 77
AND Timestamp = 12548652
```

But, Joe's update fails because, while there is still a row with an ID of 77, there is no longer a row with an ID of 77 and a timestamp of 12548652. Your code now has the opportunity to test for the error and handle the update problem with several possible options. You can offer Joe the chance to overwrite the previous update. You could compare the values in each column and find out that it's okay to write Joe's update. You can refresh Joe's application with the new set of data and let him reenter his update. The important point is that you are in control of the locking issue and you are deciding how to handle the situation. Well done!

These two techniques, updating only edited columns and using a timestamp column, don't work well together because the granularity, or scope, of the solution is different in either case. The timestamp indicates that the row has been touched. The first method is based on the column level and requires more code to update only the columns; such code involves actual changes in the user interface. Alternatively, in an update stored procedure you could reexamine the values and issue an error if the updated columns had been changed during the user session.

Deadlocks

A *deadlock* is a different type of transaction problem than those calling for transaction isolation or optimistic locking. The basic idea is that two transactions are each waiting for the other to release a lock so that they can continue. Transaction one is waiting for transaction two, and transaction two is waiting on transaction one. If nothing intervened, they would both wait forever.

While desktop databases have had considerable problems with deadlocks in the past, server-based SQL database products handle deadlocks well. The best way to demonstrate a deadlock is with a timeline, as shown in Table 9-3.

Because server-based SQL databases handle deadlocks, these problems are not as bad as they sound, and they're easily avoided with a simple technique. In your

Transaction One	Time	Transaction Two
Begins transaction	:01	
Gets a share lock on Table A, Row 123	:02	
	:03	Begins transaction
		Requests and gets an exclusive lock on Table C, row 1, and updates the row
Requests an exclusive lock on Table C, rows 1–5, is granted only an update lock, and waits for transaction two to release its exclusive lock on Table C, row 1	:04	
	:05	Requests an exclusive lock on Table A, rows 100–200, receives only an update lock, and begins waiting for transaction one to release its share lock on Table A
Both transactions are now stuck, waiting for a resource held by the other transaction.		
	:06	
A process on the SQL product detects the deadlock situation and automatically aborts one of the transactions. Transaction one has done the least amount of work, so it will be rolled back.		
Transaction one is rolled back; all locks are released. The connection is notified that the transaction failed due to a deadlock.	:07	
	:08	Transaction two's update lock is promoted to an exclusive lock. The update performs correctly.
	:09	Transaction two commits the transaction
The front-end application code attempts the transaction again	:10	

Table 9-3   *A Deadlock Timeline*

transactional code, if you always work with the tables in the same order, that will reduce the chance that two transactions are waiting for competing resources. The following suggestions will also reduce deadlocks.

Transaction Suggestions

In server-based SQL databases, you, as the database developer, have much greater control over your transactions than do desktop database developers. It's critical that you understand how SQL handles transactions and how your particular SQL product deals with isolation levels and their corresponding locks. Here are a few tips to make working with transactions and locks easier:

► The basics always apply: If you think of transactions in terms of procedural code and loops, instead of sets of data, your code will run slow and you'll find inconsistencies between what you expect and the result. Try to avoid cursors in your transactional code. Cursors are extremely slow. They tie up resources and increase the chance of a locking issue.

► Return the minimum data requested from the server in terms of rows and columns. As I mentioned before, this will also help reduce locks and improve the performance of both the database engine and the network.

► Reduce the scope, or size, of your locks. Several locked rows will have less chance of a locking than several page locks.

► Good client/server development moves the processing as close as possible to the data. Move as much code as possible to triggers and stored procedures. They offer the fastest possible execution of code against data, and speed will be on your side in the battle of the locks.

► Always test for an error after every data modification statement.

► Avoid grabbing a large set of data and holding on to the lock. Beware, views tend to grab and hold share locks.

The Basic UPDATE Statement

Although there are many transactional and locking issues behind the scenes, the syntax for the basic UPDATE statement is straightforward.

```
UPDATE table SET columns = data
FROM data_source
WHERE criteria
```

The SQL UPDATE statement will change the values in the specified columns of the selected rows of a single table. It's pretty straightforward. Multiple columns may be updated by listing the columns and the new values separated by commas.

```
UPDATE [Order] SET RequestedShipDate = '2/2/2003' WHERE OrderID = 77
```

This SQL statement changes the requested ship date for order 77 to Groundhog Day.

WHERE Is Your Best Friend

The SQL UPDATE and SQL DELETE commands are similar in that they alter a set of rows. The key concept is that they affect a "set" rather than a single row. If you have a background in procedural programming, the most important single concept for you to embrace is working with sets rather than single rows.

Regarding the SQL UPDATE command, it's vital that you use the WHERE clause to define the set of rows to be updated. There's nothing difficult or tricky about the WHERE clause, or its conditions. But if the WHERE clause is left off, then the entire table will be updated.

A common trap involves matching the data type of the WHERE parameter and the variable being used to build the SQL string. Mixing numbers with quotes or using strings without quotes is an easy mistake to make.

Another easy error is mixing the syntax between SQL and your front-end language. String concatenation operators (&,+) are often different between the SQL and the front-end language.

My one big tip is to include copious parentheses in the WHERE clause. They ensure that the execution of multiple conditions is in the order you intend, and they document your intention, so other developers, and you a year later, will readily understand your intention.

Using the FROM Clause

The initial table in the UPDATE statement identifies the table being updated. However, it may be that to specify the correct set of rows to be updated, you need to reference another table across a join. For this reason, an optional FROM clause enables you to define a complete data source, including joins.

```
UPDATE employees SET lastname = 'Smith'
FROM employees
JOIN orders
ON employees.employeeID = Orders.EmployeeID
WHERE OrderID = 10248
```

Complex SQL statements involving several joins quickly become non-updatable. In these cases, remember that the second word in the UPDATE statement determines the single table affected by the update, which keeps the UPDATE statement updatable. To demonstrate this, the following SELECT statement is non-updatable because it includes an aggregate function and GROUP BY within a subquery brought into this statement as a derived table—a rather nonupdatable mess for most SQL products.

```
SELECT * FROM employees
JOIN (SELECT TOP 10 EmployeeID FROM Orders GROUP BY EmployeeID ORDER BY COUNT(*) DESC) O
ON O.EmployeeID = Employees.EmployeeID
```

However, if the same SELECT statement is used as a data source within a SQL UPDATE statement, the update performs well. The Employees table is the single table updated.

```
UPDATE Employees SET Title = 'Top SalesPerson'
FROM employees
JOIN (SELECT TOP 1 EmployeeID FROM Orders GROUP BY EmployeeID ORDER BY COUNT(*) DESC) O
ON O.EmployeeID = Employees.EmployeeID
```

That's the power of the FROM clause in the SQL UPDATE statement.

Updating to Calculated Values

The new value isn't limited to a hard-coded value; the column can be updated to a value from another column, or from a calculation. This is how a single UPDATE statement makes smart data modifications to thousands of rows.

```
UPDATE Orders
    SET TotalAmount =
            (SELECT Sum([Order Details].Amount * [Order Details].Quantity)
                FROM Orders
                    INNER JOIN [Order Details]
                            ON Orders.OrderID = [Order Details].OrderID
                WHERE Orders.TotalAmount IS NULL
                AND Shipped = 0 AND OrderEntryComplete = 1)
    FROM Orders, [Order Details]
```

This SQL UPDATE statement first locates all orders that have not shipped. For these rows, it joins with the correct order detail rows, sums the amount from the order detail rows by multiplying the quantity by the amount, and then writes that sum to the order table. The goal of this particular SQL query is to denormalize the total value of each order into its own column. That may or may not be a good idea, depending on other database constraints. I have used this type of denormalization in inventory and inventory transaction systems. The point is that one SQL statement handles the update regardless of the number of rows affected. This type of update is critical within triggers, which fire once even if thousands of rows are affected.

The key is to think in terms of data sets. The UPDATE statement is designed to perform an algebraic update to multiple rows, moving data from one location to another. Between the WHERE clause, the second FROM, and well-designed joins that reference data in other tables, the UPDATE statement is amazingly versatile.

I've lost count how many times I've replaced multiple lines of looping code with a single SQL UPDATE statement.

Things That Prevent Updates

Every data modification action, regardless of what it might look like at a graphical front end, is actually one of three text statements sent to the database engine. Table 9-4 presents an overview of the many database design elements, constraints, and code that could affect your attempts to perform an insert, update, or delete.

Things That Might Prevent Data Modification	Insert	Update	Delete
Column definition:			
Data type / length	X	X	
Default value			
Constraints:			
Primary key	X	X	
Foreign key	X	X	X
Unique index	X	X	
No null and no default	X	X	
Check constraints	X	X	
Code:			
Triggers	X	X	X
Views with check	X	X	
Security	X	X	X

Table 9-4 *Things That Might Prevent Data Modification*

The "things that might prevent your data modification list" can be divided into three categories. The first category is the data column and the data type itself. The most problematic category is the second—the five SQL constraints. Custom code, in triggers and views, the last category, can also block a data modification either intentionally or due to a logic error. Last, security may block an attempt to modify data.

Undocumented Schemas

Before we begin working through the list, it's profitable to discuss documentation of database schemas. Knowing the database schema inside and out will greatly diminish your frustration due to blocked updates. I find that when working with a small database (under 15 tables), it takes no time at all to master the data schema and work efficiently with the design. On larger systems, over 100 tables, it may take me up to a week of development time to fully wrap my head around the design and rememorize the whole system. Keep that in mind as you switch from database to database. It takes time for the brain to dump the last schema and load the new one.

One of the biggest problems is that SQL Server has no built-in database documentation method. The cheapest solution is to build your own documentation tool by reporting schema information from the system tables or the schema_information ANSI standard views included with good database products. A couple of hours with Access or Crystal and you've built a database reporting tool to your exacting specifications. Good job.

Several shops use tools like Erwin or Visio to graphically document their database design. A seven-foot strip of 42-inch-wide plotter paper with every table and relationship is great for understanding the database design and mapping complex joins. And besides, it looks impressive to guests and bosses.

If you're using Microsoft SQL Server, there's a new product called Total SQL Analyzer, available from www.fmsinc.com, which can print several great looking reports documenting the database design.

The point is that if you're running into anything other than the listed things that might prevent data modification, chances are the real cause is that you were unaware of the constraint.

Data Type Incompatibility

Each SQL product has the standard ANSI data types and a few product-specific extended data types. SQL will automatically convert between data types if it makes logical sense. For example, converting from integer to string is easy, but converting from string to integer is not. You'll want to check the data type conversion chart in the documentation for your SQL product.

If you do need to convert data from one type to another, there are two commands in SQL for data conversion. *CAST* is the ANSI standard data conversion method. *CONVERT* is a Microsoft data conversion command similar to CAST, but it includes several data type formats.

CAST and CONVERT can be used within SQL statements. I recommended that if you reconfigure a data column, you also provide a suitable name for the new result via a column alias. For example:

```
SELECT FirstName + ' ' + LastName AS FullName,
CONVERT( NVARCHAR(50),Hiredate, 1) AS Hire
FROM Employees
```

In this example, FullName and Hire are column aliases, so that the data assembled from the concatenation and the convert function will have a nice column name.

Unique Primary Key Constraints

Primary keys are the single most important concept in relational databases. The purpose of the primary key is to provide a unique identifier for the row, and to provide primary key–foreign key linking within the database. To support this purpose, here are my rules for good primary keys:

▶ They should be unrecognizable and meaningless to end users. Users should never see a primary key. If a user sees the primary key of a table, they should wonder how the database could possibly work.

▶ Never, never, ever use a real-life value for a primary key.

▶ Primary keys should never be updated.

▶ Primary keys should be computer generated. I prefer Microsoft Unique Identifiers (Global Unique IDs or GUIDs), a 16-byte hexadecimal number, and the NewID() function for primary keys over identity fields, because GUIDs support replication. It doesn't hurt that GUIDs also reinforce my anti–user friendly rule #1 of the primary key.

When working with GUIDs, the NewID() function generates a new GUID, which is guaranteed to be unique regardless of row, table, computer, network, continent, or planet. I like the uniqueness of the unique identifier data type. Because the GUIDs are generated by the NEWID() function, the PK can be generated by code and your code then knows the ID, circumventing the possible coding difficulties with identity columns:

```
SELECT NEWID()
{619D261D-340A-4196-ABF0-EEC9714FF487}
```

Perhaps the worst primary keys I've ever seen were used on legacy databases and involved intelligent product codes. The first two digits indicated the department, and the next digit indicated the format for the following digits. The next two digits indicated the product type, and then two digits for product size, and so on. Eventually hard-coding values into a code runs out of room. So rules are generated, "If the third character is a Z, then the next two characters mean this; otherwise, it's like this other product code." What a mess. The first rule of database design is one piece of data into one data placeholder (row * column). Database indexes aren't meant to sort by the third position if the first position is "D". This whole idea of creating intelligent codes is a bad design by uneducated developers.

Using real-life data as a primary key is only one step away from such a poor design. Social Security Number, Product Number, Customer Number, EmployeeTimeClockNo, and Flight Number are all terrible primary keys. They belong in the database, of course, and with a unique constraint, but never as a primary key. You don't want the human whim of changing a number to affect the relational linking between your tables.

So, if you follow my rules, and you don't let users see the primary key, you'll never have a problem trying to update a primary key. But if for some reason you did want to update a primary key (for a conversion perhaps), you'd run into problems for one of two reasons.

First, primary keys are, by definition, unique. If you try to update a PK column to a value already in use, the action would fail. If this happens during a conversion, there is a problem with reliability of the old data. And I'd bet that the old primary key was human generated and uniqueness was not enforced.

Second, referential integrity (which is discussed in greater detail in the next chapter) could cause a primary key update to fail if there's a secondary row that's pointing to the primary key. Updating the primary key would cause the secondary rows to no longer relate to a valid primary table row. This would violate referential integrity and cause the primary key update to fail.

Some SQL products will cascade the PK update to the foreign key of secondary rows. I strongly recommend that you avoid cascading updates. It's just an easy way to cause trouble in the database. If your users want cascading updates, the first mistake was letting users know about a primary key.

Foreign Key Constraints

Foreign keys are the secondary counterpart to primary keys. Foreign keys don't need to be unique, since they are the many side of a one-to-many relationship. So, updating foreign keys to a value already in use won't cause a problem.

If a foreign key constraint has been established, and referential integrity is being enforced, then an update to a value that is not a valid primary key in the primary table would cause the foreign key update to fail. Realistically speaking, foreign keys should rarely, if ever, be updated. Perhaps during data conversion or migration, foreign keys might need to be massaged as rows are merged and data is cleaned up. But in day-to-day operations, an order detail for order 77 is seldom changed to order 78.

Unique Index Constraints

Since primary keys should never be seen by mere mortal users, it follows that other columns would contain a unique customer number, social security number, UOC code, or ISBN number. The best way to implement these columns is with a unique constraint or unique index.

If a SQL UPDATE statement attempts to update a column to a value already in use, then obviously the update will fail. In the same manner, attempting to update multiple rows to the same value will cause the update to fail.

Allow Nulls and Defaults

Null is a special term in the database world. It does not mean empty, blank, zero, empty string, or space. Null means unknown. So, here's a question: can null ever be equal to null? No, and never! If it's unknown, then it can never be known if it's equal. That's why SQL has the keyword IS for working with null.

```
IF @temp IS NULL
IF @temp IS NOT NULL
```

Regarding updates and inserts, if the column has a NO NULL constraint, then the data modification must apply some known value, or there has to be a default. If there's a default and no value is supplied by the insert, then the default will be used instead. If you try to specifically write a null value into a column that is set to NO NULLS, then the update will fail.

Check Constraints

Check constraints are useful to provide simple data validation to a column. Check constraints are fast, but the big drawback is that most database products limit the constraints to hard-coded values or other columns in the same row. SQL Server 2000 includes functions that can perform complex SQL commands and then return a scalar, or single, value into a check constraint.

Typical check constraints are (in psuedocode):

```
HireDate > Birthdate + 14years
Shipdate >= Orderdate
```

Triggers

I love triggers. *Triggers* are fast compiled SQL batches that are fired by an action to a table. Typically, triggers are used to handle custom auditing, complex data validation, custom referential integrity, calculating and updating other tables based on your update, or handling logical deletions. In Chapter 10, there's more information on triggers.

Regarding updating data, there are two primary ways a trigger may cause your update to fail, a ROLLBACK and an INSTEAD OF trigger.

Most likely, if a trigger is causing an update to fail, the trigger's logic is causing a rollback of the transaction. The only solution is to examine the trigger and to comply with the logic, or to alter the trigger. Trigger logic will cause some data to fail, but unless the trigger is faulty, it will only block some data modification actions.

Triggers can update other tables, firing other triggers, and triggers can call stored procedures, which can in turn update other tables, causing more triggers to fire. If the system lacks documentation, debugging an application with multiple triggers can quickly become frustrating.

Nested triggers reveal a deeper problem—nested transactions. Within Microsoft SQL Server, any rollback will roll back every transaction currently pending. There is no nested rollback. That means that if TableA_UpdateTrigger calls stored procedure XYZ, which then updates TableB_UpdateTrigger, and the last trigger hits an error and issues a transaction rollback, then the whole thing rolls back. The update to Table A failed, but to find the error you have to look into the trigger code in Table B.

Here are some tips for debugging triggers:

▶ Use good error handling code within all triggers and stored procedures. When you write to the error log, be sure to include the procedure name that experienced the error.

▶ Turn off recursive triggers to prevent triggers from being called twice in the same update.

▶ Nothing beats good documentation. At the top of every trigger or stored procedure, list the tables updated within the code.

▶ If you don't want a trigger to fire due to a cascaded trigger, then check the trigger_level and abort the trigger.

The second way that triggers can cause problems involves the INSTEAD OF triggers, which will always abort the original data modification action. The trigger may decide to take the data sent to the trigger and use it in its actions. However, the original action is always thrown away. Therefore, unless the INSTEAD OF trigger is in fact doing another set of actions that satisfy the intent of the user, your data modification will disappear.

Views, with Check

Chapter 14 includes further detail on the view WITH CHECK option. Basically, it means that the WHERE conditions are checked not only when reading from a view, but also when writing back through the view. If you're attempting to update data through a view, and you're changing the data used in the WHERE of the view, there's a chance that your update will fail. The only way to be sure is to check the source SQL SELECT statement used to create the view. If the view was constructed with encryption, then you'll need to refer back to the original scripts.

Security Settings

Security tends to be a problem in production systems once administrators have locked down the database; during development, however, security is rarely an issue. Just be aware that any heavy duty back-end database will have heavy duty security and that at some point you'll need to master the security schemes of your SQL product.

Summary

Update commands are typically straightforward. The majority of concerns will be incorrect WHERE condition logic, unknown schema names, or constraint violations. In each case, the best prevention is knowing the data and the data schema, and mastering the transactional integrity features of your preferred SQL database product.

Deleting Data

IN THIS CHAPTER:

The Basic DELETE Statement

Things That Prevent Deletions

Referential Integrity

Logical Deletion

Truncating a Table

D eleting data has always been a bit of a touchy subject. Every developer I know has a special take on the subject and certain practices that they will forever avoid. I suppose that's because nothing causes more headaches, or is more damaging to an application, than a user claiming that the computer lost all his or her data. Never mind that the user deleted the data, it's time to blame. Seasoned developers all have their stories, and their favorite method to prevent such disasters—"I'll give up my logical delete code when you pry it from my cold, dead fingers."

This chapter focuses on the problems you'll likely encounter when working with delete and offers some best practice solutions, including a method to manage deleted data by logically deleting data instead of physically deleting it.

The Basic DELETE Statement

The delete is a pretty simple SQL statement:

```
DELETE FROM table WHERE criteria
```

That's it. No columns are required, because the delete is affecting rows and not returning columns of data. It's so simple that it's dirt easy to delete more data than intended. And, there's no undo button in SQL Server. Once the data is deleted, it's gone.

Just in Case

If you do attempt to delete a couple of bad rows, and then find that all the Michigan dealers no longer have customers, it's time to restore from a backup. Fortunately, a good transaction log backup can be restored to any point in time. It's for this reason that I avoid shrinking the transaction log at checkpoints or using the "simple recovery plan." The transaction log is your personal safety net. Always remember, if a user destroys important information in your application, your application, and you, will be blamed, not the user. It's the database's job to protect the integrity of the data from the user.

NOTE

There's a new product for SQL Server, Log Explorer from www.Lumigent.com. While it's expensive, it opens the transaction log for browsing. In the case of accidental over-deletion, Log Explorer enables you to select any past transaction and roll it back. That's pretty cool—this third-party tool also gives you an undo button.

The Data Saving WHERE Clause

When performing any SQL statement that modifies data, the WHERE clause is your best friend—especially when deleting data!

The WHERE clause's syntax and conditions are identical for its select, insert, update, or delete uses. The difference is that the delete removes data. While inserts and updates are easily fixed, an erroneous delete is harder to recover from.

I strongly suggest that, prior to performing any ad hoc DELETE statement, you first try the statement as a SELECT * query to double-check that the correct rows are being properly filtered by the WHERE clause. I dream in SQL, yet I habitually double- check any data modification statement. It's the database variation of "measure twice—cut once."

FROM-FROM

The basic DELETE statement deletes rows from a single table. And that's perfectly okay; you wouldn't want to delete across a join. However, you may want to perform a WHERE condition on another side of the join, or use multiple tables to help determine the rows to be eliminated. To accomplish this, some SQL products include an extension to the delete that establishes the data source, including joins, in the same way a SQL SELECT defines the data source—the "second FROM."

```
DELETE FROM TableA
    FROM TableA JOIN TableB ON TableA.ID = TableB.ID
    WHERE TableB.code = 23
```

Be careful here—this SQL statement includes two FROMs. The first FROM identifies the table from which rows will be deleted. The second FROM is the data source used to identify the rows. The table in the first FROM must be in the data source of the second FROM.

In the preceding example, TableA is a secondary table to TableB. All TableA rows that point to code 23 in TableB will be deleted. It's an easier method than looking up the TableB primary key for code 23 and then using that primary key in a WHERE clause when deleting from TableA.

Here's a real-life example:

```
DELETE FROM [Order]
FROM [Order]
JOIN Customer
ON [Order].CustomerID = Customer.CustoemrID
          WHERE Customer.Active = 0
```

The intention is to delete any order for an inactive customer that's still floating around in the database. The preceding syntax is clear: wherever there's an order that matches with an inactive customer, delete the order.

Without the FROM-FROM syntax, the DELETE statement would have to be written like this:

```
DELETE FROM [Order]
WHERE OrderID IN
(Select OrderID
FROM [Order]
JOIN Customer
ON [Order].CustomerID = Customer.CustoemrID
            WHERE Customer.Active = 0)
```

This version of the delete employs a subquery to first determine which orders belong to inactive customers. Then the delete removes any rows found in the result set of the subquery. While either form will work, I prefer joins to subqueries when possible because joins are more direct and easier to read.

The FROM-FROM syntax might be confusing if you're not aware of it, but once it's understood, it actually improves readability of the SQL statement and thus raises the quality of your code.

Things That Prevent Deletions

While INSERT and UPDATE SQL statements had a long list of things that prevent data modification, deleting data has a much shorter list: foreign keys, triggers, database security. There isn't much to stand in the way of a delete, because data doesn't need to be validated, it just has to cooperate and go away.

While database security can thwart a delete action, working with security depends on the SQL database product. Instead of delving into these issues, this chapter will deal with the intricacies of referential integrity, foreign keys, and triggers as they involve deleting. Foreign keys go hand in hand with cascading deletes, so cascading deletes will be explained.

Referential Integrity

If a table is a primary table and there's a secondary table with a foreign key constraint pointing to that primary table, then primary table rows referenced by the foreign key may not be deleted. That's the rule. In plain English, it simply means that you can't delete an order if there are order details connected to the order. It would break what database architects call referential integrity.

Referential integrity means that every time a secondary row points to a primary row, that primary row must, in fact, exist. Referential integrity is broken at the primary table level by deleting the primary table row, or by updating the primary table row, so that the foreign key no longer points to a valid primary row.

Any decent relational database can automatically enforce referential integrity by refusing to execute any action that would break referential integrity. SQL Server databases do so by means of a foreign key constraint applied to the secondary table. This is often referred to as *declarative referential integrity,* or DRI.

I've heard folks who claimed to be database developers complain about referential integrity. They say that it makes it harder to input data or to fix data errors. Nine times out of ten when I'm asked to step into a database project that's failing, there's no referential integrity applied to the database. Hmmm, there seems to be a correlation here. The idea that referential integrity is only a bother and maybe it will get turned on later is a sure sign that the integrity of the data is less than paramount to that developer. That's a source of trouble, because the real role of the database developer is to position data so that it correctly models reality. Without referential integrity, the relational database model can't model reality. Whenever I design a data structure and build the tables, I apply referential integrity as I go. The data integrity rules apply at the beginning of the database construction, not at the end of the project.

Optional Foreign Keys

A common misconception is that referential integrity means that every foreign key has a related primary key, or every child row has a parent row. Referential integrity is often explained as "no orphans." This explanation is close, but it misses a subtle, but important, alternative application. It is perfectly acceptable in SQL to permit nulls in the foreign key, if the relationship is optional. Which means that it's okay to have children without parents! The rule is better explained as, "a child doesn't have to have a parent, but if it does, that parent has to be a real parent." Or more simply, "No imaginary parents."

So, in database design, it's more complicated than just the one-to-many relationship. In actuality, there are two types of foreign key relationships, required and optional. As a developer, you need to know when to use each type.

The purpose of the database is to model reality. If in reality the relationship between the primary and secondary tables is true, don't permit nulls in the foreign key; however, if the relationship is casual, and it isn't absolutely required, then allow nulls in the foreign key. Here are a few examples:

▶ An order detail row is invalid if it doesn't belong to an order. It would be wrong to have an order detail without an order. This relationship is not an option, so don't allow nulls in the OrderDetail.OrderID foreign key column.

▶ Assume there are three methods of order urgency that are optionally assigned to an order. An order is perfectly valid without an urgency method assigned. The Order-Urgency relationship is completely optional; therefore, the Order.UrgencyID foreign key should allow nulls.

▶ This example is more complex. The region is used to determine which warehouse ships the order. An order can't be shipped without a valid region. But an order might be placed and saved without a region. The solution is to make the regionID optional and allow nulls, but to place a constraint on the order complete flag so that it can't be set true if the RegionID is null.

```
Order constraint:
(OrderComplete = 1 AND NOT ISNULL(RegionID)) OR OrderComplete = FALSE
```

Referential integrity is extremely important to the success of the database project. When it gets in the way of performing a delete, it's doing its job correctly, because you've done your job well.

Cascade Deletes

The problem with referential integrity is that there are times when you want to delete an order, but you can't because the order has order detail rows assigned to it. Before the order can be deleted, you have to first delete the order detail rows. So, you go to delete those and discover that the order detail has order allocations assigned to them.

Tracing down all the required rows is a real pain, which is why so-called database developers fail to enforce referential integrity.

There's a better way to deal with this problem. When a primary row is deleted, a method called "cascading deletes" deletes the related secondary rows automatically, preventing the break in referential integrity. For example, if cascading deletes is programmed on the OrderDetail foreign key constraint that refers to the Order table, then when order number 15 is deleted, the database engine will automatically delete all order detail rows for order number 15 as well.

Cascading deletes are not limited to a single level; they "cascade" from table to table, if configured for each table in the cascade. While this can be powerful, it can be a plague as well. A user will make a simple deletion in a high-level table and hundreds or thousands of rows will be zapped into oblivion. The application will be blamed, and you just played a round of "bet your career." Be warned; don't let deleting a region cause a deletion of 1,500 customers, which in turn causes 75,000 orders to disappear. You, as the database developer, want to maintain complete control over deletions.

Here's my rule for cascading deletes. If the secondary row's data is important on its own, don't use cascading deletes. Only cascade the delete if the secondary data absolutely depends upon the primary data. In the real world, that means that it's okay to cascade deletes from orders to order details, because an order detail, without the order, is useless. On the other hand, a customer record is still important even if its region is deleted, so don't cascade from region to customer. And a shop order that is flagged as urgent is still important even if someone deletes "urgent" from the order status table. So don't apply cascade delete to the order status foreign key in the order table.

Cascade Delete Triggers

SQL products differ on how they implement cascading deletes. The best databases will feature cascading deletes as an option to the DRI/foreign key, since this is the fastest possible method; however, many databases will implement cascading deletes with a trigger. Sometimes you'll find a wizard or third-party tool that will write the cascade trigger for you. While the trigger is not complicated, it's more work than simply checking the cascade delete button.

Triggers are a special type of stored procedure code. Within the trigger, the "deleted" table mirrors the data that was just deleted. By joining the "deleted" trigger table with the cascading delete, the correct rows will be deleted in the cascade table:

```
CREATE TRIGGER Order_CascadeDelete
ON [Order]
```

```
FOR DELETE
DELETE FROM OrderDetail
FROM OrderDetail
JOIN DELETED ON OrderDetail.OrderID = Deleted.OrderID
```

One important note about the cascading delete trigger: constraints are checked before an "after trigger." This means that if you implement DRI at the database engine level, it will prevent the delete before the trigger has a chance to perform the cascade delete. Therefore, a trigger-based cascade delete method requires that you also enforce referential integrity via triggers instead of using the built-in referential integrity. The referential integrity trigger would test any insert or update actions to make sure that valid parent rows exist.

Logical Deletion

The permanence of the SQL DELETE command means that to build a robust application that can handle the day-to-day errors of the users, a more sophisticated delete system is usually needed. If you want an undo button, you have to build it yourself. As a rule, I do not permit physically deleting data in my applications, only logically deleting rows. This is not as amazing as it seems: dBase, back in the early 1980s, set a deleted flag when rows were deleted. Data wasn't physically removed until the file was packed.

Logical Delete Flag

In many tables, I include a logical delete flag called "IsDeleted." This bit column is defaulted to false, so new rows are initially set as active rows. The bit is toggled true when the row is logically deleted. The bit is set true either by the front-end app or by calling a stored procedure to delete the row. It would be nice to allow the front end to think it's deleting the row and then have a trigger convert the physical delete into a logical delete.

Unfortunately, it's not that easy. Rolling back the physical delete also removes the deleted table in the trigger. If the logical delete bit update is before the rollback, it too will be rolled back. If the logical delete update is after the rollback, then the deleted table is not available to see which rows were deleted. If you choose to implement a logical delete system, my recommendation is to use a stored procedure to toggle the IsDeleted flag.

To make this system work, every view, every stored procedure, and every SQL statement needs to check that bit to filter out all logically deleted rows.

Implementing a logical delete system requires disciplined programming, but it's worth it. Here's a sample logical delete trigger. Instead of deleting a row, the front-end application calls this stored procedure, which receives a single ID and handles the logical delete:

```
CREATE PROCEDURE Main_Delete
(@MainID UNIQUEIDENTIFIER )
AS
     UPDATE dbo.Main SET IsDeleted = 1
          WHERE dbo.Main.MainID  = @MainID
Return
```

Logical Delete Triggers

I love triggers. There is no better method of implementing complex business rules than a trigger. The whole point of client/server applications is to move the processing closer to the data, and that means putting the data manipulation and validation in stored procedures and triggers. They run lightning fast, have the fastest possible access to the data, and are completely in the control of the database developer. If you want performance and control over the application, then take the time to develop with stored procedures and triggers.

In the 1990s, n-tier design became popular, which puts business rules and complex constraints in a middle tier or object. Front-end and object-oriented programmers tend to like this practice, but database developers tend to shy away from n-tier designs. From the viewpoint of data integrity, there are two primary problems with this design. First, the code is one step removed from the database. It's faster to execute the code right inside the database engine than to pass it to another component often running on another machine. Second, with the increasing ease of distributed database technology, databases are often accessed from multiple applications and front-end tools. Applications like Access, Excel, and a host of others can easily get to the tables. This means that there's little guarantee that the client will access through the middle tier. If the rules are implemented in a middle layer, they may be only occasionally enforced. That just doesn't cut it. If the rules are implemented in a SQL trigger, they are absolutely enforced (except in the case of a few database administrative tools that sometimes bypass the triggers and transaction log).

In regard to preventing a physical deletion, a trigger, defined as "for Delete" or "after delete" for a table, will run when a delete action hits the table. The trigger can then do whatever you desire concerning the delete action. If you don't like the deletion, then raise an error and roll back the transaction. In regard to building a logical delete system, triggers serve multiple roles. I enforce the following system rules using triggers:

- ▶ Rows not logically deleted may not be physically deleted.
- ▶ Logically deleted rows may be not be updated.
- ▶ Logically deleted rows may be physically deleted only with the SA login.

These system rules are all implemented using the following triggers:

```
CREATE TRIGGER Main_LogicalDelete
ON dbo.Main
FOR UPDATE
AS
/* pn 12-20-00 version 1*/
      /* multi-row enabled */
      /* Check Logical Delete */
      IF EXISTS(SELECT * FROM deleted WHERE IsDeleted = 0)
            OR suser_sname() <> 'sa'
      BEGIN
            RAISERROR ('physical delete failed', 14, 1)
            ROLLBACK
      END
RETURN
```

This trigger simply checks for the presence of any rows not already logically deleted; if any exist, then the physical delete operation is rolled back. Additionally, the IF statement ensures that the user is logged in as "sa." If either condition (rows not logically deleted, or user not "sa") is not satisfied, then the next line, or BEGIN-END block of code, is executed. In this case, the next line is the BEGIN-END block that rolls back the delete.

The next trigger ensures that deleted rows are not manipulated or updated. The logic is that if the row's data is worth updating, then it really shouldn't be considered deleted. The problem is that if any update to a logically deleted row is rolled back, then a logically deleted row could not be undeleted, because the undelete would be rolled back. The solution is to roll back only if the row was and will be logically deleted before and after the update. This prohibits the update but permits the logical delete flag itself to be updated.

```
CREATE TRIGGER Main_LogicalDeleteUpdate
ON dbo.main
FOR UPDATE
AS
      /* multi-row enabled */
      /* Check Logical Delete */
      IF        EXISTS (SELECT * FROM deleted  WHERE IsDeleted = 1)
          AND EXISTS (SELECT * FROM inserted WHERE IsDeleted = 1)
BEGIN
            RAISERROR ('physical delete failed', 14, 1)
            ROLLBACK
      END
RETURN
```

Cascading Logical Deletes

A logical delete system is still not perfect, and it causes new questions and problems. The logical delete system has to handle a custom version of referential integrity and cascade deletes. These systems take a considerable amount of time to code and test. Managing a complete logical delete system is more complex than a physical delete system because it has to simulate cascade deletes.

The logical delete method has to indicate if the row itself was logically deleted, or if the row was logically deleted due to a cascaded logical delete. For some tables, this means that each row needs two flags, IsLogicalDelete and IsCascadeLogicalDelete. Some developers refer to the cascade logical delete as a virtual logical delete.

Logically undeleting, or restoring, is the biggest difficulty with a logical delete system. If a logical delete cascades, then a logical undelete should cascade as well. Undeleting at a lower level means determining if the lower-level row was virtually deleted because of the parent row or some other primary table row being undeleted. For example:

▶ Order 77, for Customer Acme Giants has five detail lines.

▶ Order 77 line 3 is logically deleted.

▶ Detail line 4 is for part 123. Part 123 is logically deleted, which cascades to order 77, detail line 4.

▶ Order 77 is deleted, which cascades down and virtually deletes all detail lines.

▶   If Order 77 is undeleted, which detail line should the cascade undelete?

▶   If Part 123 is undeleted, which detail lines, if any, should be undeleted?

The point is that each solution has pros and cons. Physical deletes lose data. Logical deletes are complex and open a can of worms. Many applications implement a logical delete method without any cascading effects as a balance between these two extremes.

Truncating a Table

A discussion of deletes and how they can cause trouble wouldn't be complete without mentioning the TRUNCATE TABLE SQL command. Truncating a table deletes every row in the table very quickly. The problem is that only the page deletes are logged in the transaction log; the row deletes are not. Think of this as a bulk insert, which also bypasses the transaction log, but in reverse.

```
SELECT COUNT(*) FROM Customer
77
TRUNCATE TABLE Customer
SELECT COUNT(*) FROM Customer
0
```

I strongly recommend that you avoid the use of bulk insert, or TRUNCATE TABLE. The few moments of performance gained are not worth the potential problems of trying to recover without a transaction log.

Summary

How you manage delete operations in your application is up to you. This chapter has presented the pitfalls to watch out for and a few ideas to help you think about a solution you can live with. The applications that don't consider managing deleted records are either non–mission critical, or nonsuccessful. Just remember, "WHERE is your best friend."

Grouping and Aggregating Data

IN THIS CHAPTER:

Common Aggregate Functions

GROUP BY

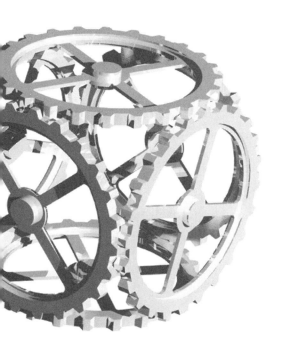

Data is just bits on a disk. When data is meaningful, then it's information. Part of the task of the database developer is turning raw data into information; in other words, finding the information hidden within the data by summarizing the data. Within SQL, the grouping by and aggregate functions are designed to do just that.

An aggregate function performs some type of mathematical function, such as sum, min, or max, on a column and returns the mathematical answer. The aggregate function is performed on the entire set. That's where the grouping function comes into play. It divides the result set into smaller sets based on values in columns. The aggregate functions are then applied to the smaller grouped sets instead of the entire result set.

The best part is that all these functions are performed quickly within the database engine—without code looping through the records. When it comes to preparing data for summary reports, aggregate functions do the trick.

The most common trouble when working with aggregates is that as soon as you use one aggregate function, the database engine wants every column to participate. For example, in the following code, the second column gathers the count of the orders, but the first column isn't a part of the aggregate functions, and there's no GROUP BY clause. As you can see, aggregates are an all-or-nothing proposition. As soon as you begin to use aggregates, the entire query must become an aggregate query. And this makes perfect sense, because the record set returned is summation data across the entire data set determined by the FROM and WHERE clauses. Returning data from a single internal row would be incorrect.

```
SELECT FirstName + ' ' + LastName, COUNT(OrderID)
FROM Employees
JOIN Orders ON Employees.EmployeeID = Orders.EmployeeID
Server: Msg 8118, Level 16, State 1, Line 1
Column 'Employees.FirstName' is invalid in the select list because it is not
contained in an aggregate function and there is no GROUP BY clause.
Server: Msg 8118, Level 16, State 1, Line 1
Column 'Employees.LastName' is invalid in the select list because it is not
contained in an aggregate function and there is no GROUP BY clause.
```

This means that as a developer, you can't afford to master only one or two aggregate functions and expect to work with them successfully. If you work with aggregates at all, you must understand and employ the entire set of aggregate and group by functions. This chapter will explain the use of aggregates and how to effectively solve problems when working with aggregates.

The chapter will begin by explaining the aggregate functions as they can be applied to an entire result set. Once the functions are understood on their own, the GROUP BY clause will be added to the code to enhance the aggregate functions.

Common Aggregate Functions

While there are aggregate functions for statistical operations, and different SQL database products add their own unique aggregate functions, these five common aggregates account for the overwhelming majority of actual uses.

► COUNT (* [ALL | DISTINCT] expression)

► SUM ([ALL | DISTINCT] expression)

► AVG ([ALL | DISTINCT] expression)

► MAX (expression)

► MIN (expression)

When using any of these aggregate functions, there are a few points to remember:

► Aggregate functions require a scan operation, which is slower than a seek.

► Aggregate functions will leave the column name as null, so you'll want to provide a column alias name.

► Every column must participate in the summation, either in an aggregate function, or as part of a group by.

► Aggregate functions that perform numeric calculations (SUM, AVG) ignore nulls. They have to; otherwise, the calculations would fail.

The COUNT() Function

The Count() function determines the number of rows in the set or grouping. Typically, this is used to count the number of secondary rows under a primary row, such as the number of orders for a customer, or the number of appointments for a professional.

```
COUNT (* [ALL | DISTINCT] expression)
```

COUNT() commonly counts the primary key, although in some cases it's useful to count some other column. Unfortunately, Microsoft's new GUID data type, which is an ideal primary key, may not be used as a count column. So, if you're using GUID primary keys, as I recommend, you'll need to use COUNT(*).

```
-- Example using *
SELECT COUNT(*)
     FROM Employees
```

```
        WHERE Country = 'USA'

-----------
5

(1 row(s) affected)

-- Example using the Primary Key
SELECT COUNT(EmployeeID)
        FROM Employees
        WHERE Country = 'USA'

-----------
5

(1 row(s) affected)
```

By default, the count function will count "all" rows in the set; however, the "distinct" keyword can be added to force it to count only unique rows. In the following code, the distinct keyword causes the count function to count only unique productIDs.

```
SELECT COUNT(DISTINCT ProductID) FROM [Order Details]
-----------
77

(1 row(s) affected)
```

Some developers will use a "COUNT(*) > 0" to check for rows in a result set. This is slow, because instead of just seeing if there are any rows, SQL Server has to determine the total count. A faster alternative is to use the EXISTS function with a subquery. The EXISTS function checks for the presence of any data in a result set. At the first row located, it stops and lets the rest of the SQL statement continue. The SELECT statement passed to the EXISTS function must SELECT *.

```
IF EXISTS(SELECT * FROM Employees WHERE (Birthdate = GETDATE()) )
```

This EXISTS function would return true (1) to the IF keyword if any employees were celebrating their birthdays today.

The EXISTS function can be combined with a NOT if you're checking for an empty result set. Just as a NOT in a WHERE clause slows performance, the NOT EXISTS will also take longer than a positive EXISTS. But slow and correct beats fast and wrong every time. If the logic calls for a NOT EXISTS, it's still faster than "COUNT(*) = 0".

```
IF NOT EXISTS(SELECT * FROM Employees WHERE (Birthdate = getdate()) )
```

Another common misapplication of the COUNT() function is using the COUNT() function to determine the number of rows in a table. While this is certainly accurate and ANSI standard, a faster method is to use a database-specific method to return the row count of a table. For example, in Microsoft SQL Server, the fastest way to determine table size is to examine the sysindexes table. The first query demonstrates the slow method. The following view dynamically returns the row count of all user tables.

```
-- Table RowCounts
SELECT COUNT(*) AS ProductCount FROM Products
SELECT COUNT(*) AS CustomerCount FROM Customers
SELECT COUNT(*) AS EmployeeCount FROM Employees
GO
ProductCount
------------
77

(1 row(s) affected)

CustomerCount
-------------
91

(1 row(s) affected)

EmployeeCount
-------------
9

(1 row(s) affected)


-- The TableRowCount View
-- a faster method of determining table rowcounts

CREATE VIEW dbo.TableRowCount
AS
SELECT TOP 100 PERCENT dbo.sysobjects.[name], dbo.sysindexes.[rows]
     FROM dbo.sysindexes
     JOIN dbo.sysobjects
          ON dbo.sysindexes.[id] = dbo.sysobjects.[id]
     WHERE (dbo.sysobjects.xtype = 'U')
          AND (dbo.sysindexes.indid = 0
          OR dbo.sysindexes.indid = 1)
     ORDER BY dbo.sysindexes.[name]
```

```
SELECT * FROM tablerowcount

name                             rows
--------------------             ----------
CustomerCustomerDemo             0
CustomerDemographics             0
EmployeeTerritories              49
Categories                       8
Customers                        91
Employees                        9
Order Details                    2155
Orders                           830
Products                         77
Shippers                         3
Suppliers                        29
Region                           4
Territories                      53

(13 row(s) affected)
```

This SQL statement, stored as a view for repeated use, joins sysindexes with sysobjects and then returns the table name plus the row count from sysindexes. It's fast and elegant.

The SUM() Function

When you need to determine the total amount for a column from a result set, then the SUM() function is the best way to go. The SUM() function simply adds all nonnull values and returns the answer. The function is rather straightforward, any problems tending to involve summing incorrect rows.

```
-- Total sales item quantity in the database
SELECT SUM(Quantity)
      FROM [Order Details]
-----------
51317

(1 row(s) affected)

-- total dollar amount sold in 1996
SELECT SUM(Quantity * UnitPrice) AS Sales1996
      FROM [Order Details]
      JOIN Orders
            ON Orders.OrderID = [Order Details].OrderID
```

```
       WHERE DatePart(yy,OrderDate) = '1996'

Sales1996
--------------------
226298.5000

(1 row(s) affected)
```

The AVG() Function

In the same way that the SUM() function calculates the numeric total of a single column in the result set, the AVG() function calculates the average of all nonnull values in a column.

```
SELECT AVG(Quantity) AS AvgQuantity1996
     FROM [Order Details]
     JOIN Orders
          ON Orders.OrderID = [Order Details].OrderID
     WHERE DatePart(yy,OrderDate) = '1996'

AvgQuantity1996
---------------
23

(1 row(s) affected)
```

As with the other aggregate functions, most problems are caused by incorrectly building the result set in the FROM clause using joins or subqueries, or an incorrect WHERE clause.

The MIN() and MAX() Functions

The MIN() and MAX() functions return the smallest or largest values in the result set. Both of these functions work well with numeric, string, or datetime data. While these functions may seem similar to the top predicate, the benefit of using min() or max() is that they may be used with other aggregate functions. The down side is that, while these functions locate the extreme values in a result set, they provide no method of returning the other data from the row containing the min or max value. In the following code, for example, the largest and smallest order detail lines are quickly located, but determining the orderID for those detail lines is not possible using this technique. Aggregate functions are useful for calculating information from the entire set. To drill into row-level details, use subqueries or the top predicate with an ORDER BY clause.

```
SELECT MAX(Quantity * UnitPrice) AS LargestOrderDetail1996,
     MIN(Quantity * UnitPrice) AS SmallestOrderDetail1996
     FROM [Order Details]
     JOIN Orders
          ON Orders.OrderID = [Order Details].OrderID
     WHERE DatePart(yy,OrderDate) = '1996'

LargestOrderDetail1996  SmallestOrderDetail1996
----------------------  -----------------------
10540.0000              7.3000


(1 row(s) affected)
```

GROUP BY

By themselves, the aggregate functions return values from the entire result set. And many times this is useful. However, as you've seen in some examples, a value had to be hard-coded into a WHERE clause to pull the correct aggregate data. To determine the count of employees in the U.S.A., "USA" had to be written in the WHERE clause.

```
SELECT COUNT(*)
     FROM Employees
     WHERE Country = 'USA'
```

This presents a problem when we want to report the employee count from multiple countries. The countries will likely be unknown during development, and as new countries are brought into the database, you'd hate to constantly rewrite the code. As a rule, hard-coding values is a poor practice.

The solution is to let the SQL database engine create smaller result sets from the whole subset based on values in a specified column. The aggregate functions in the select columns are then calculated, not on the overall result set, but on each of the smaller groups of data, as demonstrated in the following two code samples.

```
SELECT Country, COUNT(EmployeeID)
     FROM Employees
     GROUP BY Country
Country
---------------  -----------
UK               4
USA              5


(2 row(s) affected)
```

```
SELECT Country, COUNT(CustomerID)
     FROM Customers
     GROUP BY Country

Country
--------------- -----------
Argentina       3
Austria         2
Belgium         2
Brazil          9
Canada          3
Denmark         2
Finland         2
France          11
Germany         11
...
Switzerland     2
UK              7
USA             13
Venezuela       4

(21 row(s) affected)
```

Cleaning Up a GROUP BY Query

There are a few points to remember when polishing a GROUP BY query.

```
SELECT FirstName + ' ' + LastName, COUNT(OrderID)
FROM Employees
JOIN Orders ON Employees.EmployeeID = Orders.EmployeeID
GROUP BY Orders.EmployeeID, LastName, FirstName
GO
-------------------------------- -----------
Nancy Davolio                    123
Andrew Fuller                    96
Janet Leverling                  127
Margaret Peacock                 156

(9 row(s) affected)
```

   While this SQL statement returns valid data, it could use some clean-up. A polished SELECT statement involving an aggregate function will also likely include column aliases for the aggregate columns to provide a useful column name, and sometimes sorting based on the aggregate columns to emphasis the aggregate data.

```
SELECT FirstName + ' ' + LastName AS Employee,
COUNT(OrderID) AS 'NumberOfOrders'
FROM Employees
JOIN Orders ON Employees.EmployeeID = Orders.EmployeeID
GROUP BY Orders.EmployeeID, LastName, FirstName
ORDER BY 2 DESC
Go


 Employee                                   NumberOfOrders
------------------------------             -----------
Margaret Peacock                            156
Janet Leverling                             127
Nancy Davolio                               123
Laura Callahan                              104
...
(9 row(s) affected)
```

This result set, with column headers and sorted so that the top seller is at the top, is much better suited for reporting the number of sales per employee.

Aggregate functions are also commonly combined with the top predicate discussed in Chapter 7.

```
-- top 20% counties by Customer Count
SELECT TOP 20 PERCENT Country, COUNT(CustomerID) AS CustomerCount
      FROM Customers
      GROUP BY Country
      ORDER BY 2 Desc


Country          CustomerCount
---------------  -------------
USA              13
France           11
Germany          11
Brazil           9
UK               7


(5 row(s) affected)
```

One more significant point on planning aggregate queries with GROUP BYs: if the group by column is a string column and you're not also grouping by a unique index, then it's highly possible that the data will be grouped according to the text rather than the unique individual rows. To solve the potential problem, it's a good practice to always include the group by table's primary key even if you don't need it in the output columns.

The SQL Order with Aggregates

When working with aggregate functions, a natural question is, "How does the WHERE clause filter rows, before or after the grouping?" It's a good question. How we write SQL queries depends heavily on the answer. The best answer to that question is to walk through the process of aggregate query.

1. **From**   The first step in a SQL aggregate query, as with any query, is the creation of the data set from the tables and joins listed in the FROM clause.

2. **Where**   The second step is filtering the correct rows from the tables. Use the WHERE clause to select the correct initial set of data.

3. **Aggregate functions / group by**   The grouping occurs after the WHERE clause.

4. **Having**   The HAVING clause filters out groups based on the having criteria.

5. **OrderBy**   The remaining groups are then ordered according to the ORDER BY clause.

6. **Select columns**   As a final step, the columns are positioned and the result set is sent to the client.

In this code example, the HAVING clause is used to remove those countries with less than five customers:

```
SELECT Country, COUNT(CustomerID)
     FROM Customers
     GROUP BY Country
     HAVING COUNT(CustomerID) > 4
     ORDER BY Country

Country
--------------- -----------
Brazil          9
France          11
Germany         11
Mexico          5
Spain           5
UK              7
USA             13

(7 row(s) affected)
```

By combining aggregate functions, groupings, the top predicate, WHERE clauses, and the HAVING clause, you can easily present critical information from a large set of data.

Generating Cube Subtotals

Once data is presented in subgroups, someone will ask for subtotals and grand totals. The cube option will add a row for every group, with a null value and an overall total. If you are grouping by two or more columns, the cube option will add an extra row for each group for each column, and a grand total row. The grand total row will have a null in every group by column.

Most report writers and front-end tools don't know how to handle rows that include subtotals, so for most production applications, I recommend you avoid the cube option and calculate the subtotals and grand totals in the report writer. Nevertheless, the cube option can be useful if you're quickly selecting data in an ad hoc query.

In the first example, the last row reports a null as the country—this row is the total of all countries.

```
-- Simple Cube
SELECT Country, COUNT(CustomerID)
    FROM Customers
    GROUP BY Country WITH CUBE


Country
--------------- -----------
Argentina       3
Austria         2
Belgium         2
. . .
USA             13
Venezuela       4
NULL            91

(22 row(s) affected)



-- Large Cube
-- All Sales by Country and Product Category
SELECT ISNULL(Customers.Country, 'all countries') AS Country ,
    ISNULL(Categories.CategoryName, 'all categories') AS Category,
    SUM([Order Details].Quantity * [Order Details].UnitPrice) AS Sales
    FROM Orders
    JOIN [Order Details]
        ON Orders.OrderID = [Order Details].OrderID
    JOIN Customers
        ON Orders.CustomerID = Customers.CustomerID
    JOIN Products
        ON [Order Details].ProductID = Products.ProductID
```

```
JOIN Categories
    ON Products.CategoryID = Categories.CategoryID
GROUP BY Customers.Country, Categories.CategoryName WITH CUBE
ORDER BY Customers.Country, Categories.CategoryName


Country          Category          Sales
--------------  ---------------  --------------------
all countries    all categories   1354458.5900
all countries    Beverages        286526.9500
all countries    Condiments       113694.7500
all countries    Confections      177099.1000
all countries    Dairy Products   251330.5000
all countries    Grains/Cereals   100726.8000
all countries    Meat/Poultry     178188.8000
all countries    Produce          105268.6000
all countries    Seafood          141623.0900
Argentina        all categories   8119.1000
Argentina        Beverages        1798.0000
Argentina        Condiments       907.0000
Argentina        Confections      2135.1000
Argentina        Dairy Products   1143.5000
Argentina        Grains/Cereals   390.0000
Argentina        Produce          1139.0000
Argentina        Seafood          606.5000
Austria          all categories   139496.6300
```

In the large cube example, the ISNULL() function is replacing the nulls in the cube subtotal rows with a more readable and meaningful phrase.

Recap

Aggregates allow you to turn massive amounts of data into useful information. To summarize, these are the keys to using aggregates:

▶ As soon as you use one aggregate function, every column must participate in the aggregate.

▶ COUNT() will include rows with nulls, while SUM() and AVG() will ignore null values.

▶ Data typing must be observed. Numeric aggregate functions are limited to numeric columns. MIN and MAX may be applied to string columns.

▶ When grouping, include the primary key, even if you're not selecting the primary key, to ensure that you actually group on unique rows.

► When grouping, the WHERE clause is executed before the grouping, the HAVING is executed after the grouping.

Summary

This chapter has focused on using the most common of the aggregate functions. It has covered what aggregation is and how to use the most common functions. It has also shown some of the common pitfalls associated with grouping and aggregation. As an example of a complex aggregation problem, we have examined computing summary statistics for a three-dimensional table.

Using Joins

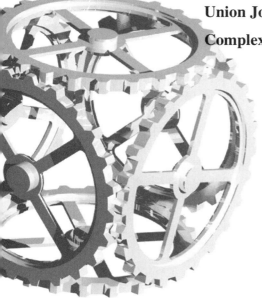

A relational database divides the data into several tables of similar or related data. Often these tables by themselves are completely meaningless. A properly normalized order detail table with data about the line items of an order, for example, will include a foreign key to the order table, and not include any data about the order. The order detail table simply points to the order table. When retrieving order detail data, to determine the order number, or even the customer, a connection must first be made between the order detail row and the corresponding order row so that data from the order table can also be viewed.

NOTE

If you are unfamiliar with the common Customer—Order—OrderDetail—Product structure, the Northwinds sample database includes these tables. Admittedly, there are several flaws with Northwinds, but it is commonly available, so you can try these queries on your own.

In an older ISAM (indexed sequential access method) database, code would have to loop through the order detail table or seek the correct order row to locate and display corresponding data. But SQL is designed for relational databases and excels at connecting, or joining, data between multiple tables. The key to developing relational database applications is thinking in terms of data sets rather than thinking in terms of individual rows. Developing relational database applications that run well requires complete fluency in the ways that SQL joins data from multiple tables.

SQL databases, and the front-end access methods, all include some mechanism to move through a recordset row by row for those cases when it's absolutely necessary, such as SQL cursors, ADO recordsets, or Jet recordsets. However, these methods are painfully slow compared to an elegant SQL statement that allows the query optimizer and database engine to perform the join as a set. When data from multiple tables must be viewed as a single set, the join is a developer's best tool.

Mastering the SQL join is critical for the database developer. I was called in to rescue one project that was failing when performing a complex search based on several criteria from about a dozen tables. The search would take 5 to 20 minutes and often fail. The search procedure was constructed using about 200 lines of nested loops. Rebuilding the search with a SQL statement including the appropriate joins reduced the search to about one minute, and it never failed. Further optimization of the tables and indexes reduced that search to one to three seconds for every search. Moving as much of the processing as possible from code to the database engine is where the performance gains are found.

The Join Within the SQL Statement

The *join* is used within the FROM clause of the SQL statement to connect, or link, two tables into a single resultset used by the rest of the SQL statement. In a strict sense, a join is simply a better way to say, "Select from TableA and from TableB where TableA.id = TableB.id and then view it as a single recordset."

In the example of the order and order detail tables, the two tables can be connected using the common "OrderID" column. In the order table, OrderID is the primary key. The order detail table includes OrderID as a foreign key. The join connects rows from the two tables with the same OrderID.

Inner Joins

By far the most common join is the *inner join,* sometimes called an equi-join in some database products, or a natural join in some textbooks. It produces a resultset of all matching, or corresponding, rows between the two tables The basic syntax for an inner join is:

```
SELECT {columns} FROM TableA JOIN TableB ON TableA.column = TableB.comlumn
```

The join operation will limit the number of rows returned. Rows from either side of the join without matches will not be included in the resultset. In a sense, the inner join functions as a WHERE clause. In fact, earlier versions of SQL and some database products specified the join using the following syntax:

```
SELECT {columns} FROM Tablea, TableB where TableA.PK = TableB.FK
```

Changes in the Resulting Row Count

Joins typically increase or decrease the number of rows returned compared to the original table without the second table joined to it.

Because the inner join creates a resultset by matching rows, if there are multiple rows on one table that match the other table, a row is returned for each combination. In the case of a join between two tables in a one-to-many table relationship, a single row will be returned for each row in the many side. The rows from the one side will appear to be repeated for each matching many-side row. This increases the number of rows returned. For example, order 77 has one row in the order table. And that's enforced because OrderID is the primary key. But, in the order detail table, there are five line items for order 77. An inner join between Order and OrderDetail, looking for order 77, is written like this:

```
SELECT Order.OrderID, OrderNumber, LineNumber, PartID
FROM Order
INNER JOIN OrderDetail
ON Order.OrderID = OrderDetail.orderID
WHERE OrderID = 77
ORDER BY LineNumber
```

This SQL statement returns the following resultset:

OrderID	OrderNumber	Line Number	PartID
77	123-456	1	q-123
77	123-456	2	w-234
77	123-456	3	e-345
77	123-456	4	r-456
77	123-456	5	t-567

Even though there is only one row in the order table for order 77, the select statement returned five rows, because the matches to OrderDetail required that each of the five rows in OrderDetail is returned in the resultset.

Sometimes joins will have the opposite effect, causing rows to disappear from the resultset. Inner joins exclude rows from either side that don't have a matching row. A common example of this effect is a join between customers and orders that eliminates customers without orders. It is a good idea to check the SQL statement with an outer join to find any mismatched or dropped rows. Outer joins are explained later in this chapter.

Working with Graphic Query Tools

When you first begin working with complex queries involving several joins, you'll find that graphically diagramming the joins will improve your experience. Most SQL databases and front-end tools provide a method to place tables on a graphic surface and draw the joins between the tables. In addition, the properties of the join can often be specified, creating an outer join.

The downside is that graphic tools often generate SQL that, while technically correct, is difficult to read and debug. For example, if a SQL statement requires joining six tables, the graphic tool might not list the join columns in sequence with the join table. Debugging this type of SQL statement in text form quickly becomes a nightmare. Often a more direct solution is to redo the join portion of the SQL statement in text.

When developing SQL within stored procedures and embedded SQL, the graphic tool may not be available or useful even though these are often the most complex SQL statements in the database application. The SQL extensions that are desired within stored procedures will not work in the graphical query tool. Learning to write SQL joins without the aid of a graphic tool will make debugging the more complex portions of the application easier.

Execution Order of the SQL Statement

At what point the join takes place in the execution of the SQL statement is important. The basic task of the join is to merge two recordsets into what looks like a new resulting recordset. Because the role of the join is to produce a new recordset, the join is used within the "from" portion of the SQL statement. While the basic SQL statement makes sense when read left to right, it's not performed in that order. A better way to think of the SQL statement is:

▶ **FROM... JOIN**   Join these tables into a recordset

▶ **WHERE**   Filtering the rows to be retrieved by the criteria

▶ **SELECT**   View these columns from the new recordset

▶ **ORDER BY**   And place them in this order

Because the SQL engine will first join the tables into the recordset, it's critical that the joins be defined properly to produce the correct resulting recordset. If the joins are incorrect, then the WHERE clause has no chance to select the correct rows.

Because of the execution order, understanding how the query optimizer works in your database product is important. Some query optimizers, such as MS SQL Server, are cost based and will design a query plan that requires the least amount of processing to work given the joins, WHERE clauses, SELECT columns, and index statistics. When writing SQL statements for cost-based query optimizers, you'll find that when hitting the same data, the query plan will be the same even if the query is written dramatically different. However, if the data or indexes change, the query optimizer may generate a very different query plan. The SQL Server Query Analyzer graphically displays the estimated and actual query plans.

The Oracle query optimizer allows you to choose between cost-based and rule-based optimization. Rule-based optimization generates the query execution plan in terms of how the query is written. Understanding how to write efficient queries for the Oracle query optimizer is critical for Oracle developers.

Self Joins

Some database projects will include a relationship involving only one table. One column becomes a foreign key, which points back to that same table's primary key. Two examples of this type of relationship are the classic employee table and a real-world example of an item system with item versions.

Most employees report to another employee. If the employee table's primary key is EmployeeID, then a good way to express the relationship between an employee and his or her boss is to include the boss's primary key in the employee's row in a column called ReportsToID. To enforce referential integrity, a foreign key constraint should be applied to ReportsToID so that only valid EmployeeIDs can be inserted into ReportsToID. But there's at least one employee who's at the top of the pyramid and who doesn't report to anyone, so it's logically valid to permit the ReportsToID column to contain a null. And that's exactly how the column should be set up: same data type as EmployeeID, Foreign Key constraint to EmployeeID, and allow nulls.

From this single-table schema, a self-join can extract a list of every employee and that employee's boss.

```
SELECT E.FirstName + ' ' + E.LastName AS Emp,
B.FirstName + ' ' + B.LastName AS Boss
FROM Employee E
LEFT OUTER JOIN Employee B
     ON E.ReportsToID = B.EmployeeID
```

Because SQL statements' execution begins with the data source in the FROM clause, I'll walk through this statement starting with the Employee table. In the FROM clause, the employee table is listed twice. The "E" and "B" are named ranges.

They provide an alias for the table so that the same table can be referenced multiple times in the SQL statement. The "E" instance of the Employee table will be used for the employees, and the "B" instance will be used to extract bosses. A left outer join is crafted between E and B so that employees without bosses will still be listed in the resultset. If an inner join were used here, the top boss would be dropped from the report!

The SQL statement is completed by concatenating the first and last names from the E, giving it the alias of "emp," and assembling the bosses' full names and applying the alias of "boss."

The second example of a self-join comes from a real-world material specification system. Each item can go through several versions of specifications. Each version is tracked as a unique stand-alone item, yet it must always relate back to its original item for compatibility and ordering. The main columns of the item table look like those shown in Table 12-1.

The business rules for the item specification insist that when an item is originally created as version 1.0, the OriginalItemID is set to ItemID. As new versions of an item specification are created, the new version is given a new unique ItemID, but the OriginalItemID remains the same. The logic of applying the OriginalItemID is best handled in the stored procedure creating the new version. An abbreviated sample of the table is shown in Table 12-2.

Column	Constraint	Data Type	Default
ItemID	Primary Key, No Nulls	GUID (Global Unique Identifier)	newid()
OriginalItemID	Foreign Key— to ItemID, No Nulls	GUID	
ItemVersion	No Nulls	Number 4.2	1.0
ItemName	No Nulls	nVarChar	
IsActive	No Nulls	bit	1

Table 12-1 *Item Specification Table Design*

ItemID	OriginalItemID	ItemVersion	ItemName	Active
A123	A123	1.0	WidgetOne	0
A124	A123	1.1	WidgetOne	1
A125	A125	1.0	ThingamaGiggy	0
A126	A123	2.0	WidgetOne	1
A127	A125	1.1	Thing-a-Gig	1

Table 12-2   *Item Specification Data*

The Widget item has three versions of the specifications. Of those, two are still active, but version 1.0 has been retired from production. The ThingamaGiggy is in its second version, and this version has seen a name change.

From this single-table schema, there are lots of creative SQL statements waiting to happen.

To find all active item specifications:

```
SELECT ItemName, ItemVersion
    FROM Item
    WHERE IsActive = 1
```

To list all original item specifications:

```
SELECT ItemName, ItemVersion
    FROM Item
    WHERE ItemID =  OriginalItemID
```

To retrieve all item specifications for the item originally known as the "ThingamaGiggy" takes a little more work. The "one" side of the join will locate the original item specification. The "many" sides of the join will find all the item specifications.

```
SELECT I.ItemName, I.ItemVersion, I.IsActive
    FROM Item O
    JOIN Item I
        ON O.ItemID = I.OriginalItemID
    WHERE O.ItemName = "ThingamaGiggy"
        AND O.ItemID = O.OriginalItemID
    ORDER BY I.ItemVersion
```

The basis of this task is to join between the original item and all the subsequent versions of that item. To perform a self-join requires two instances of the table, so the first instance will locate the original item specifications. It will have the range variable, or table alias, of "O." The second instance of the Item table, called "I," is used for the item versions.

In the preceding SQL statement, "ItemID = OriginalItemID" was used in the WHERE clause to filter only the initial item specifications for any item. The same WHERE condition is applied here with the additional condition of ItemName.

An inner join between O and I will now limit all rows from the I table to only those with OriginalItemIDs equal to the initial ItemID of any rows in O. Since O has already been filtered to the single row for ThingamaGiggy version 1.0, the join will filter I to only those item specifications derived from ThingamaGiggy version 1.0 (A125 in the OriginalItemID column). Even the version 1.0 specification has A125 in the OriginalItemID column, so it too will be listed.

To complete the SQL statement, the columns are listed in the SELECT, and the sort is applied in the ORDER BY.

Outer Joins

Outer joins return a larger set than an inner join by including all the rows from one of the tables, even those "outside" the set of matches between the two tables. This type of join can be extremely useful in cases where the data is less symmetrical or has mismatched data.

Outer joins are declared as either left or right outer joins. The difference is which table's rows are included outside the join. A *left outer join* means that the table listed first (reading left to right) in the text of the SQL is the table supplying the additional, or mismatched, rows. From the earlier example, an inner join between customers and orders would ignore customers without orders; however, this outer join solves the problem:

```
SELECT Customer.CustomerName, [Order].OrderNumber
FROM Customer
LEFT OUTER JOIN [Order]
ON Customer.OrderID = [Order].OrderID
ORDER BY CustomerName
```

This SQL statement would return all customers, whether or not a given customer had any orders. If an inner join were used, then only customers with orders would have been returned. For customers with multiple orders, they would be listed for each order. Customers without orders would be listed once and have a null in the OrderNumber column. Here's an abbreviated example data set typical of an outer join:

CustomerName	OrderNumber
Alpha Graphics	123
Best Advertising	124
Best Advertising	456
Creative Thinking	<null>
DuckBeak Animation	567
DuckBeak Animation	678
English Tea and Crumpets	654
Fantastic Doodles	<null>

Right Outer Joins

If you manually type your SQL statement, chances are you'll seldom build a right outer join. But if you drop your tables on a graphics query builder, then the order of the outer join will likely be based on the order the tables were dropped on the graphic surface.

A *right outer join* is essentially the same as a left outer join except that the table listed on the right side of the join is the outer side of the join. In our example, a right outer join would have returned only customers with orders, the orders, and any orders that don't match up with customers. With proper referential integrity, that would never be the case. Unfortunately, legacy data is seldom as clean as is hoped. Using an outer join to locate mismatched rows is a standard data conversion and data scrubbing technique.

Data Scrubbing with Nulls

Since outer joins find mismatched rows, it's a perfect tool for locating faulty rows. A straightforward method for singling out the mismatched rows combines an outer join with an "is null" WHERE condition to return only mismatched rows:

```
SELECT Customer.CustomerName, [Order].OrderNumber
FROM Customer
```

```
LEFT OUTER JOIN [Order]
ON Customer.OrderID = [Order].OrderID
WHERE CustomerID IS NULL
ORDER BY CustomerName
```

This code is nearly the same as the previous example. The outer join includes all customers whether there's a matching order or not. The difference is that this time customers with orders are filtered out in the WHERE clause. Only those customers with a null in OrderID are returned:

CustomerName	OrderNumber
Creative Thinking	<null>
Fantastic Doodles	<null>

As you search questionable data for patterns and attempt to clean the data, thinking of the data in terms of joins and nulls will prove to be an effective and impressive method. Several loops of code, nested views, or subqueries can be eliminated using this powerful technique.

Full Outer Joins

The *full outer join* returns every row from both tables regardless of matches. Rows with matches will contain data from both data sources, while rows from either side of the join without a match will result in nulls in place of the missing values. Microsoft SQL Server implements a full outer join; however, with most other SQL-based databases you'll need to perform a left outer join and a right outer join and then union the results.

In practice, the full outer join is rarely used. In the past couple of years, I can remember building only one query within an application with the full outer join. However, a full outer join is useful for quickly searching for mismatches in either side of the join.

An Eighteenth-Century Analogy

Here's an easy way to picture the different types of joins. Imagine an eighteenth-century church with the genders segregated. Women are sitting on the left side, and the men are on the right. Some of the congregation are married couples, some are single. Each side of the church represents one table, and there are different ways to join and select from that two-table database.

▶ **Inner join**   If every married couple came together in the center aisle and left the church walking hand in hand, leaving all the singles in the church building, that would represent an inner join. Only matches are in the resulting set.

▶ **Left outer join**   If all the women, married or single, stood and left the church taking their husbands along and left the bachelor men in the church, that would look like a left outer join. If a woman is single, her partner space in line would be empty.

▶ **Right outer join**   A right outer join would look like all the men leaving the church with their spouses, and leaving the single women behind.

▶ **Full outer join**   If everyone leaves regardless of their marital state, that would represent a full outer join. Every married couple is walking together, but singles are walking alone. The space normally occupied by their spouse is empty.

Legacy Joins

If you're working with a relatively new database project on a new SQL database engine, this section will seem strange. But if you're maintaining an older SQL database application, you may come across an old-style syntax for an outer join. Because a join is in fact nothing more than selecting from two tables where the values are equal, the original ANSI SQL syntax for a join looked like two tables and a WHERE clause.

```
SELECT …
     FROM TableA, TableB
     WHERE TableA.ID = TableB.ID
```

Outer joins were expressed within the WHERE comparison operator by adding an * on either side of the equal sign. For example, a left outer join looked like this:

```
SELECT …
     FROM TableA, TableB
     WHERE TableA.ID *= TableB.ID
```

With any luck, you'll never see one of these, and if you do, chances are you've already asked if you can upgrade, so I won't bother suggesting it here. But, I wanted to warn you.

Cross Joins

The *cross join* is a different kind of join altogether. Instead of merging the two tables into a single recordset by matching rows, the cross join actually multiplies the two tables together, producing a large Cartesian resultset.

Assume TableA has two rows with the values "Red" and "White." TableB has three rows with the values "1," "2," and "3." A cross join between TableA and TableB would be written as:

```
SELECT * FROM TableA CROSS JOIN tableB
```

The resultset would be:

Red	1
Red	2
Red	3
White	1
White	2
White	3

Each value is matched with every value in the other table. Two rows in TableA are multiplied by three rows in TableB, resulting in six possible combinations in the resultset, thus multiplying the rows.

Often cross joins are used with insert queries to generate data or prepopulate tables. In some applications, a certain number of rows must exist prior to editing the rows. A cross join is an effective method of generating the required rows.

Cross joins are also used to generate sample data for load testing. After all, you can't very well tune an index with 15 rows in the table, but 15 rows and three cross joins later and the table could have 2.5 billion rows.

Union Joins

A *union join* does exactly what it sounds like it would do. The result of one SQL SELECT statement is appended to another SQL SELECT statement. The two resultsets are simply pasted, or stacked, together.

The two SELECT statements must have the same number of columns, and the columns must line up with compatible data types. Although the columns are often the same, they need not be. If the two tables have different columns, the resultset will use the column names from the first table. Union join queries may be sorted by specifying the ORDER BY on the last SQL statement.

A single union join may include multiple SQL statements, each joined with the union join.

```
SELECT StudentID, Name FROM Student
UNION
SELECT TeacherID, Name FROM Teacher
UNION
SELECT EmployeeID, Name FROM Employee
ORDER BY Name
```

The union join handles unique rows differently than the single SELECT statement. A single SQL select will, by default, return duplicate rows unless the DISTINCT command is stated following the SELECT. DISTINCT causes the SQL engine to generate the resultset and then compare all the rows, eliminating any extra rows that are complete exact duplicates. It's similar to doing a "group by" on every row. This slows down the query. The union join, however, is the opposite. By default, the union join will perform a scan and eliminate any duplicate rows. It's seldom that a union will include duplicate rows. If this is the case, the UNION ALL join will perform a simple append without scanning for duplicates and improve performance.

Complex Joins

Out of 1,000 joins, 999 will match rows from two tables where the data in one table equals the data in the joined table. Whether the join is an inner join or an outer join, the ON condition is nearly always equal, just as in this standard example:

```
SELECT *
FROM TableA JOIN TableB ON TableA.ID = TableB.ID
```

In the real world, however, there are times that a query requires more than two tables and a single equal condition.

Multiple Tables

Once you get the hang of it, building a query with more than a dozen tables is pure fun. There's no fixed limit on the number of joins within a SQL statement other than any limit an individual SQL database engine imposes. From my experience, a typical complex join will merge four to seven tables. The syntax is pretty simple: just keep listing the joins. As long as every joined table is somehow connected to another table with an ON condition, it really doesn't matter in which order the tables are listed.

```
Select {columns}
From Table1
Join Table2 On Table1.PKID = Table2.FKID
Join Table3 On Table2.FK = Table2.PKID
Join Table4 On Table1.ID = Table4.FKID
```

Multiple Join Conditions

In the same way that a WHERE clause can use multiple conditions, a join may connect two tables using multiple connections. If you make it a practice to use single-column primary keys (recommended), then you may never need to build a join that uses multiple join conditions. However, if you're working with a legacy database that used multiple columns for a primary key, then you'll need to list both of those columns in the join:

```
SELECT *
FROM AS400Orders O
     JOIN AS400OrderLines L
     ON O.CustomerNo = L.CustomerNo
     AND O.OrderNum = L.OrdNumber
```

You'll notice that not only are two columns required to match rows between the legacy order and order detail tables, but the columns have dissimilar names.

Non-Equal Join

Developers tend to think of joins in terms of tables, because the columns tend to be obvious and the condition is rarely other than "equal." But there's no written requirement that the join condition be "equal." A join is basically a WHERE clause between two tables. In that sense, the condition of the join could be a different comparative operator, or multiple operators. Although the application is rare, I have solved problems with nonequal joins.

While building an MRP inventory application, I needed to locate inventory from the purchasing tables that was scheduled to arrive before the customer's required ship date. The first part of the join matched the Inventory ItemID.

The date requirements were handled by joining the order table and the purchasing table where the order required date was after the purchasing scheduled receive date.

```
SELECT …
FROM OrderDetail
     JOIN PODetail
     ON OrderDetail.PartID = PODetail.PartID
     AND OrderDetail.RequiredDate > PODetail.ProjectedReceivedate
```

A Readable Style

When writing complex joins as text, I have found that the following formatting makes reading them easier:

```
Select CustomerName,
       CustomerNumber,
       OrderDate,
       OrderNumber,
       OrderPriority,
       OrderStatus,
       SalesPerson.FirstName + ' ' + SalesPerson.LastName as SalesPerson
   From Customer
           Join Order
               On Customer.CustomerID = Order.CustomerID
           Join SalesPerson
               On Order.SalesPersonID = SalesPerson.SalesPersonID
           Join OrderStatus
               On Order.OrderStatusID = OrderStatus.OrderStatusID
           Join OrderPriority
               On Order. OrderPriorityID = OrderStatus.OrderPriorityID
```

When building joins, some SQL databases allow the keywords INNER or OUTER to be optional. Most SQL developers write the full-join syntax for clarity. I tend to drop the word INNER, recognizing that 80 percent of my joins are inner joins, but I include the full syntax for the outer join for readability.

Summary

The world of relational databases is a world of sets. If you can think in terms of data sets as you program, your applications will work with, rather than against, SQL.

The heart of SQL is the join. Merging, twisting, combining, and segmenting data sets is what being a database developer is all about. To accomplish that, the SQL join is the right tool. Live it, eat it, breath it. Because SQL joins are fun.

Using Subqueries

S ometimes the solution to a data query problem lies somewhere between a complex set of nested views and a standard join in a simple query—maybe you need to look up some data and use it inside a SQL statement. Often overlooked by SQL developers, subqueries are extremely powerful because they let you work with data from multiple sources in nearly any way you can imagine without being tied to the structure of the join. The subquery is an embedded SQL statement that passes data to the main, or outer, query. Subqueries enable the SQL developer to dynamically substitute any variable portion of the main, or outer, SQL statement. The query within the subquery can only be a SELECT SQL statement, so you could think of the subquery as a "subselect" or a "substitute query." Because subqueries open up the use of multiple data within the SQL statement, they are closely related to joins. In fact, all inner joins may be rewritten as subqueries, but not all subqueries may be rewritten as inner joins.

This chapter explains the simple subquery, how to substitute subqueries within a SQL statement, and then how to use the more complicated correlated subqueries. Along the way, several examples and cautions will point you in the right direction with your subqueries.

Subquery Basics

Subqueries are flexible because they can substitute so many portions of the SQL statement, but they fall into two broad categories based on how they share data with the outer SQL statement: simple subqueries and correlated subqueries.

A simple subquery is a stand-alone query that could run by itself. Simple subqueries run once and the result is then used in the outer query. The internal flow of a simple subquery is:

1. The subquery executes.

2. The result, or result set, is substituted within the outer query.

3. The outer query then executes using the result of the subquery.
   Total queries executed: 2

Correlated subqueries are a bit more complicated in that the subquery refers to a data element from the outer query. Because the subquery depends on data from the outer query, the subquery must execute once for every row from the outer query:

1. The outer query executes.

2. For every row in the outer query result set, the subquery executes using the data passed to it from the outer query. Total queries executed: row count from outer query + 1

    While a subquery can contain only a SELECT SQL statement, you can insert a subquery into any type of SQL statement—INSERT, UPDATE, DELETE, or SELECT. Because a subquery is nothing more than a SQL SELECT statement, it too can include a subquery. Theoretically, there's no limit to the number of nested subqueries other than the text limit of a SQL statement and the limit to the number of tables referenced within a SQL statement. SQL Server, for example, is limited to 32 total tables within any statement. Admittedly, nesting subqueries is not for the faint of heart. If the nesting becomes complex (more than subqueries), I recommend moving some of the deeper subqueries to views.

Substituting Subqueries

Chapter 7 pointed out that the only mandatory keyword in the SELECT statement is the word SELECT. Everything else is optional. The same is true of subqueries. Even the most basic SELECT statement can serve as a subquery. For example, the following SELECT statement is a valid SQL statement and subquery. Even though hard-coding a single value is relatively useless, it serves as a first test subquery.

```
Select (Select 3)
-----------
3
(1 row(s) affected)
```

Inside the parentheses, the "SELECT 3" is a subquery. It passes the value of 3 to the outer query.

    A subquery can be used as a substitute for any variable portion of the SQL statement. This rules out keywords such as SELECT, TOP, and FROM, as indicated in the subquery substitution chart shown in Table 13-1. A subquery can return a single value, a single column data set, or a full data set. How much data the subquery returns determines if the subquery is a legal substitution in a given portion of the SQL statement.

    Of this list of possibilities, from my experience, the most common use for a subquery is dynamically providing a WHERE condition, followed by substituting a column value, and providing a data source as a derived table.

SQL Element	Use of Subquery	Subquery Returns:		
		Single Value	Single Column	Data Set
Select	No, keyword			
Predicate (Top n, %, Distinct)	No, keyword			
Column names	Yes,	OK		
Column values	Yes, subquery returns single value	OK		
From	No, keyword			
From data source	Yes, subquery returns data source as derived table	OK	OK	OK
WHERE	No, keyword			
WHERE condition	Yes, subquery returns single column name, or single value condition, or values "IN" condition list	OK	OK	
ORDER BY	No, keyword			
ORDER BY column	Yes, for column names	OK		
GROUP BY	No, keyword			
GROUP BY column	Yes, for column names to group by	OK		

Table 13-1   *Subquery Substitutions*

SQL is so flexible that there are often several possible methods to accomplish the same task. The best option depends on you, your style, and the method that seems the most straightforward to you. Personally, I prefer joins to subqueries when possible. However, there are some situations when building a subquery feels better than building a join.

Substituting a Column Name

The first place in a SQL statement permitting the use of a subquery is in the column names. Why would you want to change the column? Why not just use a case in the outer query? The two methods are very similar. The case would modify the values passed from the query without changing the output column name or alias. Changing the column name from within the subquery actually changes the column used in the outer query. If no alias is used, then the column name changes as well as the values.

Personally, I don't recommend changing the column names, because it can break the front-end application. Additionally, substituting the column name with a subquery is bizarre enough that your code will be more difficult to decipher. With those cautions, this technique does work, so let me explain how to use it if you should decide to do so.

When substituting the column name, a single value from the subquery becomes a column name. Multiple subquery substitutions are okay, so long as each subquery substitutes a single column name with a single system name. While the first example is correct, several other possible syntaxes that seem as if they might work in fact fail, as the following examples will demonstrate:

```
SELECT (SELECT lastName), (SELECT Firstname) AS First FROM employees
LastName                First
--------------------    ----------
Davolio                 Nancy
Smith                   Andrew
Leverling       Janet
...
(9 row(s) affected)
```

The best application of this approach would combine the column substitution with other logic, such as case, to alter the column used. For example, additional logic in the case statement could dynamically alter the column name returned.

```
DECLARE @ColSelected INT
SELECT @ColSelected = 1

SELECT (SELECT CASE @ColSelected
            WHEN 1 THEN lastName
            WHEN 2 THEN FirstName END),
     (SELECT Firstname)
     FROM employees

LastName                FirstName
--------------------    ----------
Davolio                 Nancy
Smith                   Andrew
```

```
…
(9 row(s) affected)
```

So far, so good, but subquery column name substitution fails in many cases. The easiest way to break this application of the subquery is to use quotes around the column names. This changes the substitution from column name to column value, and the string is simply passed on to the outer query.

```
SELECT (SELECT 'lastName') AS Last, (SELECT 'Firstname') AS First
FROM employees
Last     First
-------- ---------
lastName Firstname
lastName Firstname
…
(9 row(s) affected)
```

It's also important that the subquery returns a single value. If the subquery attempts to insert a data set into the column position, the SQL statement will not execute. Each column name must be returned from its own subquery.

```
CREATE TABLE SQname
(ColumnName SYSNAME
--note: SYSNAME is a data type that maps to a nvarchar(128)
--and is useful when referencing system names within SQL Server.
GO
INSERT SQname VALUES ('LastName')
INSERT SQname VALUES ('FirstName')
GO
SELECT * FROM Sqname
ColumnName
------------------------
LastName
FirstName

(2 row(s) affected)

SELECT (SELECT * FROM SQname) FROM Employees ORDER BY lastname

Server: Msg 512, Level 16, State 1, Line 1
Subquery returned more than 1 value. This is not permitted when the
subquery follows =, !=, <, <= , >, >= or when the subquery is used as
an expression.
Drop table SQname
```

Even selecting a single column name from a table does not substitute the column name properly:

```
CREATE TABLE SQname
(      SQPK            INT IDENTITY,
     ColumnName       SYSNAME,
     Selected      BIT)
GO
INSERT SQname (ColumnName, Selected) VALUES ('LastName', 1)
INSERT SQname (ColumnName, Selected) VALUES ('FirstName', 1)
GO
SELECT * FROM Sqname

SQPK             ColumnName                      Selected
-----------      ---------------------           --------
1                LastName                        1
2                FirstName                       1
(2 row(s) affected)
SELECT (SELECT ColumnName FROM SQname WHERE Selected = 1 AND SQPK = 1)
AS Last FROM Employees ORDER BY lastname

Last
 --------------------------------------------
LastName
LastName
LastName
...
(9 row(s) affected)
```

Substituting the column name with a subquery is not common code, but it holds possibilities. If you have an application that could benefit from this technique, then perhaps knowing the method that works, the possible logic, and the limitations will benefit you.

Substituting a Column Value

A subquery is the best way to return a single look-up value within a column. In the same way that a column could return the sysuser, server time, or string literal, a subquery that returns a single value can pass that value back to the outer query, which is then passed on within the result set. Each row will see the same value. If you don't care about the network overhead—and it's probably too small to worry about—then this technique works well.

```
SELECT 'string literal', GETDATE(), SUSER_SNAME(), ( SELECT 3 )
---------            ------                    ------          ------
string literal     2001-07-01 14:12:49.220              PAUL\Paul          3
(1 row(s) affected)
```

The rule when performing this method is that the subquery must return only one value; multiple values will cause the SQL statement to fail. Otherwise, any legal SQL SELECT statement will work within the subquery.

If you're having trouble getting a column substitution subquery to work, the best way to troubleshoot is to copy, paste, and execute the subquery by itself. You'll be able to see if the query is working as a stand-alone query and how many rows it's passing back. Once you get the subquery to work on its own, it will work in the same manner with the outer query.

What do you think will happen if the subquery returns no rows? The outer query will see a null and pass the null on within the outer result set. A simple string literal is used in the example to force the return of at least a single row.

```
-- with a value
SELECT 'hard coding is bad.',
    ( SELECT lastname FROM employees WHERE employeeID = 1 )
-------------------         --------------------
hard coding is bad.        Davolio

-- without a value returned by the subquery
(1 row(s) affected)

SELECT 'hard coding is bad.',
    ( SELECT lastname FROM employees WHERE employeeID = 10 )
-------------------         --------------------
hard coding is bad.        NULL

(1 row(s) affected)
```

This technique is especially useful for gathering several pieces of status information for inclusion within reports, such as system user and domain or row counts.

Alternatively, from a stored procedure, a SQL SELECT statement, the front-end application could gather the data separately and store it within a variable. Tucking the data into the outer query enables the database developer to provide additional features for the query and saves work for the front-end programmer.

Dynamically Setting the Top Row Count

As a subquery, this can't be done. It would be nice to store a value from a user report definition dialog box and then use that value to determine the number of top rows listed in the report, but the subquery is the wrong tool to dynamically alter the top row count.

```
SELECT TOP (SELECT 3) LastName FROM Employees ORDER BY lastname
Server: Msg 170, Level 15, State 1, Line 1
Line 1: Incorrect syntax near '('.
Server: Msg 170, Level 15, State 1, Line 1
Line 1: Incorrect syntax near 'LastName'.
```

SQL batches and stored procedures are covered in Chapter 15, but they offer the best solution to dynamically altering the top value in a SQL statement. The natural inclination is to substitute a local variable for the top row count. Within SQL Server this, too, fails.

```
DECLARE @TopCount INTEGER
SELECT @TopCount = 3
SELECT TOP @TopCount LastName FROM Employees ORDER BY lastname
Server: Msg 170, Level 15, State 1, Line 4
Line 4: Incorrect syntax near '@TopCount'.
```

The solution within SQL Server is to use the SET ROWCOUNT function. Just like the Top predicate, SET ROWCOUNT will run the entire query, apply the ORDER BY, and then return the top number of rows.

```
DECLARE @TopCount INTEGER
SELECT @TopCount = 3
SET ROWCOUNT @TopCount
SELECT LastName FROM Employees ORDER BY lastname
LastName
--------------------
Callahan
Davolio
Dodsworth
(3 row(s) affected)
```

So, while the subquery won't let you dynamically set the number of rows returned, the SET ROWCOUNT command is a suitable alternative.

Referencing a Derived Table

Perhaps the most interesting use of a subquery is as a derived table. The result set of the subquery is simply used like any other table or view in the "from" portion of the outer query. This is cool. It means that instead of nested views (with their inherent performance problems), a custom data source can be assembled to fit the exact needs of the query. Unlike the column substitution, which can substitute either a column name or a value, the FROM clause will accept only a data set.

There is one significant trick to using a derived table. The subquery must be given a "Table Alias" or named range. And this makes sense, because the data source must have a name so that its columns can be properly referenced.

```
SELECT lastname FROM ( SELECT * FROM employees ) As E
lastname
-------------------
Callahan
Davolio
Dodsworth
...
(9 row(s) affected)
```

In this SQL statement, the SELECT statement within the parentheses is the subquery. It returns a data set to the outer query with the named range "E". From the data set now known as "E", the outer query extracts the lastname column and returns the result set to the calling application.

Because the derived table is a data source, there's nothing stopping you from performing any SQL function you might use with a regular table; inner joins, where conditions, outer joins—they all work well. To put this to the test, this SQL statement finds all orders for items from France that were handled by sales employees and sold to customers in France.

```
-- Using Three Subqueries
SELECT OrderID
    FROM
            (SELECT * FROM Employees WHERE Title LIKE 'Sales %') E
        JOIN      (SELECT * FROM Orders WHERE shipcountry = 'France') O
            ON E.EmployeeID = O.EmployeeID
        JOIN      (SELECT * FROM Customers WHERE Country = 'France') C
            ON O.CustomerID = C.CustomerID

-- Using Joins
```

```
SELECT OrderID
    FROM Orders O
    JOIN Employees E
        ON O.EmployeeID = E.EmployeeID
    JOIN Customers C
        ON O.CustomerID = C.CustomerID
    WHERE E.Title LIKE 'Sales %'
        AND O.ShipCountry = 'France'
        AND C.Country = 'France'

-- using 1 subquery
SELECT S.OrderID
    FROM
(SELECT O.OrderID, E.Title, C.Country, O.ShipCountry FROM Orders O
    JOIN Employees E
        ON O.EmployeeID = E.EmployeeID
    JOIN Customers C
        ON O.CustomerID = C.CustomerID ) S
    WHERE S.Title LIKE 'Sales %'
        AND S.ShipCountry = 'France'
        AND S.Country = 'France'
```

As we read these three SQL statements, they appear to be very different approaches to the same task. Not surprisingly, the SQL Server query analyzer generates the exact same query plan for every query. Which version is best? It depends upon which is most obvious to you.

Derived tables based on subqueries are a powerful and flexible addition to the basic SQL statement. Creating a custom data source opens a world of possibilities for creative queries.

Building a Dynamic WHERE Clause

The most common use of subqueries involves dynamically altering a WHERE condition. There are two basic methods techniques, WHERE conditions comparing single values and WHERE conditions that match within multiple rows from a result set. The difference between a standard WHERE condition and a WHERE condition with a subquery is that the comparison operator must handle searching for a value in a data set.

Here's how it works. As a general rule, the WHERE condition will test a column in the outer query against the single column returned from the subquery to see if a value in the outer query is "in" the data set returned from the subquery. "In" is the keyword. But, if you're absolutely sure the subquery will return a single data value, then an "=" is permitted.

- ▶ **Standard WHERE clause**   WHERE (value comparison value)
- ▶ **WHERE clause with data set**   WHERE Column IN (subquery)

Here's a simple example demonstrating a dynamic WHERE clause using a single value from a subquery. Because we know the subquery will return only a single value, it's safe to take advantage of the performance benefits of the equal comparison operator.

```
SELECT Lastname
     FROM Employees
     WHERE EmployeeID =
     (SELECT EmployeeID FROM Orders WHERE OrderID = 10250)

Lastname
-------------------
Peacock

(1 row(s) affected)
```

The query works fine and is more robust with the "in" operator. If the subquery should return a multirow data set, the outer query will not fail.

```
SELECT Lastname
     FROM Employees
     WHERE EmployeeID IN
     (SELECT EmployeeID FROM Orders WHERE OrderID = 10250)

Lastname
-------------------
Peacock

(1 row(s) affected)
```

The next example will make use of the multirow searching nature of the IN operator by returning all orders to France from the subquery. The subquery will prepare a data set of every EmployeeID from the Orders table according to the WHERE clause. The data set is then passed to the outer query, which checks every one of its rows to see if they are "in" the subquery result set.

```
SELECT Lastname
     FROM Employees
     WHERE EmployeeID IN
     (SELECT EmployeeID FROM Orders WHERE ShipCountry = 'France')

Lastname
-------------------
Davolio
Fuller
Leverling
...
(9 row(s) affected)
```

You can reverse the effect of the IN comparison operator with a NOT.
For example,

```
WHERE EmployeeID NOT IN (subquery)
```

Performance becomes a factor when dealing with "nots." Imagine that you are searching a phone book to determine if anyone named "Arnold" lives in Hickory, NC. If the search is a positive search, then it concludes with the first Arnold found. But, if you're searching to make sure no one named Arnold lives in Hickory, NC, then logically you have to search through every record to prove there are no Arnolds. The same is true for the database engine. A positive search is significantly faster than a negative search. If you can rewrite a negative search as a positive search, the performance gains are worth the development time.

Altering the GROUP BY and ORDER BY

The column names used in the GROUP BY and ORDER BY portions of the SQL statement may be set via a subquery in the same manner, and with the same rules, that the column names are set. Although it can be done, I have never found a use for this application of subqueries. When I want to dynamically set the ORDER BY, I use a view, and the calling SQL statement supplies the ORDER BY, or a case statement within the WHERE clause.

GROUP BYs must be carefully designed, and I do not recommend dynamically changing the grouping of a query. If I needed to develop three sets of possible groupings, I would opt for developing three queries. However, if you do desire to alter the ORDER BY or GROUP BY with a subquery, follow the same rules and suggestions as when setting the column names via a subquery.

Correlated Subqueries

Moving into more complex territory, it's possible to pass a column from the outer query rows to the subquery. A correlated subquery references a column from the outer query and is run once for every row in the outer query. While a simple subquery will run as a stand-alone query, a correlated subquery will not run by itself.

Correlated subqueries are sometimes called repeating subqueries because the subquery is executed for every row in the outer query. For example, this query locates all orders that were shipped to the home state of the person taking the order:

```
SELECT * FROM Orders WHERE employeeID IN
(SELECT employeeID FROM Employees WHERE Region = Orders.ShipRegion)
```

Here's how this query executes:

1. The outer query executes and finds all orders.

2. For each outer query row, the subquery is executed using the shipregion from the outer query row.

3. If the employeeID is passed back as a match, then the outer query order row is kept; otherwise, it is excluded from the final result set.

Because correlated subqueries depend on matching values between the outer query and the inner subquery, many correlated subqueries can be rewritten as inner joins. In this case, the matching values are the region and the employee. The previous query could be stated as:

```
SELECT Orders.* FROM orders
    JOIN Employees
        ON Orders.ShipRegion = Employees.Region
        AND Orders.EmployeeID = Employees.EmployeeID
```

Personally, I enjoy working with joins over subqueries when possible. The syntax of the join makes the relationships between the two tables obvious. However, both queries have the same result set, and the same query optimization plan, so use the query form that suits you.

Summary

This chapter has focused on subqueries, which enable you to build SQL statements with custom data sets and data look-ups. If you regularly develop with subqueries, your code will be flexible and robust.

You need to watch out for several issues. Be wary of negative searches within subqueries. Try to change the NOT IN to an IN for the performance gains. Positive searches run significantly faster. Be careful with the type of data set returned by a subquery. If the portion of the SQL statement accepts only a single value as a substitution, a subquery that returns a single column list data set will cause the outer query to fail. The trick to debugging a subquery is to run it by itself. In the case of a correlated subquery, run it with sample data.

If the subquery nesting becomes too complex, consider breaking out the deeper subqueries into views if the query is not a high-demand query. Views will hurt performance, but they can increase the readability of the logic. Correct beats "fast but wrong" every day of the week. Once you can prove that the query is generating the correct data, you can always go back later and optimize. The optimization will be much easier with a known correct value.

Subqueries are similar to joins; decide which to use based on what you find most readable. A smart cost-based query optimizer is going to convert a subquery into a join.

CHAPTER

14

Using Views

IN THIS CHAPTER:

Using Views

Nesting Views

Partitioned Views and Federated Databases

Views as Security

Problems with Views

Views are the most misunderstood part of SQL databases—they are avoided like the plague by some and used to the point of abuse by others. Views are sometimes explained as virtual tables, causing some developers to think that views store data in a temporary location someplace. I've spoken with developers who think that views dramatically improve performance. I've even read that views are a great way to provide row-level or column-level security. None of that is true.

A view is a stored SQL SELECT statement with a name. Period.

Views are used as data sources within SQL SELECT statements just like tables. So complex joins, aggregates, or other SQL SELECT statements may be predefined for ease of use. For example, the following SQL SELECT statement may be stored as a view using the following syntax:

```
CREATE VIEW SalesByRegion AS
SELECT Region.RegionName, SUM(OrderDetail.Amount) AS SalesAmount
FROM OrderDetail
JOIN Order ON OrderDetail.OrderID = [Order].OrderID
JOIN Region ON [Order].RegionID = Region.RegionID
GROUP BY RegionID, RegionName
```

This SQL SELECT statement groups together all the OrderDetail rows joined to region and then calculates the total sales grouped by region. By creating the SQL SELECT statement as a view named SalesByRegion, the statement is stored, and data may be retrieved by simply selecting from SalesByRegion:

```
SELECT * FROM SalesByRegion ORDER BY RegionName
```

Selecting * from this view returns a result set with two columns, RegionName and SalesAmount. The calling SQL statement adds the sort order to the result set.

RegionName	SalesAmount
California	923
Eastern	535
MidWest	482
NorthEast	893
Southern	378
Western	358

While views may contain only SELECT-type SQL statements that retrieve data, a view may be used in any type of SQL statement where a table may be used, with some restrictions on updatability. The resulting data set from a view may be used within a join, and tables and views may be mixed in joins.

By definition, a view is not sorted. However, some SQL databases will permit AN ORDER BY clause if the SQL statement also includes top 100 percent predicate. Since a view is only a stored SQL statement and is typically referenced from within another SQL statement, sorting within a view is questionable. Views will make use of indexes on the underlying tables, but views themselves may not be indexed. An exception to this is MS SQL Server 2000 Enterprise Edition. But this is a specialized exception primarily intended for federated databases (discussed later, under "Partitioned Views and Federated Databases").

Using Views

Any SQL SELECT statement can be saved as a view, so any SQL solution can be created as a view for users. A common practice is to create a view that prepares an entire set of data. The view is then called with a WHERE clause to select the row or rows required. This lets the end user or client application work with complex SQL statements without constantly building a complex SQL statement.

The view created in the preceding section, SalesByRegion, returns all the sales regions. Adding a WHERE clause to the calling SELECT statement limits the rows returned:

```
SELECT * FROM SalesByRegion
      WHERE RegionName = 'California' OR RegionName = 'NorthEast'
ORDER BY RegionName
```

This SELECT statement pulls from the view only the sales from California and the northeast.

```
RegionName          SalesAmount
California           923
Eastern              535
MidWest              482
NorthEast            893
Southern             378
Western              358
```

Views to Project Columns

Views are excellent at converting data from an unfriendly state to a readable state. String functions and concatenations can rearrange the data in the columns into a format better suited for the user:

```
CREATE VIEW SalesRepNames AS
SELECT FirstName + ' ' + LastName AS SalesRep
      FROM Employees
      WHERE Title = 'salesrep'
```

Another typical application for a view is to denormalize or flatten several tables into a single data set. This shields the end user from building SQL statements with multiple joins. (Or rather, it shields your data from an end user.) In either case, it's better to build and store a correct SQL statement than to expect an untrained end user to properly control an outer join.

Nesting Views

Because any view can be used as a data source in another SQL statement, it's even possible to nest views within views. These can be thought of as building block views, or stored subqueries. Technically, a nested view is similar to a subquery used as a derived table.

I've met very few developers who make use of nested views; however, I've found them very useful and solved some complex data logic problems with a series of nested views. Nested views are great for complex aggregate analysis type problems. I remember one report I programmed that required seven elaborate levels of nested views. The flow began from a single table, branched out, and then merged back together again. When diagrammed, it looked like a cut diamond. If you work at thinking through data analysis problems with nested views, you'll find that this is an extremely powerful technique.

Here's a recent real-life example. The database already had an audit table, recording every insert and update for every table at the column level of detail. The request was to gather usage data from the audit table and inventory transaction table to produce a report that showed the average number and max number of data modifications per minute per day. The data had to go through several stages of massaging, selections, groupings, and unions. The final view pulls from eight nested views, five levels deep. The user needs only select from the final view to benefit from all nine SQL queries.

The process begins with two streams, one from the audit table, and the other from the inventory transaction table, as shown in Figure 14-1. The first section prepares

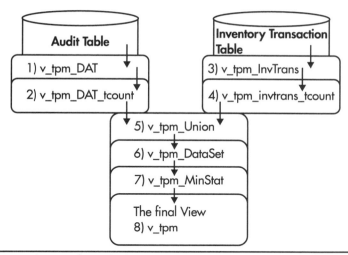

Figure 14-1 *Nested views for calculating application activity*

the two different data formats for a common format in the data set view. The audit rows need to be aggregated by actual row update because several fields may be updated to a single row and each column update has a row in the audit trail. Views 1 and 2 handle the audit trail. Views 3 and 4 massage the inventory transactions. View 5 merges the audit data with the inventory transaction data so that it can be accepted by View 6, the main data set with the transaction count for each minute. From the data set, two sets of statistics are prepared for each day. View 7 calculates the day's total count, the day's average transactions per minute from every minute that had transactions, and the maximum transactions per minute for that day. The final view, v_tpm, performs the last task of clean-up and provides aliases for the columns.

The code for this process follows:

```
--1
CREATE VIEW dbo.v_tpm_DAT
AS
SELECT CONVERT(nvarchar(20), AuditDateTime, 101) AS tDate,
    CONVERT(nvarchar(20), AuditDateTime, 100) AS tmin,
    TableName, RowGUID
FROM dbo.s_Audit
GROUP BY CONVERT(nvarchar(20), AuditDateTime, 100),
    CompanyContactID, TableName, CONVERT(nvarchar(20),
    AuditDateTime, 101), AuditDateTime, RowGUID
--------------------------------------------------------
--2
CREATE VIEW dbo.v_tpm_DAT_tcount
```

```
AS
SELECT tDate, tmin, COUNT(TableName) AS tcount
FROM dbo.v_tpm_DAT
GROUP BY tDate, tmin
--------------------------------------------------------
--3
CREATE VIEW dbo.v_tpm_InvTrans
AS
SELECT CONVERT(nvarchar(20), InventoryTransactionDateTime,
    101) AS tdate, CONVERT(nvarchar(20),
    InventoryTransactionDateTime, 100) AS tmin,
    'data' AS Expr1
FROM dbo.InventoryTransaction
--------------------------------------------------------
--4
CREATE VIEW dbo.v_tpm_invtrans_tcount
AS
SELECT tdate, tmin, COUNT(Expr1) AS tcount
FROM dbo.v_tpm_InvTrans
GROUP BY tdate, tmin
--------------------------------------------------------
--5
CREATE VIEW dbo.v_tpm_Union
AS
SELECT v_tpm_DAT_tcount.*
FROM v_tpm_DAT_tcount
UNION
SELECT v_tpm_InvTrans_tcount.*
FROM v_tpm_InvTrans_tcount
--------------------------------------------------------
--6
CREATE VIEW dbo.v_tpm_DataSet
AS
SELECT tDate, tmin, SUM(tcount) AS tCount
FROM dbo.v_tpm_Union
GROUP BY tDate, tmin
--------------------------------------------------------
--7 calculating the total daily count from the data set view
CREATE VIEW dbo.v_tpm_Stats
AS
SELECT tDate, SUM(tCount) AS tCount, AVG(tCount) AS t_avg, MAX(tCount) AS t_max
FROM dbo.v_tpm_DataSet
GROUP BY tDate
--------------------------------------------------------
--8 the final view, pulling the daily stats and the minute stats
CREATE VIEW dbo.v_tpm
AS
SELECT dbo.v_tpm_MinStat.tDate AS Date,
```

```
    MIN(DISTINCT dbo.v_tpm_DayCount.tCount) AS day_count,
    MIN(DISTINCT dbo.v_tpm_MinStat.t_avg) AS tpm_avg,
    MIN(DISTINCT dbo.v_tpm_MinStat.t_max) AS tpm_max
FROM dbo.v_tpm_Stats
GROUP BY dbo.v_tpm_MinStat.tDate
```

To run this set of nested views, the user needs only select from the final view.

```
Select * from v_tmp where tdate between 1/1/2001 and 1/7/2001

tdate               day_Count            tmp_avg      tmp_max
----------          ----------           ----------   ----------
1/1/2001                     2                    1            1
1/2/2001                12,249                   13          148
1/3/2001                 6,428                    6           23
1/4/2001                 8,736                    4           35
1/5/2001                 8,674                    5           12
1/6/2001                    35                    2            8
1/7/2001                     0                    0            0
```

Because the result is calculated only from minutes with actual entries, the averages aren't lowered due to inactivity. This type of activity report indicates the actual load the users experience. From the data set view, peak hours of activity could also be easily determined.

As this example demonstrates, nested views enable you to twist and manipulate the data though several stages. While some of these steps could be performed using subqueries, it would be nearly impossible to code all eight views in a single SQL statement. And if you did get it to work, you'd spend hours figuring it out when you later had to make a change.

As you'll see in the section "Problems with Views," nested views are not a panacea and should be used only when required. But when the problem calls for a complex series of data manipulations, nesting views turns a single huge problem into several smaller, bite-sized problems.

Partitioned Views and Federated Databases

An advanced application of views spreads, or partitions, the data horizontally (by rows) across multiple tables. If you've never worked with partitioned tables, the concept will seem impossible or bizarre at first. The idea of partitioned views is that if a very large table is broken down into multiple smaller tables with identical schemas, and if data is spread across the multiple tables according to a value in the row, then each table would contain a subset of the rows from the larger data set. I call the column used to separate the data the partition key, but that's not a standard.

Data is typically split by sales region, sales year, or active data versus archive data. The benefit is that when selecting from one of the tables, a higher percentage of the now smaller table can be cached in memory, and database performance can be improved.

Since SQL databases work best when data pages are cached in memory, this idea actually works well. The key is to segment the data according to how it is retrieved. If the client application or reporting tool regularly selects certain segments of data, you'll see a performance gain.

To create a partitioned system, you must follow strict rules concerning the design of the partitioned tables and the partitioned view. The requirements for that each partitioned table are these:

▶ Each table's schema must be identical.

▶ The value used to segment the data rows must be a part of the primary key.

▶ Each table must include a check constraint so that it can receive only the data intended for that table.

▶ While not a requirement, the naming schema for the partitioned tables should make the segmentation obvious, such as EastCoastCustomers, and WestCoastCustomers.

If creating the separate tables was all there were to partitioning data, coding the application would be very messy. Just getting data into the correct table would be laborious. Fortunately, partitioned views solve the problem of working with partitioned data.

A partitioned view, actually a union all SQL statement combining all the partitioned tables, is used to retrieve data from any table and store data into the correct table. What's amazing is that this partitioned union view is updatable! Rows can even be inserted into the union view. The trick is the check constraint. When working with a partitioned view, the query processor uses the check constraint to insert or update using the correct table.

Let me show you how this works. In this example, the sales data will be partitioned into separate tables—one for each year's worth of data. The first step is to create the tables and the partitioned view:

```
CREATE TABLE [Sales2000] (
    [SalesID]  UNIQUEIDENTIFIER ROWGUIDCOL NOT NULL,
    [YearID] [INT] NOT NULL,
    [SalesAmount] [MONEY] NULL,
    CONSTRAINT [PK_Sales2000] PRIMARY KEY CLUSTERED
    (
```

```
            [SalesID],
            [YearID]
      )  ON [PRIMARY] ,
      CONSTRAINT [CK_Sales2000] CHECK ([YearID] = 2000)
) ON [PRIMARY]
GO
CREATE TABLE [Sales2001] (
      [SalesID]  UNIQUEIDENTIFIER ROWGUIDCOL NOT NULL,
      [YearID] [INT] NOT NULL,
      [SalesAmount] [MONEY] NULL,
      CONSTRAINT [PK_Sales2001] PRIMARY KEY CLUSTERED
      (
            [SalesID],
            [YearID]
      )  ON [PRIMARY],
      CONSTRAINT [CK_Sales2001] CHECK ([YearID] = 2001)
) ON [PRIMARY]
GO
CREATE TABLE [Sales2002] (
      [SalesID]  UNIQUEIDENTIFIER ROWGUIDCOL NOT NULL,
      [YearID] [INT] NOT NULL,
      [SalesAmount] [MONEY] NULL,
      CONSTRAINT [PK_Sales2002] PRIMARY KEY CLUSTERED
      (
            [SalesID],
            [YearID]
      )  ON [PRIMARY] ,
      CONSTRAINT [CK_Sales2002] CHECK ([YearID] = 2002)
) ON [PRIMARY]
GO
-- Partitioned View
CREATE VIEW "All_Sales"
AS
      SELECT SalesID, YearID, SalesAmount
      FROM Sales2000

UNION ALL
      SELECT SalesID, YearID, SalesAmount
      FROM Sales2001
UNION ALL
      SELECT SalesID, YearID, SalesAmount
      FROM Sales2002
GO
```

Now that the structure for the partitioned view is created, including the three partitioned tables and the partitioned view, it's time to test it with some data.

```
INSERT INTO Sales2000 (SalesID,YearID,SalesAmount) VALUES(newid(),2000, 1)
INSERT INTO Sales2001 (SalesID,YearID,SalesAmount) VALUES(newid(),2001, 1)
INSERT INTO Sales2002 (SalesID,YearID,SalesAmount) VALUES(newid(),2002, 1)
GO
SELECT * FROM All_Sales
GO
SalesID                               YearID       SalesAmount
------------------------------------  -----------  ---------------------
CF3FCCFE-879E-496C-9BBD-ECB3681C6417  2000         1.0000
18D5A976-13DF-4D2F-9C8E-73834B9DE654  2001         1.0000
5F80C504-B284-4386-A19C-614FDFF41260  2002         1.0000
(3 row(s) affected)
```

Inserting directly into the individual tables worked fine, but that was expected. When the SELECT statement pulls from the All_Sales view, the UNION ALL combines the sales data from the three tables as needed.

The real test will be inserting rows through the partitioned union view, All_Sales. These rows will have a sales value of 2, so they'll be easy to spot later.

```
INSERT INTO All_Sales (SalesID,YearID,SalesAmount) VALUES(newid(),2000, 2)
INSERT INTO All_Sales (SalesID,YearID,SalesAmount) VALUES(newid(),2001, 2)
INSERT INTO All_Sales (SalesID,YearID,SalesAmount) VALUES(newid(),2002, 2)

SELECT * FROM All_Sales
GO
SalesID                               YearID       SalesAmount
------------------------------------  -----------  ---------------------
34C6A22D-0BB1-45D3-8ABE-02B028F436B3  2000         2.0000
CF3FCCFE-879E-496C-9BBD-ECB3681C6417  2000         1.0000
18D5A976-13DF-4D2F-9C8E-73834B9DE654  2001         1.0000
6356D5A2-575A-48FC-80FD-C85F7DF6B83C  2001         2.0000
5F80C504-B284-4386-A19C-614FDFF41260  2002         1.0000
A3B85FD5-CA3C-4083-B0F1-61AFAADFF0F5  2002         2.0000

(6 row(s) affected)
```

It worked. When data is entered, the database engine writes to the correct underlying table, based on the constraint.

The down side of partitioned views is that they involve hard-coded values requiring regular maintenance. Since the most common form of partitioned views is to separate the tables by year, each year a table must be created and the partitioned view modified, or else the application fails. If the partition is by region, then you know the regions will change. Another problem with partitioned views is that you can't update data to move it from one underlying table to another. You have to delete the row and reinsert it with a new value in the partition key.

A federated database uses partitioned views to spread the data not only across tables but across servers as well. Federated databases are used in the most demanding cases for scalability. Using linked servers and views, the servers will assign the SQL statement to the appropriate server and merge the results. Inserted data goes to the correct server. Update actions will move data from one server to another as the data changes from one partition to another. This is the technique used in the database wars to get those incredible benchmarks running on several million dollars' worth of multiprocessor clustered servers.

Views as Security

I mentioned at the opening of this chapter that views are sometimes used to secure columns or rows. It's true that a view can be used to expose, or "project," only certain columns, and that views can return selected rows according to a WHERE clause.

Column-level security is less of an issue to be solved with views now that SQL database products are implementing column-level security within the database engine. If security is offered by the engine, that's the fastest and best place to enforce the security. Otherwise, I recommend that you use views to enforce column-level security.

Using the WITH CHECK Option

Views can also enforce row-level security by limiting the result to certain rows. In addition, the WITH CHECK option on a view will enforce the criteria of the WHERE clause so that nothing can be written to the table through the view that's not also valid when retrieved by the view. It's as if the WHERE clause is a two-way check—pretty cool. If a view returns only East Coast Region sales data, then only East Coast Region sales data can be inserted through the view.

However, the old adage "today's solution is tomorrow's problem" is in full force with this particular solution. Unless you completely lock down the tables and provide access to the tables only through the views (raising the problems with locks and the performance issues described in the next section), the end user will still have access to the table through some other means. As new data patterns require additional views with new WHERE conditions, using views for row-level security becomes a maintenance nightmare.

A better practice is to use the database's built-in security or custom stored procedures. If the requirement is to restrict certain columns, then use column-level security. If the intention is to permit access only to certain rows, it's much better to write stored procedures that dynamically restrict the rows based on a custom security look-up table than to build and hard-code an ever-increasing number of views.

Problems with Views

Views are a convenience, by letting the developer store a few powerful SQL statements, but this convenience is at a cost. I want to point out eight key problems to watch out for when working with views. The problems are listed in the descending order of significance based on severity and likelihood.

Speaking of Locks, Updates, and Views

By far the biggest potential nightmare when working with views is the potential for held share locks. Reading data via a view is just like selecting from a raw table with a bound record set. The view grabs a share lock and holds on to it until the view's record set is released. SQL locks are tighter than an average desktop database-locking scheme. If any connection has a share lock (meaning "I'm looking at this data"), then no connection can gain an exclusive lock (meaning "I'm changing this data").

To further exacerbate the situation, locks are not handled sequentially. To walk through a situation, connection 1 has a share lock, and connection 2 wants to gain an exclusive lock. While connection 2 is waiting, connection 3 comes along and grabs a share lock and then connection 1 drops its share lock. Connection 2 is still waiting for a chance to get an exclusive lock. Updates simply wait and wait. And if the data being locked is commonly accessed by views, then the update will likely time out because the exclusive lock has to wait until all connections release all share locks. It's like trying to pull out of a parking lot into a busy boulevard. Views run fine, but the update times out and returns an error.

So, views don't present a problem for reading data, but they can block updates. The more reads from the views, the greater the update problem. Another aspect of the locking problem is the isolation level of the transaction. In a nutshell, the isolation level determines which changes may be seen between transactions during different stages while being committed. The issues involving updating, isolation levels, and locks are discussed in greater detail in Chapter 9, but here are some view-specific tips.

The duration of the share lock is dependent on the type of record set used in the front-end application. It's possible to read from a view and immediately release the lock. I've developed applications that retrieved data only through views and had no locking problems because the front end used snapshot record sets. If a similar option is available to you, it's better than holding on to a share lock.

Another possible solution to the view/locks problem is to carefully add table lock hints within the views. Lock hints are not ANSI standard, so you'll want to check your SQL database for the right syntax and rules. If the view is intended to retrieve data without updating data, then a NOLOCK hint is appropriate. If the view is going to update data, then you may want to consider a ROWLOCKhint. NOLOCK hints should still honor and apply exclusive locks, so updates will still work correctly. The ROWLOCK hint should keep the database lock manager from escalating a lock from row to data page to extent to table, which helps solve the locking problem.

Performance

The second most significant issue with views is the performance hit compared to using stored procedures to retrieve data. Here's how this works: When a view is referenced by a SQL statement, the view's stored SQL statement is retrieved and a new SQL statement is assembled that combines the two SQL statements, probably involving a subquery or a SQL statement that includes an additional WHERE clause. The query optimizer then creates a query plan in the same way it would if the SQL statement were submitted by the client application, often going through several lengthy steps. If the view is rehit using the exact same parameters, there will likely be some optimization from a saved query plan; however, several steps are still required to prepare the SQL statement for execution. In contrast, stored procedures and functions are precompiled and optimized, thus yielding significant performance benefits when compared to views.

While a single-table, nonnested view won't experience a significant hit, the performance problem is exacerbated with nested views. I built a large database with a complex method of logical deletes and filtered the logically deleted rows using views. Deletes need to be cascaded, even logical deletes, right? So, I also initially implemented checking the parent rows for the deleted flag using nested views. Big mistake. It killed performance. Rebuilding the views with every table within a single view, instead of nested views, to check for the cascading logical deleted flag solved the problem.

The best way to avoid the performance hit with views is to simply avoid views. Make views available for some ad hoc queries to ease selecting data from multiple tables (with the proper locking hints, of course), but it's best to use stored procedures as the primary means of retrieving and updating data in the client/server application.

Views Are Often Nonupdatable

Nearly any view other than a simple single-table query will often be nonupdatable, depending on your SQL database product and the construction of the view. A number of SQL elements in a view, or anywhere in the chain of nested views or subqueries within the view, will cause the resulting data set to be nonupdatable:

- ▶ Joins
- ▶ Aggregates and Group bys
- ▶ Unions

While these are the most common causes of nonupdatable views, the list for each database product is long and specific. Because views are so easily made nonupdatable, many client application programmers end up building separate SQL statements in the front-end application to update the data retrieved from views. While this solves the problem, I don't recommend this practice for high-usage areas of the application, because client-side SQL statements receive no optimization benefits compared to stored procedures.

Microsoft has provided a unique solution to this difficulty. Code may be attached to tables as triggers, which fire based on insert, update, or delete actions. MS SQL Server 2000 adds triggers that fire "instead of" the insert, update, or delete action. The idea of an "instead of" trigger is that the triggering action is abandoned and another set of code is executed "instead of" the calling action. For instance, if a user executes an insert command on the inventory table, an "instead of" trigger would look at the inserted rows and throw them away. The trigger could then decide to perform the same insert or do something else altogether.

The cool thing is that while "after update" triggers can only be applied to tables, "instead of" triggers can be applied to tables or views. This means that an "instead of" trigger may be applied to a view and your code handles the update. For applications that depend on complex views, this is a feature that you'll want to explore.

Schema Changes

Views break easily if the underlying table structure changes. The best way to prevent this difficulty is to use an option called "with schema binding," if your implementation of SQL offers such an option. If the view is created with this option, any attempt to change the underlying tables or views generates an error:

```
CREATE VIEW CurrentProductList
WITH SCHEMABINDING
AS
SELECT p.ProductID, p.ProductName
FROM dbo.Product p
WHERE (((p.Discontinued)=0))
```

Schema binding requires that the data source object referenced (table or view) is completely and distinctly referenced. Simply calling the table by its name is insufficient, because it's possible that multiple users may create tables with the same name. If a user has created the table "Product," then that table would be referenced. If the user has not created a "Product" table, then the database owner's "Product" table is referenced. Therefore, to specifically reference the correct "Product" table for schema binding, the table must be referenced using the complete naming scheme:

```
Server.Database.Owner.Object
```

Within the current database, the owner and table name will suffice, using "dbo" as the alias for the database owner:

```
dbo.Product
```

Debugging Difficulties

Views might present difficulties in debugging a complete database for several reasons:

▶ Computers generate well-formatted, orderly results. This lulls users into accepting the results as factual even when they are erroneous. Testing with well-known sample data will help find errors.

▶ Since views hide the underlying SQL SELECT statement, which often includes some SQL operation that modifies the rows returned, it's easy to miss rows without realizing it.

▶ Debugging a front-end query with a view is difficult for an end user who is unfamiliar with views. A complex set of nested views can create a situation that transforms even a seasoned database developer into a detective.

If your database uses views, implement a careful naming convention and document the purpose of each view. In the case of nested views, diagram the nesting flow and carefully test each view. Creating views that simplify the data structure will work only if the users properly understand the purpose of each view.

Multiple Table References

Another problem with views occurs within a chain of complex, deeply nested views in which the same underlying tables may be referenced at various levels of the nesting. I've seen this cause query optimization problems with strange results, or the SQL Server Query Optimizer simply refusing to attempt the view.

Anytime you're selecting data from a table, manipulating it in some way, and then rejoining it back with the same original table (or another view based on the same table), you should carefully test each step of the view nesting with a small set of predictable data.

Editing Views

If a view needs to be altered on a production database, you'll want to edit and test the new view on a development/test database before implementing the change into the production database. We've all seen applications that ran great in a small separate development environment and then failed miserably in production. "It ran fine in the office" is the programmer's version of "The check's in the mail." That's why the development environment should be as close to the production environment as possible. If the production machine has the hard drive space, I recommend that you install a separate instance of your SQL database product on the production server for development purposes. This way, the server performance will be identical between development and production. The development load is typically so small that it will not impact the production requirements. I recommend against simply having two databases on the same server; by having a full separate instance, you ensure that development can test server options without affecting the production environment.

As you edit stored SQL statement of a view, many graphic view and query editors will generate code to drop and re-create the view. This may be okay in development, but in a production environment dropping and creating an object will also drop any permissions that have been set for the object. You want to avoid creating security problems. Because views are embedded within another SQL statement, the security error message may not even point you in the right direction.

To avoid these problems, use the ALTER VIEW command instead of drop and create. The ALTER VIEW command syntax is similar to that for CREATE VIEW.

```
Alter View vCustomers as
Select CustomerID, CompanyName, Contact
From Cdbo.Customer
```

Rebuilding Database Objects from Scripts

Once the view is edited and tested, you'll need to move the new version of the view to the production environment. Because views are embedded within the server's database, copying a new version of the front-end application will not deliver the view. The easiest way is to take the text file, called a SQL script, of the ALTER VIEW command and run that on the production database.

It's critical that you keep safe copies of every change script, as well as the original database creation scripts. Many shops use a version control system to house the database scripts.

As you work with SQL scripts, the order of object creation is important. If the database schema includes nested views, then you must be careful to create the views in the correct order. Just as a view cannot be created on a table that does not yet exist, if a referenced view does not exist, then creating a view that depends on the nested view will fail. This may seem obvious, but Microsoft SQL Server 7.0 has a problem generating scripts that consider nested views.

Summary

Views can solve certain problems by replacing complex SQL statements as a single data source. End users and client-side developers like views because the data can be denormalized and made to look recognizable, but views present performance problems and can cause lock problems. The primary method of data retrieval and modification, especially for heavily accessed portions of the application, should be stored procedures. While views should be avoided as the structural pillar of the application, if used judiciously, they can contribute to the success of your project.

PART III

Solving Complex Problems

OBJECTIVES

▶ Examine the use of stored procedures

▶ Compare triggers and stored procedures

▶ Learn how to use parameters

▶ Understand transaction processing requirements

▶ Examine locking strategies used with transactions

▶ Understand the differences in transactions on Microsoft and Oracle databases

▶ Learn to use cursors to manipulate data

▶ Practice with exception handling while using cursors

▶ Understand how to implement tree data structures using SQL

▶ Practice with tree operations

Triggers, Stored Procedures, and Parameters

IN THIS CHAPTER:

Fundamental to understanding stored procedures is the notion that SQL uses a *declarative* query language. From a programmer's point of view, this is a major change, as the majority of computer languages are procedural. The difference between the two types of language is essential, and yet simple to understand. Procedural developers use languages such as T-SQL, PL-SQL, SPL, C, C++, and Java. The language(s) supported for authoring a procedure depends on the DBMS. In a traditional procedural programming language, for example C, the programmer gives step-by-step instructions to attain her desired result. In contrast, a SQL programmer gets information by requesting data that meets specific criteria; the programmer does not give elaborate instructions on how the data is to be retrieved—that is the job of the database.

Use of a declarative method is helpful in the reduction of software problems; anyone who has ever used a procedural language knows that a small collection code can become burdensome quickly if it is not managed properly. One aspect of SQL and its declarative nature is that problems are rarely elusive and can be readily fixed without much trouble.

Another added benefit of SQL is that declarative queries are not dependent on the data representation. This means that the database is free to store data in its own way. In other words, the folks at Microsoft, Oracle, or any other vendor have made the decision for you as to how and where to store the data, making your job's scope more defined.

In short, instead of writing a procedure to turn some input into output, in SQL you simply "declare" the output you want, and the database does the rest. As a result, declarative languages such as SQL often require a more limited level of expertise to accomplish some very sophisticated tasks.

But what happens when an added level of sophistication is needed? Often triggers can do the job. *Triggers* are fragments of code that run automatically in a database before or after a table is modified. Triggers function at the row level of a database.

Alternatively, stored procedures can be the answer to a developer's needs. *Stored procedures* are collections of SQL statements that can be saved and applied in future cases. The objective of stored procedures is to enable developers to write more complex programs in the database using a single query. Stored procedures are a welcome tool for anyone who has ever experienced writing individual SQL statements; he knows that such methods can become a backbreaking task when a high level of processing is occurring in a DBMS. To avoid the limitations of declarative languages, databases with stored procedures afford a full procedural programming language within the database. An important and useful addition to stored procedures are *parameters*. Parameters are values passed to a stored procedure that customize the program for a particular purpose—these are discussed in greater detail later in this chapter.

Why Use Triggers and Stored Procedures?

The primary advantage to using triggers and stored procedures is that they enable users to create and sustain a more manageable set of code for use by all existing and forthcoming applications associated with the database. The power of having one set of code to accomplish this task is very great. To understand this concept better, consider the following:

A bank wants to keep track of how frequently its customers access their accounts. To accomplish this, its programmers create a local customer control so that each time a customer visits the bank to check a balance or to make a deposit, a withdrawal, or a transfer, the bank's database is updated to note the visit. The real-time tracking of customers enables the bank's management to know when are the busiest times of the day, how much money should be available, how many staff members should be helping customers, and so on.

Assume that the bank builds this table and audits it frequently. If the bank's ambitions for this table never change and no other features need to be added, then code from almost any procedural language could be written and attached to the database. This method of data gathering could simply be written so that the local customer control code would execute an UPDATE statement to mark each transaction visit.

For most organizations that use a DBMS, however, change is a frequent occurrence; banks are no exception. For instance, consider if the bank decided to offer online banking in addition to its existing offerings. The bank could use Java servlets to give users this access, but by doing it this way it would now have two copies of code to maintain, one for the local customer control and another for online access.

Eliminating Code Troubles with Triggers and Stored Procedures

In the long run, having multiple sets of code can lead to several problematic issues. For a problem such as the one that the bank faces, using a stored procedure could eliminate the potential trouble down the road. Use of triggers or stored procedures is thus a favorable alternative. Allowing all applications that need to access the database to use stored procedures as an intermediary, rather than independently manipulating the tables, can over the long term save thousands of hours. Another advantage is that using a stored procedure allows the bank to write just one code set. The upcoming examples will illustrate just how valuable it is to keep code to a minimum. In the following examples, the triggers and stored procedures work not only for the local customer control and online applications, but also for any future applications that may be added.

When you are learning to troubleshoot stored procedures, it is important to begin by understanding the context in which they are typically used. The following section reviews some of the larger issues in troubleshooting stored procedures. To accomplish this, we will set up an example application that will provide the functionality needed for the bank's goals.

This section will focus on understanding why one would use a stored procedure to troubleshoot a major task such as application enhancement. Further, this section will address how incorporating triggers and/or stored procedures into an application could improve performance. Later, and in the following chapters, some specific troubleshooting issues and various mutations of triggers and stored procedures that are interesting and relevant are addressed.

Scenario

To put the problem into perspective, consider the following code that would be used at the bank each time a customer withdrew funds from his or her account. You might imagine that a bank would want to set up some utility functions to interact with the database, for example, through ODBC. In this example, those functions are expressed as DB_*.

DESIGN TIP

Many databases, including Oracle and SQL Server, have integrated code libraries to allow for easier integration and increased portability of application and database code. The two most common libraries are ODBC and JDBD; when choosing a database and application, it is important to consider how these products integrate and utilize these useful code libraries.

The purpose of the bank's system is to enable auditing of its records. There are three basic ways to approach this. The following sections review each approach to show where it would be used and to understand the problems and pitfalls that are inherent to it.

This example begins by creating a table in SQL; this will be the backbone of the bank's auditing system. Next comes a common approach to creating an audit table that integrates the system into code. To make the code work with SQL, we show the steps involved in modifying the code to make the application code functional. Next, the example shows how triggers can offer an alternative to the finite process of code modification. Last, an example of an alternative to code modification and/or triggers, stored procedures, is shown.

Without using stored procedures and triggers, organizations are forced to constantly update code manually. The reason this is a less desirable option stems from the inherent need to create an audit log table in each section of code. As discussed, for each customer account there are four transactions that can take place, and the application code for doing the four functions consists of these actions:

▶ Query the balance of an account

▶ Deposit some amount into an account

▶ Withdraw some amount from an account

▶ Transfer some amount from one account to another

To begin, a table in SQL appears as:

```
CREATE TABLE accts (
 acct_id  INTEGER NOT NULL PRIMARY KEY,
 balance  INTEGER NOT NULL,
 .
 .
 .
);
```

With a simple table built in SQL, the developer is free to write the application in any procedural language. The purpose of this code is to provide a way for code to call SQL through an ODBC link. For this example, we use C code:

```
/* Query */
int query (int acct_id) {
    int balance;
    balance = DB_get_int ("SELECT balance FROM accts"
                          " WHERE acct_id = :1", acct_id);
    return balance;
}
/* Deposit */
```

```
int deposit (int acct_id, int amt) {
    int balance;
    /* Check for positive amount */
    if (amt <= 0) {
        return 0;
    }
    DB_dml ("UPDATE accts SET balance = balance + :1"
            " WHERE acct_id = :2", amt, acct_id);
    return 1;
}
/* Withdrawal */
int withdrawal (int acct_id, int amt) {
    int balance;
    /* Check for positive amount */
    if (amt <= 0) {
        return 0;
    }
    DB_begin_transaction ();
    balance = DB_get_int ("SELECT balance FROM accts"
                          " WHERE acct_id = :1"
                          " FOR UPDATE OF balance", acct_id);
    /* Check for sufficient funds */
    if (balance < amt) {
        DB_abort_transaction ();
        return 0;
    }
    DB_dml ("UPDATE accts SET balance = balance - :1"
            " WHERE acct_id = :2", amt, acct_id);
    DB_end_transaction ();
    return 1;
}
/* Transfer */
int transfer (int src_acct_id, int dest_acct_id, int amt) {
    int src_acct_balance;

    /* Check for positive amount */
    if (amt <= 0) {
        return 0;
    }
    DB_begin_transaction ();

    src_acct_balance =
        DB_get_int ("SELECT balance FROM accts"
```

```
                      " WHERE acct_id = :1"
                      " FOR UPDATE OF balance", src_acct_id);
    /* Check for sufficient funds */
    if (src_acct_balance < amt) {
        DB_abort_transaction ();
        return 0;
    }
    /* Perform the transfer */
    DB_dml ("UPDATE accts SET balance = balance - :1"
            " WHERE acct_id = :2", amt, src_acct_id);

    DB_dml ("UPDATE accts SET balance = balance + :1"
            " WHERE acct_id = :2", amt, dest_acct_id);
    DB_end_transaction ();
    return 1;
}
```

Once the appropriate code is established to make it possible to access and audit the accts table, the next step is to create a table in SQL that will store the auditing information. This is where the individuals who are interested in viewing their audited information will access their data. Before they can see the data, a table must be built to store it. A CREATE SEQUENCE command is used to build an audit table in SQL:

```
CREATE SEQUENCE accts_audit_id_seq;
CREATE TABLE accts_audit (
    audit_id            INTEGER NOT NULL PRIMARY KEY,
    audit_time          TIMESTAMP NOT NULL,
    acct_id             INTEGER NOT NULL REFERENCES accts,

access_type VARCHAR(20) NOT NULL
        CHECK (access_type IN ('query', 'insert', 'update')),
        old_balance     INTEGER,
        balance         INTEGER NOT NULL,
        notes           VARCHAR(1000)
    );
```

There are several fundamental problems with the approach described. First of all, there is an over abundance of logic in the application that will be duplicated if another application needs to access the same data. Fundamentally, this is an issue of maintenance and convenience. If other applications need to access the database but need to perform the same functions (for instance, online transactions, site visits,

ATM transactions), then the result will be that you must duplicate the application's functionality. This is problematic if the application's functions change, because then the code for each of these functions must also be changed.

As you can see, there is a nontrivial amount of coding needed to assure that the data is properly handled. That issue aside, the developer now needs to make it possible to audit the customer's use of the bank's services. The developer has a choice to make about which option to use to establish an audit table.

The first option is to modify the application code. This method consists of adding new rows tov the audit table at set times. Alternatively, the developer can choose to add a trigger to the table inside the database; or as mentioned, the developer can add a stored procedure to accomplish this task. The next few sections review how each of these options will play out.

Option 1: Modifying the Code

If we choose to modify the code, the query function we used will look like this:

```
/* Query */
int query (int acct_id) {
    int balance;

balance = DB_get_int ("select balance from accts"
                " where acct_id = :1", acct_id);

/* Update the audit table */
DB_dml ("insert into accts_audit"
" (audit_id, audit_time, acct_id, access_type,"
"  old_balance, new_balance, notes)"
" values (accts_audit_id_seq.nextval,"
"         sysdate,"
"         :1,"
"         'query',"
"         NULL,"
"         :2,"
"         :3)",
acct_id, balance, "normal query");

return balance;
}
```

Take another look at the original code that addressed the query function:

```
/* Query */
  int query (int acct_id) {
      int balance;
      balance = DB_get_int ("select balance from accts"
                            " where acct_id = :1", acct_id);
      return balance;
  }
```

As you can see, a significant amount of code has been added to the original version of the query function. Rather than our laboring through each of the four functions that require modifying, suffice it to say that a similar modification would be needed for each.

Reviewing the elements of the preceding code should reveal that maintenance of application code could become very complicated very fast. Consider that the programming must be individually updated on each of the four procedures and must be correct; in other words, a single syntax error in any section of the code can cause the entire program to fail.

With so much work to build and maintain an application using a procedural coding system, it becomes desirable for an alternative method to be used that would more efficiently and effectively meet the needs of database users. SQL provides such a method, called triggers.

Triggers

A *trigger* is a fragment of code that runs automatically in a database before or after a table is modified. Triggers are commonly used alternatives to stored procedures.

Uses of triggers include:

▶ Ensuring that a column receives adequate default information

▶ Creating an audit row that is inserted into a separate table

▶ Assuring data consistency

For an example of data consistency, consider what happens if newly entered data is inconsistent with other information in the database, such as in the case of a key conflict. A trigger will create an error that will roll back the faulty transaction.

For troubleshooting purposes, triggers can be very handy. Anyone who has ever administered a database will know that auditing data input is a crucial task. All too frequently, a user of the database enters erroneous information into the database that requires fixing. Triggers can help in the identification of potential errors, and they can help identify the origin of the error by creating an audit table.

DESIGN TIP

It is important to note that triggers work at the row level—this fact has major implications that will become clear later, after we review stored procedures.

Structure of Triggers

Triggers are commonly associated with INSERT, UPDATE, and DELETE operations within specific tables.

When using PL/SQL, the trigger looks like:

```
CREATE TRIGGER trigger_name
ON
FOR (INSERT, UPDATE, DELETE)
BEGIN
  ;
END;
```

Goals of Triggers

It is important to clarify that triggers are not stored procedures; their purpose is much more narrow in scope, since they are tied to individual tables. However, while they are not as global as stored procedures, their power is quite valuable, particularly for the purpose of auditing. Other uses include regulating data consistency, performing rollback functions if an error is made in the database, and performing actions in one table when changes occur in another, associated table. The primary capabilities of triggers include enabling code to access:

▶   All new data in INSERT operations

▶   All new data and old data in UPDATE operations

▶   All deleted data in DELETE operations

Additionally, triggers perform functions similar to constraints (see Chapter 8) by ensuring that data in a table agree with rules defined by the database developer.

Option 2: Using a Trigger

Now back to our example. Recall that three solutions are posited for handling the application problem. The second utilizes triggers.

The trigger function that is used to update the accts table appears as:

```
CREATE TRIGGER accts_audit_sql
BEFORE UPDATE ON accts
FOR each row
BEGIN
INSERT INTO accts_audit
(audit_id, audit_time, acct_id, access_type,
old_balance, new_balance, notes)
VALUES
(accts_audit_id_seq.nextval,
sysdate,
:old.acct_id,
'update',
:old.balance,
:new.balance,
'normal update')
END;
```

As can be seen when comparing this with option 1, a trigger is a less error-prone solution that enables the application to interact with a single piece of code that is a simple SQL transaction.

DESIGN TIP

In an effort to troubleshoot, avoiding trouble in the first place is always an ideal method. Triggers enable developers to simplify their code.

Option 3: Using Stored Procedures

Stored procedures are generally broken down into three parts. The first section identifies all declarations of the variables that will be used in the section where commands are executed. Next is the executable command section. And the third section is where exception handling occurs.

The ultimate goal for most developers who look at stored procedures is to attain the ability to build an API into tables. The mission here is to automate updates rather than have applications update after the code within the applications has been restructured. Stored procedures offer yet another and even more powerful alternative to the two approaches that have been discussed so far in this chapter.

Here is a look at what a stored procedure would consist of in PL/SQL for the query function that has been discussed in our example:

```
CREATE FUNCTION query
(v_acct_id IN integer)
RETURN integer
IS
 v_balance  INTEGER
BEGIN
 SELECT BALANCE INTO v_balance
 FROM accts
 WHERE acct_id = v_acct_id;
 RETURN v_balance;
END;

CREATE FUNCTION deposit
 (v_acct_id IN integer, v_amt IN integer)
RETURN void
IS
BEGIN
  SELECT BALANCE INTO v_balance
    FROM accts
    WHERE acct_id = v_acct_id
    FOR UPDATE OF balance
  IF (v_amt <= 0)
    ABORT
  ELSE
    UPDATE accts SET balance = balance + v_amt
      WHERE acct_id = v_acct_id
END;

CREATE FUNCTION withdrawal
 (v_acct_id IN integer, v_amt IN integer)
RETURN void
IS
  v_balance    integer
BEGIN
  -- Check for positive amount
  IF (v_amt <= 0)
```

```
      ABORT
  ELSE
    SELECT balance INTO v_balance
      FROM accts
      WHERE acct_id = v_acct_id
      FOR UPDATE OF balance;

    -- Check for sufficient funds
    IF (v_balance < v_amt)
      ABORT
    ELSE
      UPDATE accts SET balance = balance - v_amt
        WHERE acct_id = v_acct_id
    END IF
  END IF
END;

CREATE FUNCTION transfer
 (v_src_acct_id IN integer,
  v_dest_acct_id IN integer,
  v_amt IN integer)
RETURN void
IS
  v_src_balance    integer
BEGIN
  -- Check for positive amount
  IF (v_amt <= 0)
    ABORT
  ELSE
    SELECT balance INTO v_src_balance
      FROM accts
      WHERE acct_id = v_src_acct_id
      FOR UPDATE OF balance;

    -- Check for sufficient funds
    IF (v_src_balance < v_amt)
      ABORT
    ELSE
      -- Perform the transfer
      UPDATE accts SET balance = balance - v_amt
        WHERE acct_id = v_src_acct_id
      UPDATE accts SET balance = balance + v_amt
        WHERE acct_id = v_dest_acct_id
```

```
        END IF
      END IF
    END;
```

NOTE

The "dual" table is just a mock table (in Oracle) that keeps the SQL parser from generating an error.

Now the C (application) code for the query becomes:

```
int query (int acct_id) {
int balance;

balance = DB_get_int ("SELECT query(:1) FROM dual", acct_id);

return balance;
 }
```

Using a stored procedure instead of modifying the application code or using a trigger include the following benefits:

▶ Stored procedures give the user better control over the transaction vs. triggers of applications.

▶ Triggers can only operate on row-level events, for example: "$5 was removed from Joe's checking account," whereas with a stored procedure, the result can be more true to the scope of the transfer. For example, the result might say, "$5 was removed from Joe's checking account and placed into his savings account." The triggers live deep down in the database and only see the rows.

Procedures operate much higher up in the database, with a much broader scope—in the case of Joe's account, several rows are affected as a result of a transfer from one account to the next. For the same level of granularity to be available in triggers, several triggers would need to be written.

Syntax and Types of Stored Procedures

While stored procedures are immeasurably valuable, there are some limiting factors. The syntax of stored procedures varies considerably from one DBMS to the next.

For all practical purposes, attempting to write completely portable stored procedures is not feasible. Fortunately, most organizations have only a single DBMS to administer, thereby avoiding potential conflict. However, in the case of a DBMS transfer, it is possible for the calls of most stored procedures to be transferred—calls include the name schema and method for data transfer. As a result, much, but not all, of the client application code can remain if the DBMS is changed.

The next section looks at some of the more common methods for constructing stored procedures. It is important not only to talk about but also to show the differences between stored procedure methods offered by assorted vendors. The construction of a stored procedure in SQL Server, for example, is unlike that in PL/SQL. Having a thorough understanding of different databases is an effective way to help users recognize issues and effectively troubleshoot problems.

Stored procedures are created with the CREATE PROCEDURE statement. The purpose of the CREATE PROCEDURE statement is to create an identifier in Transact-SQL for SQL Server or PL/SQL in Oracle. By including an identifier, you assure that the statement is saved for later use. If you write a statement without the CREATE PROCEDURE statement, then it will run just like any other query, but it will not be stored.

The creation of stored procedures is far more complex than most other operations in SQL, but with that in mind, it is possible to learn how to effectively learn, use, and of course troubleshoot stored procedures. To get to this point, however, it is important to become familiar with the structure and applications of stored procedures.

The structure of a stored procedure consists of the following:

```
CREATE PROCEDURE procedure_name
[@parameter_name datatype [(length)], …]
AS
SQL statements
```

As mentioned earlier, the goal of a stored procedure is to enable users to create and sustain a single set of code for use by all existing and forthcoming applications associated with the database. In the case of the bank's procedure, the goal is to allow a single set of code to oversee its customers' access to their accounts whether by a walk-in visit to the bank or via an online transaction.

When writing stored procedures, it is important to remember to place elements of the procedure in the proper sections. The most common failure to observe this rule involves declarations. All DECLARE statements for programs should be found in the declarations section of the program. This method delivers some key benefits, including these:

- ▶ It prevents users from exercising variables prior to their initialization.
- ▶ It enables users to rapidly view the variables list that is associated with a stored procedure.

Debugging Stored Procedures

Any stored procedure that you build and use is only as good as its reliability. Having a plan to recognize, diagnose, and treat errors is key to successfully administering an application over the long term. Factors to keep in mind include knowing how and when to check for problems in a program, which can be done through a variety of ways. Many error diagnostic programs are designed to monitor program execution and alert the developer if or when an error is incurred. However, not all diagnostic programs are created equal, so in the next sections we review some of the most common debugging tools and offer some suggestions on how to use them most effectively.

Oracle Examples

PL/SQL does not always tell you about compilation errors because, as a language, it is not particularly well designed for producing output, unlike many other procedural languages. Instead, it gives you a cryptic message such as "procedure created with compilation errors." As a rule, if the error is not obvious within the first few minutes of glancing over the code, a good start to the troubleshooting process begins with the following command:

```
SHOW ERRORS PROCEDURE <procedure_name>
```

This command will print any errors that are generated during the compilation of a query.

Similarly, you can get the errors associated with a trigger you have created by using:

```
SHOW ERRORS TRIGGER <trigger_name>
```

Alternatively, "SHO ERR" is an abbreviation for "SHOW ERRORS," and you can omit "PROCEDURE ..." or "TRIGGER ..." if you just want to see the most recent compilation error.

A second method employs the DBMS_OUTPUT command. This package of tools provides a command available to the user for displaying output on the console—in effect, this tool mimics other languages that have built-in statements to allow output to be sent directly to the console in a window or other readable format.

This is the DMBS_OUTPUT package's first command:

```
SET SERVEROUTPUT ON
```

This command prints the string argument that describes the error.

Microsoft Examples

Transact-SQL is the language used for writing stored procedures in SQL Server. The process of executing Transact-SQL code follows a sequence of executed statements. The output of these statements is sent to the user whenever a GO keyword is encountered. Users of Transact-SQL must get used to seeing frequent GO statements throughout their code. However, there is a caveat to this rule in the case of stored procedures. Since the output of a stored procedure is held until it has concluded its execution, GO statements are not necessary.

DESIGN TIP

The GO statement marks the boundary of a query batch. Only the statements delimited by the GO statement are sent to the DBMS for processing. The statements appearing between two GO statements cannot share variables or the results of statements that appear prior to the GO block. If GO appears in a stored procedure, it is typically the last statement.

Error Handling Techniques for Transact-SQL

As discussed, the differences between declarative and procedural techniques can give rise to several challenges, one of which is detecting and resolving errors. In Transact-SQL, users have the responsibility to determine how and when the code should be scanned for errors. Once errors are detected, a user must also choose the most appropriate way to deal with them.

Unlike with other forms of SQL, troubleshooting with the PRINT statement is not the only useful method in Transact-SQL. The problem with PRINT is that it does not truly debug the culprit error, nor will it stop the execution process. Furthermore, it will not inform the database that an error has occurred—here the database continues to execute until the end of its procedure, at which point it will deliver an error message. Fatal severity levels are an exception to this rule; if a table referenced within a stored procedure does not exist, then processing within the stored procedure is stopped. Caution severity levels from 20 through 25 are considered fatal. If a fatal severity level is encountered, the client connection is terminated after receiving the message, and the error is logged in the error log and the application log.

An alternative is the RAISERROR command. RAISERROR will exit a program and report error conditions in accordance with user-defined specifications. The command will also set a system flag to record that an error has occurred. By utilizing RAISERROR, the client gains the ability to either retrieve an entry from the sysmessages table or build a message dynamically with user-specified severity and state information. Following the definition of a message, it is sent back to the client as a server error message.

In its simplest form, the syntax of the RAISERROR command looks like this:

```
RAISERROR ( { msg_id | msg_str } { , severity , state }
   [ , argument] )
   [ WITH option [ ,...n ] ]
```

Typically, the RAISERROR command in SQL Server displays as a specified error number or an error message, where system-defined error messages have values of 50,000 or less and user-defined error messages have values greater than 50,000. In the case that an error number goes unspecified, SQL Server automatically assigns 50,000 as the error message by default. An error that contains a number without a description is referred to as an ad hoc error.

SQL Server contains a second argument that functions as a method to gauge the severity of the error. Severity settings indicate the type of error. In addition to identifying errors, severity settings can also be used to offer suggestions for an action that the program can take.

Using Parameters

The final section of this chapter focuses on parameters and explains how they can be used to work within stored procedures. This section will show what parameters are capable of and how they apply to stored procedures. The chapter also explores some examples of how one might use parameters to accomplish certain tasks. But first, a review of the fundamentals of parameters in SQL is appropriate.

What Are Parameters?

Parameters are values that are passed to a stored procedure from the developer or by another program (or stored procedure). Parameters customize the action of the stored procedure for a particular purpose. A parameter may be any entity within a database. For instance, a parameter can be a filename, a range of values, a string representing a block of code, or a specific value such as a monetary amount. Depending on the situation, parameters may be required, they may be optional, or they may not be appropriate at all; determining when to include a parameter depends on factors such as complexity, the skill level of the programmer, speed requirements, and convenience. Parameters are often entered as a series of values following the program name when the program is loaded. Not all parameters need be complex. To put them into perspective, for instance, consider a DOS switch. In the DOS DIR command dir /p, the DOS switch /p (pause after every screen) is a simple but easy-to-understand parameter.

In their most reduced form, parameters require five items to be created. First, they require the name of the field in the stored procedure. Second, they require that the type of field be defined. Next, parameters require the direction of the data be unknown (0), input (1), output (2), inputoutput (3) or returnvalue (4). Fourth, they require that the maximum size of the field be defined. And last, they require the value of the field that is going into the stored procedure, which is generally supplied by calling a subroutine.

Perhaps an easier way to think about parameters is to consider that any value passed to a subroutine or any function created for processing is considered a parameter. At its most complicated level, however, programming an application in SQL, T-SQL, or PL/SQL can require knowledge of hundreds, or even thousands, of parameters.

In most circumstances, SQL parameters are single-value variables. However, parameters can be linked together to create much more complex strings of values. If a multivalue string parameter is passed, its pieces are linked into a parenthetical, comma-separated list before being passed to the SQL engine.

As you may suspect, when parameter strings increase in number of values, the opportunity for errors also rises. Accordingly, it is important to have a strong foundation to start with. To begin, a review of the general structure and protocol of using parameters in stored procedures is appropriate.

DESIGN TIP

It is important to note that multivalue links are limited to occurring only when varchar (string) parameters are present. Also, care must be taken with non-SELECT statements, to avoid inadvertently changing the value for an insert or update.

Parameter Fundamentals

This example will explain how to pass a parameter into a stored procedure and how to perform some simple inserts and updates. Consider the following table:

```
SampleTable
PrimeKey INT IDENTITY (1,1)
Field1 CHAR(10)
Field2 CHAR(10)
Status CHAR(8)
```

Consider that the goal here is to pass two parameters to the stored procedure:

▶   The old primary key value

▶   The new status

Assume that the PrimeKey field is an identity column and therefore does not need a new value.

A CREATE PROCEDURE statement will be used to pass both of the parameters; it appears as:

```
CREATE PROCEDURE spNewValue  @pPrimeKey int, @pStatus char(8) AS
```

The primary key of the record that will be updated and the new status value are both available. Observe that each parameter's data type is identified next to it. The next step is to create the new record. This is accomplished by using an INSERT/SELECT statement that appears as:

```
INSERT SampleTable
SELECT Field1,
  Field2,
  'Working' AS Status
FROM SampleTable
WHERE PrimeKey = @pPrimeKey
```

Here the parameter is used in the WHERE clause to indicate which record is wanted. A variable can generally be used on either side of the equal sign in a WHERE clause, since the variable is used to compare a column to a constant value. When it is necessary for table names or column names or an entire WHERE clause to be stored in the variable, the placement of variables becomes more complicated.

Once the new record has successfully been created, the developer needs to update the record on hand with the new status value. This statement appears as:

```
UPDATE SampleTable
SET Status = @pStatus
WHERE PrimeKey = @pPrimeKey
```

A variable can also be used as the value for the SET clause in the UPDATE statement, as shown in the preceding code.

The complete stored procedure with the parameters appears as:

```
CREATE PROCEDURE spNewValue  @pPrimeKey int, @pStatus char(8) AS
INSERT SampleTable
SELECT Field1,
  Field2,
  'Working' AS Status
FROM SampleTable
WHERE PrimeKey = @pPrimeKey
UPDATE SampleTable
SET Status = @pStatus
WHERE PrimeKey = @pPrimeKey
GO
```

As with the stored procedures shown in the previous section, the EXEC statement for this procedure looks like this:

```
EXEC spNewValue @pPrimeKey = 1, @pStatus = 'Not Work'
```

Since the parameters are set within a stored procedure, specifying the parameter names when you call the procedure is not required. However, the parameters must be in the same order as they were specified in the CREATE PROC statement.

Summary

This chapter discussed the benefits of using triggers and stored procedures. It evaluated how they can reduce potential database problems by increasing performance and overall organization in the system. These are important factors to consider. Both triggers and stored procedures offer security by creating a buffer between application developers and the database structure. If not for stored procedures, users would be required to manipulate tables directly, which can be complicated and problematic. However, if changes to data take place in a stored procedure model, then data is updated to signal those changes, but the applications used to call the stored procedure go unmodified. The chapter concluded with an evaluation of parameters and explained how they can be added to stored procedures to increase functionality. The upcoming chapters will build upon the knowledge gained in this chapter, offering more proactive and reactive troubleshooting strategies that aid in assuring a stable database.

Transactions

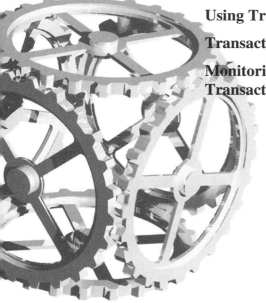

IN THIS CHAPTER:

To begin understanding transactions, take the example of bank transactions used in Chapter 15. In this case, imagine a typical bank and think about how many transactions are processed on any given day—depending on the size of the institution, the number can be quite large. Now imagine the processes that are involved in a single transaction for an electronic deposit done via an online banking system or at an ATM. Generically speaking, from a customer's point of view, the process of making a deposit follows these steps:

1. She enters her personal identification number (PIN).
2. She selects that she wants to make a deposit.
3. She enters the amount of the deposit.
4. The monies deposited are credited to her account in the bank's database.
5. She selects to either execute another transaction or get a receipt of the deposit and end her business.

In most cases, these steps go through flawlessly without a second thought. But, what if a power outage or a hard drive failure were to occur between steps 3 and 4? Is it possible that the woman would lose out on the money she had just deposited? Thankfully, the answer to the second question is no—as long as the bank's developers who assembled the database followed some important rules. In essence, the rule is to assure that in all transactions, if any of the statements within the transaction fail to execute, then none of the changes made in the transaction are applied to the database.

From the perspective of the database, the process of a customer making a deposit follows these steps:

1. The transaction begins by the user being identified by her PIN.
2. The database learns the transaction type (for example, deposit, withdrawal, transfer; in this case a deposit is chosen).
3. The monies are deposited.
4. The user is asked if any other transactions are needed.
5. a) If other transactions are needed, then step 2 is repeated.

    b) If no other transactions are needed, then a receipt is printed for the user.
6. The transaction ends and the changes are applied to the database.

Unlike in the first scenario, the preceding process guarantees that the user will not lose the record of her deposit if there is a problem midway through the transaction.

This chapter will discuss how to prevent problems associated with transactions from occurring in the first place. This discussion will include coverage of the ACID test, also treated in Chapter 9. ACID is an acronym for Atomic, Consistent, Isolated, and Durable—a set of properties that make up what is considered an adequate system for handling transactions. The discussion of transactions will begin with a breakdown of the ACID test. Later the focus will shift to show how to implement databases that successfully pass the ACID test.

Essentially, transactions consist of three actions. First is the initiation. Next is the commit action. Once a transaction is committed, the final action is to end the transaction. At the point of initiation in a transaction, all of the succeeding SQL statements are included as part of the transaction until the transaction concludes.

Transaction Processing Requirements

The ACID test helps database developers determine whether or not a database management system can reliably handle transactions. Each part of the test is explained in the sections that follow.

Atomic

The success of a transaction is an all-or-nothing scenario: either all of the SQL statements commit or all are rolled back. All changes take effect, or none do. For instance, if a bank customer makes an account transfer from his checking account to his credit line, then either both his balances are adjusted or neither is.

Consistent

Most databases include a set of user and/or database constraints that are implemented to prevent distinct types of errors from occurring. Constraints allow developers to work in the database with the understanding that if they violate a rule of a constraint, it will be pointed out to them and they will be allowed to correct it without a tremendous amount of effort. In the use of transactions, one such constraint assures that changes to the database occur by transforming it from one valid state to another valid state. Accordingly, a legal transaction is defined by its capacity to obey user-defined and database-defined integrity constraints. When integrity constraints are violated, the transaction is rolled back. For example, suppose that the bank is required to track any transactions of monies over $100,000 for FDIC purposes. To accomplish this, the developer defines a rule that adds a row to an audit table. Possibly for security or performance, the audit table is separated from the rest of the tables and stored on a different disk from the rest of the database. A potential hazard could exist in this scenario if the audit table's disk is offline and can't be written to. However, with proper constraints set to ensure consistency, the transaction will be aborted, preventing an error.

Isolated

As a rule, until a transaction has been committed, none of the changes made in the transaction are visible to others using the database—for instance, if the bank were auditing their customer account balances as a customer were making a deposit, only the balance before the deposit would be visible. However, once the transaction was committed, the bank's auditing system would recognize the new balance.

Durable

Once a transaction is committed, the outcome of the transaction will stay etched into the database even if there is a system or media failure. In other words, once a customer deposits $10 into an account, the customer's account will forever remember that $10 was deposited to that account on such a day at such a time.

The next section will discuss some of the fundamental areas that are involved in making a database that passes the ACID test. The bulk of the attention will focus on Atomic, Consistent, and Isolated—Durable will also be discussed, but some of the hardware issues that are involved, such as RAID and other backup methods, will not be covered here.

Transaction Fundamentals

Principally, transactions are SQL statement groups that are treated as single units for the point of processing. At a minimum, a transaction consists of just one statement, when that is sufficient to carry out a specific task; alternatively, a transaction can comprise several statements. As mentioned, the fundamental attribute of transactions mandates that if *all* statements within a transaction are not executed, then no changes made within the transaction be applied.

Database Locks

Whether it is in networks, telephony, or databases, concurrent access to shared resources has always been an issue for information technology. In networks, if one person is accessing a specific file, no other users can access it. Most databases operate on the same principle; however, this is not always the case. For instance, when one user is viewing or modifying a record, some databases fail to lock out all other users from that particular field. The results can range from a simple annoyance in the case of a non–mission critical database to serious data corruption in a mission critical database. However, more often than not, failure to lock a database when a user is accessing it can have some serious ramifications. Imagine what might happen at a bank if multiple users had access to records simultaneously—it would not take long for some serious problems to arise.

Thankfully, most relational databases are created to support locks for multiuser systems. The locks in databases are used to direct concurrent access to resources within the database. In a lockable database, when a user has a record open or is creating a new record, others are unable to access that record, which is how things should be. The reason why this is so good is worth discussion. When a database lacks locks to prevent multiple users from accessing records simultaneously, that database often loses a substantial number of records over time.

Understanding Locks

Consider our banking scenario again. Most banks have multiple access points for customers to access the services offered by the bank. Customers can walk into a bank location; use the drive-through; or access telephone banking, ATM, or online services. All of these access points are concurrently linked to a database on the back end that can access any customer's account data at any time. This feature is used to track individual customer transactions as well as all customer transactions, allowing the bank to stay on top of the overall number of transactions completed and the monies that are exchanged during all transactions.

Upon the completion of each customer transaction, the individual transaction (deposit, withdrawal, transfer) is summed with the running total number of transactions. So far things seem relatively straightforward, but what if two customers simultaneously complete deposits to their accounts? Suppose a husband and wife share a bank account and both are logged on to their online banking systems from different locations at the same time. At the same time, each of them decides to do some banking tasks, transferring funds, paying bills, etc. Assume that the database they are using does not have locks. Since they have both logged in at the same time, they are both going to see the same balance before any transactions have occurred. But it is entirely likely that the two customers will execute different transactions to meet each of their specific needs. What if, for example, one of them were to make a transfer of funds from their checking account to their savings account just as the other was about to pay the mortgage for their house? Consider Figure 16-1.

Clearly one of these two users will not get the results from these transactions that he or she expects. In this case, the transactions done by user 2 will overwrite the transactions performed by user 1—the individual result will likely end in a missed mortgage payment. But obviously, the problems with databases that fail to lock go way beyond the risk of bouncing checks—virtually every industry that uses a database will be at risk for some seriously damaging ramifications. The conclusion: locks are an important way to prevent update errors from occurring. To see how they work, consider again the example just used but this time with a lock applied to the database, as shown in Figure 16-2.

With a lock in place, the developer has eliminated any room for error that could occur if concurrent transactions were to happen involving user 1 and user 2 by ensuring that the resource can be occupied by only one transaction at a time.

User 1	User 2
Log in and read from database Account balance: $3,000 Savings account balance: $1,000	Log in and read from database Checking account balance: $3,000 Savings account balance: $1,000
Modify record Pay mortgage from checking: $2,300	Modify record Transfer $1,000 from checking to savings
Complete transactions Ending balances: $700 in checking, $1,000 in savings Log out	Complete transactions Ending balances: $1,200 in checking, $2,000 in savings Log out

Figure 16-1   *A set of conflicting transactions*

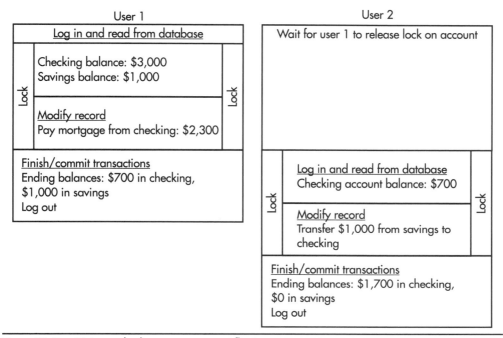

Figure 16-2   *Using a lock to manage conflicting transactions*

Using Locks

Now that a general understanding of locks has been developed, it is time to go a bit further and learn about the different types of locks that are available to developers. In relational databases, there are generally two types: row-level and table-level.

Table-level locks are offered in nearly all databases. The implications of table-level locks include locking the entire table when a user is accessing any portion of it. For instance, in the preceding example, if user 1 is accessing the savings account, user 2 or anyone else can access no other parts of the account. While this feature is good for situations such as multiple users performing banking transactions, it can cause severe disruptions to databases that see a high level of traffic. For instance, in an organization with a database that hosts multiple users who need to access common tables, table-level locks can be very inhibiting to work efficiency.

To alleviate the problems associated with table-level locks, some databases offer a more granular solution called row-level locks. Row-level locks offer a more accommodating solution to the needs of users. Unlike table-level locks, row-level locks concern only the row at which a transaction is being processed. This results in a much more efficient and effective level of control.

Using Transactions

Databases such as Oracle or SQL Server are built to work with transactions and have a specific library of commands for beginning, committing, and recalling changes made by transactions. Oracle's SQL*PLUS utilizes the COMMIT and ROLLBACK keywords, while SQL Server's Transact-SQL uses the BEGIN, SAVE, COMMIT, and ROLLBACK keywords.

Transactions in Oracle

The differences between the syntaxes found in different databases are subtle but noteworthy. In the SQL*PLUS database, the lack of a BEGIN statement implies that when one transaction ends, another begins if it is situated after the first; the next transaction begins regardless of whether the previous transaction ended through a rollback or a commit. Committing changes to the database can occur as a result of several different actions, such as creating or releasing tables or views; or, using any other commands such as ALTER, CONNECT, or, DISCONNECT can automatically commit changes in the existing transaction to the database. Concurrently, exiting SQL*PLUS automatically commits any modifications made to the database during a transaction. But if the database unexpectedly terminates, as through the loss of power or a hardware failure, then the current transaction will roll back automatically.

Here is an example of the syntax of a transaction in SQL*PLUS:

```
SELECT CustId, CustName
FROM Customers

CUSTID    CUSTNAM
-------------------------------
1      Leah Spielberg
2      David Agraz
3      Chris Nguyen
4      Michael Knapp
5      Justin Redak
6      William Romo
7      Nathaniel Raymond
```

```
8       Itai Yanai
9       Sue Huntley
10       Diane Deckert
10 rows selected
```

Suppose that at the end of each month the database administrator is required to remove all customer accounts that have been closed during the month. To accomplish this, a DELETE statement is used. During the database session, the rows specified for deletion will appear as such. For example:

```
DELETE FROM Customers
WHERE CustID IN (4, 8, 9)
3 rows Deleted
SELECT CustId, CustName
FROM Customers
CUSTID    CUSTNAME
-------------------------------
1       Leah Spielberg
2       David Agraz
3       Chris Nguyen
5       Justin Redak
6       William Romo
7       Nathaniel Raymond
10       Diane Deckert
7 rows selected
```

Once removed, the rows are not visible from this user's session. However, since the action has not been committed, the changes are not viewable to any other users who are accessing the tables. In other words, other users will still see the names of ten customers.

Should the user who executed the DELETE statement wish to abandon this transaction, the ROLLBACK command can be used. Use of the ROLLBACK command would appear as:

```
ROLLBACK
Rollback complete.
SELECT CustId, CustName
FROM Customers

CUSTID    CUSTNAME
-------------------------------
1       Leah Spielberg
```

```
2        David Agraz
3        Chris Nguyen
4        Michael Knapp
5        Justin Redak
6        William Romo
7        Nathaniel Raymond
8        Itai Yanai
9        Sue Huntley
10         Diane Deckert
10 rows selected
```

When the ROLLBACK command is used, the Customers table returns to the condition in which it was found prior to the DELETE statement.

Alternatively, if the COMMIT command is used, then the Customers table will appear as it did after the DELETE statement. Furthermore, if other users access the database after the COMMIT command is used, they too will see the changes made.

When troubleshooting a database, the COMMIT command can be very useful, as it allows the administrator to accomplish row-level changes to the database, see the results, and have the option of either committing or rolling back the transactions after reviewing the results. In many cases, however, the COMMIT command becomes a nuisance if the user is required to execute it each time he or she wants to commit a transaction. To alleviate this problem, most databases offer an autocommit option. Autocommit automatically commits transactions in the database whenever a SQL statement is executed. In SQL*PLUS, the command that turns on the autocommit mode is:

```
SET AUTOCOMMIT ON
```

To add even more functionality, the administrator can set limits to the number of transactions that she would like to commit automatically. This is accomplished by:

```
SET AUTOCOMMIT X
```

where X is equal to the number of transactions that should be automatically committed. For instance, if the developer were to write SET AUTOCOMMIT 7, then a commit would be issued after every seven SQL statements executed.

To end the autocommit mode, the developer must issue:

```
SET AUTOCOMMIT OFF
```

Finally, if the developer wishes to see the current setting for autocommit, it can be displayed using the command:

```
SHOW AUTOCOMMIT
```

The next section will review some of the similarities and differences found between SQL*PLUS and SQL Server's Transact-SQL.

Controlling Transactions

As a rule, only the developers are responsible for determining which types of actions should be grouped together in each transaction. Developers should concern themselves with keeping all of the transactions properly defined to ensure that the work is executed logically and that the database remains consistent. Keeping each transaction within the limits of its purpose is a good way to avoid problems; in other words, one transaction should consist of just the necessary parts for one logical unit of work. With regard to maintaining a clean database when using transactions, it is important that the data in all referenced tables be in a consistent state before the transaction begins and after it ends.

Returning to our example, when a customer transfers funds from one account to another, the process should consist of the debit to one account (one SQL statement) followed by the credit to the other account (a second SQL statement). To pass the ACID test, each of the statements will either fail or succeed together as a unit of work; the debit should not be committed without the credit or vice versa.

Transactions in Transact-SQL

Much as in SQL*PLUS, a transaction in Transact-SQL is a statement that produces a measurable unit of work by retrieving, inserting, deleting, or modifying data. Contrasting with SQL*PLUS, Transact-SQL databases by default operate by handling SQL statements individually on a per-transaction basis. All transactions must explicitly be declared, and one of four statements, BEGIN, SAVE, COMMIT, or ROLLBACK, must be used. Notice that a new statement, BEGIN, is identified. The BEGIN TRANSACTION statement activates another transaction. When using BEGIN statements, the developer can spell out a name for a transaction and then commit or roll back the transaction by its given name later. A good place to use this method is in nested transactions that exist within an existing transaction.

In addition to these statements, Transact-SQL supports savepoints and named transactions. Both of these give the developer more leverage for performing rollback operations to specific points in the database. Suppose the developer wished to roll back, for instance, five transactions. He could set a savepoint just before the first of those five transactions, and if he chose to roll back after the five transactions had executed, he could call the savepoint instead of rolling back each transaction individually.

Also new in Transact-SQL is the SAVE statement. The SAVE statement can be thought of in the same way as BEGIN with one exception: SAVE protects the transaction's status at a specified point within the transaction as determined by the administrator or user. Savepoints can be particularly useful for troubleshooting very large sets of transactions—breaking up and then rolling back parts of statements in a transaction can be done by identifying the name of the savepoint rather than the transaction name.

COMMIT statements in Transact-SQL generally serve the same purpose as they do in SQL*PLUS—they end a transaction and apply any changes that occur within the transaction process. Once a transaction is committed, statements within the transaction are applied to the database, at which point the user responsible for the changes and all others who access the database will see the changes. Once a transaction has been completed, the database will automatically return to autocommit mode and wait for another transaction.

The final transaction statement used in Transact-SQL is ROLLBACK. Much as in to SQL*PLUS, the ROLLBACK command in Transact-SQL is used to abandon any changes that result from a recent transaction. Unlike in SQL*PLUS, the ROLLBACK command in Transact-SQL can also be used to revert to the last savepoint.

Transactions and Stored Procedures

The preceding chapter discussed how stored procedures are used to encase and save a package of SQL statements. Using stored procedures in conjunction with transactions can be a very effective method for accomplishing a number of different tasks.

Since the purpose of stored procedures is to hold a set of SQL statements and execute the set as a group, using them for executing tasks such as tallying a group of transactions can be a far more efficient system than attempting to do so manually. Consider how a bank may use this technique to analyze their business practices: by incorporating a stored procedure into an account program that audits transactions, the bank's manager can identify specific trends that characterize transactions. The alternative would be to manually write and execute several transactions. Of course, there is a time and a place for manual instances; however, in many large databases use of stored procedures can be a major time saver.

In addition to their efficiency features, stored procedures also offer the advantage of reusability. As discussed in Chapter 15, once a stored procedure has been written, it can be saved and used again and again—in sum, one stored procedure can save hundreds of programming hours. Moreover, when using a stored procedure, the developer needs to debug the program only once; after he has done so and it satisfies its users and the database rules, it is capable of working indefinitely.

Monitoring Transactions: Using the Transaction Log

Using the rollback feature was discussed earlier in this chapter. But what if the developer needs to reverse a transaction well after its execution? It can be difficult to reverse a specific transaction, as it requires the developer to return to the database and actually seek out what effects that transaction gave rise to in what places. To alleviate this problem, an alternative to the rollback feature exists—the transaction log.

The transaction log contains a record of every change made to the database since a time set by the administrator, generally that of the last backup of the database. It collects every step that was taken to modify each record. When an administrator backs up the transaction log, he is backing up a period of activity. When he restores the transaction log backup, he is in essence replaying that documentation of activity. As a side benefit, backing up the transaction log frees room in the log for reuse to manage expansion of the database.

The transaction log literally records all modifications to a table. For instance, if a particular record in a table has been modified hundreds of times, then each change is logged and can be audited for verification. Furthermore, if an administrator wished to do so, he could perform a restore to reapply any or all of the modifications that have been made. While this is a labor-intensive proposition, in certain cases such as tracking highly sensitive data like banking records, the capacity for finite restorations is a nice reassurance, not to mention a valuable tool for troubleshooting. Frequently an administrator will wish to replay just a portion of the database. This can be accomplished by performing a restore using the STOPAT option.

Suppose at 4:20 someone inadvertently deleted a table of data the administrator could restore to 4:19. Consequently, any work done after the time of restore would be lost. The syntax for a STOPAT command is:

```
STOPAT = date_time | @date_time_var
```

This command indicates recovery to the specified mark, containing the transaction that contains the mark. If a variable is used for STOPAT, the variable must be of the varchar, char, smalldatetime, or datetime data type.

Summary

This chapter discussed some of the primary issues involved in successfully executing and managing transactions. You should now have a strong knowledge of the key requirements involved in developing low-maintenance transactions. The chapter also covered locks, how they apply to transactions, and how they can prevent problems down the road. Examples of transactions in this chapter can be used as models for future planning, and understanding transactions' interrelationships with stored procedures can help you build reliable and reusable tools.

Using Cursors and Exceptions

IN THIS CHAPTER:

Understanding Cursors

Creating and Using Cursors

Cursors for Transact-SQL

Understanding Cursors for PL/SQL

Exceptions in PL/SQL

Exception Handling

T his chapter begins with a discussion of cursors, explaining what their purpose is, how they are used in SQL, and how to avoid or fix problems that can arise when they are used. In the second part, we go in a different direction to talk about exceptions. Exceptions provide a clean separation of error handling code and provide an improved reliability of error handling. Exception handling creates a built-in mechanism for handling errors (exceptions) in PL/SQL for use with cursors and many other program elements that were also discussed in Chapter 15.

Understanding Cursors

Developers are frequently faced with the need to perform various operations on a range of records in a database. Most developers are familiar and comfortable with queries that return all of their data in the form of a single table. For instance, when an UPDATE or DELETE function is performed, the affected rows are placed in temporary tables until a commit or rollback is performed. Typically these temporary tables are used within triggers and to get the latest value for an identity column. A parallel example is found in SELECT statements. When a select is called, all the rows in a database that are returned by the query are simultaneously displayed.

Performing assorted operations on different records in the database is indeed quite useful. This task is most commonly done by writing several SQL statements using WHERE clauses that segregate each group of rows with operations that have particular requirements. While this is a satisfactory solution for many challenges, it can get out of control if the problem requires that a high number of WHERE clauses be included. As an alternative, sometimes it is easier to write a single query that addresses each of the rows individually as they are returned. You corral the rows into a holding pen, and then you work on each row in sequence to perform the work you have to do. Cursors offer this alternative approach. However, this latter method will, except in very rare cases, cause performance degradation. Using cursors is not recommended unless there is absolutely no alternative to row processing. Cursor processing is expensive.

Database applications commonly reclaim the sum of the outcome of queries, and the calling program processes the results individually one record at a time. If you are using a client program written in Visual Basic, for example, you can issue the query using the ActiveX Data Objects. You establish the connection using a connection object, create the query in a command object, and receive the results of the query in a recordset object. Your client program can then manipulate the records as it wishes. Sometimes, however, such client side processing involves intolerable overhead, as when you must return 50,000 records over a 56 Kbps WAN connection. Under these circumstances, performing all the processing on the server side is the better choice. Cursors can supply this same level of functionality at the database server at much less expense in overhead.

Consider how a standard select query is processed. The query goes from the developer to a database where each row is graded against the contents of any existing WHERE clauses. When a row meets the criteria of a WHERE clause, it is returned; if it does not meet the criteria, it is discarded. Sometimes an ORDER BY clause is also included to sort the results prior to returning them.

By contrast with traditional queries, cursors send their request to the database but receive feedback from the database not as one large package, but as single rows of information. The benefits of this method include allowing developers to manipulate the returning data either manually, in the case of small batches, or by writing programs and stored procedures within the database that can modify the output according to criteria established by the developer.

This chapter includes a review of some of the most common ways to identify how and when to use cursors, how they can be helpful, and how to troubleshoot problems that occur with them. The chapter will give examples of methods for using cursors in PL/SQL and Transact-SQL.

Creating and Using Cursors

When creating cursors in an application, it is important for you to remember that several steps are involved. The schema that follows can be used as a reference for developers; it summarizes the four major steps used to create a successful cursor:

1. Declare
2. Open retrieve
3. Fetch, update, and delete
4. Close

The details of this schema follow a simple logic, and each step will be described later with examples, but first a brief description will bring you up to speed if you are unfamiliar with cursors.

Declaration or definition of a cursor is done to create the cursor in the first place. Concurrently, declaring a cursor associates it with a SELECT statement. Once created, the cursor needs to be opened for use. The purpose of an opened cursor is to retrieve specific rows; once they are retrieved, any actions in the form of external programs, stored procedures, or manual data manipulation may take place. Retrieving specific rows affords the capacity to return, update, and delete the data that is returned; cursors allow the developer to accomplish this at the row level, individually. As a final step, the cursor must be closed.

Knowing and understanding the steps just described will help you make more informed decisions when using cursors. Furthermore, insight into how to recognize the problems that can arise with cursors will aid you in making proactive actions when troubleshooting. The following section will delve into the syntax of these five steps and aid you as a user or a developer in understanding cursors at the command-line level.

Cursors for Transact-SQL

The following examples will give you a context in which to learn about cursors, how they are structured, and where potential problems can occur within them.

Creating SQL Cursors

Cursors are created in SQL using the DECLARE statement. The DECLARE statement serves a dual purpose. First, it describes the properties of a cursor. Second, it ties the cursor to a SELECT statement. Cursor declarations can be thought of as much like variable declarations in a stored procedure. The syntax for declaring a cursor in SQL appears as:

```
DECLARE GetCustomers CURSOR
For SELECT customer_account_id, CustomerName, BranchID
FROM Customers
```

In this declaration, the example of a bank's database is used. The cursor, named GetCustomers, is tied to a select statement that is designed to retrieve a customer's account number, the customer's name, and the branch at which that customer does his or her banking. At the point of declaring a cursor, you have the option of specifying whether to allow updating of rows through the cursor. Furthermore, the developer can specify which columns can be updated.

DESIGN TIP

The DECLARE statement differs from one DBMS to the next; if using a database other than SQL Server, be sure to verify use of the proper statement.

General syntax for a DECLARE CURSOR statement appears as:

```
DECLARE name Cursor
FOR A_Select_Statement
[ FOR [ READ ONLY | UPDATE [ OF A_Column] ] ]
```

Note that the SELECT statement offers two options for a cursor: FOR READ ONLY and FOR UPDATE. Cursors using the FOR READ ONLY option are capable of returning data from operations performed within the cursor. This option is useful when you would like to give access to users but do not want those users to have the capability to make changes to any data.

Meanwhile, the other SELECT statement option, FOR UPDATE, is capable of offering many more functions and much greater authority. Use of the FOR UPDATE option enables the user to read, update, and delete rows. Use of the OF option allows developers to limit which columns can be updated by way of the cursor. This tool can be highly valuable in troubleshooting situations where you don't want users to have the capacity to modify certain data while having access to other areas. For instance, if you wanted users of the bank's database to have the capability to modify the customer's branch information but for security reasons did not want them to have the ability to modify the names or account numbers of customers, then a declaration would appear as:

```
DECLARE GetCustomers CURSOR
For SELECT customer_account_id, CustomerName, BranchID
FROM Customers
FOR UPDATE OF BranchID
```

Opening Cursors

The next step is to learn about opening cursors. Cursors are opened using the OPEN CURSOR statement; in the case of our example, it would appear as:

```
OPEN GetCustomers
```

Once it is opened, there are three main actions that can be taken with a cursor:

▶ Fetching

▶ Updating

▶ Deleting

Cursor data can be accessed using the FETCH statement, where FETCH specifies which rows shall be retrieved, where they shall be retrieved from, and where they shall be stored after being retrieved. By default, the FETCH statement will retrieve rows individually; however, you can specify to increase the number of rows to be retrieved at one time.

Upon opening, a cursor is placed in the first row of the result set. As each fetch retrieves a row from the result set, a new row is added; once all rows have been fetched from the cursor, a code is returned to denote completion.

The FETCH statement to be used in a cursor appears as:

```
FETCH CursorName
```

Here is code that shows how a cursor would appear when used with a FETCH statement. These three examples show a simple FETCH statement, *FETCH GetCustomers*, which returns a single row each time it executes:

```
FETCH GetCustomers
CustomerID          CustomerName          BranchID
1                   Johnson, Michael             1
(1 row(s) affected)

FETCH GetCustomers
CustomerID          CustomerName          BranchID
2                   Nguyen, Christopher          2
(1 row(s) affected)

FETCH GetCustomers
CustomerID          CustomerName          BranchID
3                   Spielberg, Leah              1
(1 row(s) affected)
```

As you can see, each FETCH causes the database to return one row, with the announcement that one row was affected.

When a cursor is empty, FETCH informs you that the cursor is empty by placing the result code 2 in the system variable @@FETCH_STATUS, making the cursor a useful tool for stored procedures that iterate over the rows retrieved using a cursor. For instance, in the preceding example the stored procedure can be set to use a loop that will fetch rows until the cursor is empty, thereby returning a code 2, which will cause the program to end. Keep in mind that you can check the value of @@FETCH_STATUS simply by including it in an equality. The system makes it available to you at all times.

DESIGN TIP

While it is always good to check your particular version, the OPEN CURSOR statement is supported by most DBMSs.

Updating and Deleting Cursors

Unlike fetches, updates and deletes do not have a special command for cursors. This fact simplifies things a bit by allowing developers to utilize the same commands used for other operations. However, rather than being used simply, UPDATE and DELETE commands are paired with a special WHERE clause when used with cursors. Also, CURRENT OF is used to designate which of the rows in the cursor is to be the object for the UPDATE or DELETE statement. Here is an example of the use of CURRENT OF as it is applied to a WHERE clause:

```
UPDATE customers
Set CustomerName =  'Michael Johnson'
WHERE CURRENT OF GetCustomers
```

The purpose of this operation is to provide the CURRENT OF construct with directions to specify that the CustomerName field in the record where GetCustomer resides is to be updated.

Alternatively, if the aim of the cursor is to remove the row, then a DELETE statement is paired with CURRENT OF to look like this:

```
DELETE FROM customers
WEHRE CURRENT OF GetCustomers
```

To provide consistency, the cursor is automatically moved to the next row or group of rows once CURRENT OF is used within an UPDATE or DELETE statement.

Closing Cursors

The most common method used to conclude a cursor command is to issue the CLOSE statement. By calling the CLOSE statement, all fetches, updates, and deletes that have been opened by an OPEN statement will be drawn to an end. The result of the CLOSE statement is that rows with the cursors are no longer addressable. However, once the cursor has been opened, it remains declared.

The syntax of the CLOSE statement appears as:

```
CLOSE CursorName
```

An alternative to the CLOSE statement is the DEALLOCATE statement. Deallocating goes a step beyond a CLOSE statement by revoking the declaration of a cursor in addition to removing the opportunity to address the rows within the cursor.

The syntax of the DEALLOCATE statement appears as:

```
DEALLOCATE CursorName
```

An example of the CLOSE statement appears as:

```
DECLARE  GetCustomers CURSOR
FOR SELECT CustID, CustName, BranchID
FROM Customers
OPEN GetCustomers
FETCH GetCustomers


CustomerID              CustomerName        BranchID
1                       Johnson, Michael           1
(1 row(s) affected)

CLOSE GetCustomers
OPEN GetCustomers
FETCH GetCustomers


CustomerID              CustomerName        BranchID
1                       Johnson, Michael           1
```

Note that when a closed cursor is reopened, the first row in the query is returned as a result. Now the same query is shown, only this time a DEALLOCATE statement is added and another attempt is made to open it:

```
DECLARE  GetCustomers CURSOR
FOR SELECT CustID, CustName, BranchID
FROM Customers
OPEN GetCustomers
FETCH GetCustomers


CustomerID          CustomerName      BranchID
1                   Johnson, Michael         1
(1 row(s) affected)


DEALLOCATE GetCustomers
OPEN GetCustomers


Msg 16916, level 16, State 1
A cursor with the name 'GetCustomer' does not exist
```

Unlike with the CLOSE statement, when the DEALLOCATE statement is used, the query is not available when using the OPEN command. However, it is good practice to first issue a CLOSE statement prior to a DEALLOCATE statement.

Understanding Cursors for PL/SQL

Cursors in PL/SQL are created in the declarations section of the program and are used in the program's executable commands section. This section will explain what is involved in successfully incorporating cursors into a PL/SQL program.

Declaring a Cursor

The syntax of declaring a cursor in PL/SQL departs from the conventions used in Transact-SQL and appears as:

```
DECLARE
CURSOR CursorName IS
```

```
SelectStatement;
[FOR UPDATE {OF column [,column….]] [NOWAIT]];
```

PL/SQL cursors offer a SELECT statement to rerun multiple rows to execute; the developer can then iterate each of the rows by employing a loop. As you learned from the CLOSE and DEALLOCATE examples from the last section, statements for cursors can be referenced in their temporary file and do not need to be referenced again after the cursor is opened once.

Recalling the example used earlier, the syntax would appear as:

```
DECLARE
CURSOR GetCustomer IS
SELECT CustID, CustName, BranchID
FROM Customers;
CustomerRecord GetCustomer%ROWTYPE
```

Note the presence of a new keyword, %ROWTYPE. %ROWTYPE is used to specify that a record be created where the names and data types of the fields in a record match the names and data types of a row in a table. Using %ROWTYPE allows the creation of a variable to hold the records extracted from a declared cursor. Where a normal variable receives a value passed into it, %ROWTYPE receives all the records returned by the cursor. The two processes are equivalent, except that the payload sent to a variable is the value of a SQL expression, whereas the payload sent to %ROWTYPE is a set of records.

The declaration section concludes when the keyword BEGIN indicates the beginning of the executable commands section.

Executing a Cursor

To execute a cursor, follow this template:

```
DECLARE
CURSOR GetCustomer IS
SELECT CustID, CustName, BranchID
FROM Customers;
CustomerRecord GetCustomer%ROWTYPE
BEGIN
```

```
OPEN GetCustomers;
FETCH GetCustomers INTO CustomerRecord;
CLOSE GetCustomers;
END;
.
/
PL/SQL procedure successfully completed.
```

The previous code introduces us to a new feature in PL/SQL, the assigning of attributes to the outcome of fetch operations. The assignment of attributes and their subsequent values affect the output that is returned after the program is executed.

Here are the four attributes that are associated with cursors in PL/SQL and their possible values.

▶   **%FOUND**   This attribute informs the program if a row of data is returned. There are three possible values in this situation:

   ▶   TRUE: indicates that the earlier FETCH returned a data row

   ▶   FALSE: shows that the earlier FETCH did not return a data row

   ▶   NULL: indicates that the cursor is open but has not executed a FETCH

▶   **%NOTFOUND**   This attribute is the opposite of %FOUND and shows if data in a row has not been returned. The three values are:

   ▶   TRUE: shows that no data was returned in the FETCH and that all rows have been returned

   ▶   FALSE: indicates that the earlier FETCH returned a data row

   ▶   NULL: shows that the cursor is open but has not executed a FETCH

▶   **%ISOPEN**   Here the attribute indicates if a cursor is open. This attribute has two possible values.

   ▶   TRUE: shows that the cursor is opened

   ▶   FALSE: indicates that the cursor is not opened

▶ **%ROWCOUNT** As mentioned earlier, this attribute shows the number of tows that have been returned by the cursor as it executes. There are two values associated with this attribute:

▶ 0: shows that the cursor is open but FETCH has not been executed

▶ Positive integer: presents the number of rows that have been retrieved through a FETCH operation.

Looping Cursors

FETCH statements are useful for returning a row of data via the cursor. However, unless a loop is used, a program that uses fetches will only return the first record from a table—recall the last example, where FETCH returned the first record from GetCustomers. But what happens if you want all of the rows of data without having to execute the same program over and over? If you are interested in obtaining all rows of data, then you can add the %NOTFOUND attribute; doing so ensures that a true variable will be coupled with the loop, and %NOTFOUND will guarantee that all rows will be processed. To demonstrate this, we embellish an example used earlier to show what a loop looks like with a %NOTFOUND attribute added:

```
DECLARE
CURSOR GetCustomer IS
SELECT CustID, CustName, BranchID
FROM Customers;
CustomerRecord GetCustomer%ROWTYPE;
BEGIN
OPEN GetCustomer;
LOOP
FETCH GetCustomer INTO CustomerRecord;
EXIT WHEN GetCustomer%NOTFOUND;
END LOOP;
CLOSE GetCustomer;
END;
.
/
```

In this example, the LOOP statement is used to commence the loop. To end or exit the loop, an EXIT WHEN command is used, thereby closing the looping process. In the above case, the loop will continue until the GetCustomers%NOTFOUND attribute is true. The statement END LOOP indicates that no further statements shall be executed within the loop.

Exceptions in PL/SQL

Exceptions are a part of PL/SQL to handle errors and other situations that happen during the execution of a program. When dealing with errors in PL/SQL, know that there are generally two varieties of errors addressable with exception handlers:

▶ **PL/SQL runtime errors**   These are predefined exceptions that are designed to address the most frequent errors.

▶ **User-defined conditions**   In addition to the predefined exceptions that are built into programs such as Oracle, users can write exceptions of their own. In order to make these exceptions functional, the developer must define the exception.

Declaring and implementing an exception follow this syntax:

```
exception_example EXCEPTION
```

The keyword EXCEPTION is a declaration that designates a user-defined exception. Note that user-defined conditions do not always meet the criteria to be considered an actual error; however, they generally can be fixed by using exception handlers.

Building on the preceding EXCEPTION example, note the PRAGMA EXCEPTION_INIT command. This command is used to associate an exception with a specific Oracle error using the error number as the connection.

Exception Types

In PL/SQL running on Oracle, an error is reported in the format ORA-xxxxx. Here are a variety of examples of exceptions that occur in Oracle:

▶ **ORA-00001: DUP_VAL_ON_INDEX**   Points out that a unique constraint has been violated when an update or insert statement attempted to insert a duplicate key. The database will urge the user to either remove the unique restriction or refrain from inserting the key.

► **ORA-01001: INVALID_CURSOR** Indicates an illegal operation. Sources of this exception range from a simple typing error to misappropriation of memory within the program. The latter source is difficult to isolate and often requires analysis of the program.

► **ORA-01422: TOO_MANY_ROWS** This error is given when the SELECT statement returns more than the requested number of rows.

► **ORA-00061: TRANSACTION_BACKED_OUT** This issue occurs when the shared instance being started is using DML locks, and the running instances are not, or vice versa. To remedy this problem, the developer can either:

  ► Not use DML_LOCKS by setting DML_LOCKS to zero in all instances, or

  ► Use DML_LOCKS by setting DML_LOCKS to a positive integer in all instances.

► **ORA-01476: ZERO_ATTEMPT** This error is delivered when a divisor is equal to zero and is repaired by correcting the expression, then retrying the operation.

► **ORA-01404: ALTER COLUMN** This is caused by an increase in the length of a column resulting in the combined lengths of the columns specified in a previous CREATE INDEX statement surpassing the highest index length (255). The index length is computed by adding the width of all indexed columns to the number of indexed columns. The remedy to this problem is to alter the columns by eliminating the affected index.

► **ORA-01722: INVALID_NUMBER** This error indicates that a conversion, either implicit or explicit, has failed in a SQL statement.

► **ORA-06502: VALUE_ERROR** This is the result of a conversion error in a procedural statement. Two reasons can account for why this error may occur:

  ► The developer is attempting to insert a character value in a number field.

  or

  ► An attempt is being made to insert a value in a variable that is larger than its size. For instance, if the developer tries to insert 'abcdefg' in a variable declared as varchar2 (3), the result here will be:

```
A conversion error occurred in a procedural statement
```

To remedy this problem, the developer should change the data, how it is controlled, or how it is declared so that the values do not violate constraints.

▶ **ORA-06501: PROGRAM_ERROR**   This is an internal error message that suggests that an error has been detected in a PL/SQL program. Unlike many errors, this one requires the developer to contact Oracle for further assistance.

▶ **ORA-06500: STORAGE_ERROR**   Occasionally an internal error message will be generated when memory has been exhausted or corrupted within the database. Much as with a PROGRAM_ERROR, the developer must contact Oracle to resolve this issue.

When an exception is raised, it occurs in one of two ways. The first is as a predefined exception, such as those just listed. Alternatively, user-defined exceptions are raised when the RAISE command is executed. Regardless of how an exception is raised, once it does occur the program abruptly shifts from the executable section to the exception handler. A point of note is that all shifts occur in only one direction; in other words, once an exception is handled, it will not run again without an intervention. The developer can return to the executable section in either of two ways: by manually running the executable after the exception has been handled, or, and most often preferably, by inserting nested PL/SQL blocks that can pass the exception back to the execution.

Learning how to deal with exceptions is a key way to master the troubleshooting process; the last section will analyze some of the best methods for accomplishing effective exception handling.

Exception Handling

The exception handling section of a block fits toward the end of the executable section of the query, situated just before the END statement. The syntax for the exception section of a PL/SQL block is:

```
EXCEPTION
     [WHEN exception_name THEN
          pl.sql_statements
     [WHEN exception_name THEN
          pl/sql_statements…]]
     [WHEN OTHERS THEN
```

```
            pl/sql_statements]
END;
```

The WHEN and WHEN OTHERS keywords characterize a receptacle where exception handlers can execute if no other exceptions apply. The following example shows how an exception can be utilized to retrieve the account number and name of a bank customer:

```
DECLARE
cust_name cust.cname%type;
cust_acct cust.acct%type;
custno_to_find NUMBER := 9999;
BEGIN
SELECT cname, acct
INTO cust_name, cust_acct
FROM cust
WHERE CUSTNO = custno_to_find;
EXCEPTION
WHEN NO_DATA_FOUND THEN
INSERT INTO error_log (custno, error_message)
VALUES (custno_to_find, 'Missing customer record');
END;
```

In this example, if the record of a specified customer is not found, then the error log table receives a new row.

RAISE and RAISE_APPLICATION_ERROR Statements

Earlier in this chapter, we touched upon the subject of raising exceptions in a PL/SQL block. This section will go into further coverage of the RAISE statement and how it is best used for troubleshooting situations. There are three possible ways to raise an exception in a PL/SQL block. The first is performed upon an Oracle error, which automatically triggers an exception. The next is through the explicit use of a RAISE statement—an example of this is shown in the text that follows. The last method to raise an exception is accomplished by calling the RAISE_APPLICATION_ERROR procedure.

RAISE and RAISE_APPLICATION_ERROR statements can either be placed directly within the execution section of a PL/SQL block or be presented as exception handlers—this option offers the opportunity to raise an exception several times or to include multiple raise statements in the same handler. When the RAISE_APPLICATION_ERROR option is chosen, the developer can purposefully cause a trigger or other program to fail in a specified place. For instance, if a developer were to create an employee database, a RAISE_APPLICATION_ERROR could be used to cause an application failure if a person failed to insert a first name for a new employee. Obviously, the user can simply bypass the RAISE_APPLICATION_ERROR by being sure that all required fields in the database are correctly filled out.

The syntax of a raise statement appears as:

```
RAISE exception_name
```

The exception_name can be either a user-defined exception or a predefined exception.

The next example shows how a RAISE statement is applied. Building on the context of the previous example, here the developer's application attempts to add a new customer; however, if the user neglects to enter an opening balance for the customer's new account, the procedure fails and an error is generated.

```
CREATE
Procedure create_cust (cust_num IN NUMBER,
                cust_name IN VARCHAR2,
                cust_bal IN NUMBER)
IS
no_salary EXCEPTION;
PRAGMA EXCEPTION_INIT (no_balance, -20000);
BEGIN
IF NVL (cust_bal, 0) = 0 THEN
RAISE  no_balance;
END IF;
INSERT INTO cust (custnum, custname, sal)
Values (cust_num, cust_name, cust_bal);
EXCEPTION
WHEN no_balance THEN
END;
```

In this example, the user is forced to put a value greater than 0 for cust_bal in create_cust. If the user puts a balance of 0 or null into the cust_bal record, then the no_balance exception is raised. Once the no_balance exception is raised, control of the program is transferred to the associated exemption handler. Once in the exception handler, the RAISE statement evaluates and raises the exception once more, which returns the code that calls upon the procedure.

DESIGN TIP

When defining user-defined exceptions, choose numbers between −20,000 and −20,999 to assign to the error via the ERROR_NUMBER keyword. By using this convention, the developer is assured that the user-defined exceptions will not conflict with predefined exceptions in Oracle.

The RAISE_APPLICATION_ERROR syntax appears as:

```
RAISE_APPLICATION_ERROR (error_number, error_text [,keep_errors]);
```

This statement is different from the `RAISE` statement in that it presents a way to define error numbers and messages in PL/SQL that are not ordinarily handled by Oracle's error index.

The RAISE_APPLICATION_ERROR performs well within a trigger (see Chapter 15). An example of a RAISE_APPLICATION_ERROR in a trigger follows:

```
CREATE OR REPLACE TRIGGER cust_instert
BEFORE INSERT ON cust
FOR EACH ROW
BEGIN
    IF :new.cname IS NULL THEN
    RAISE_APPLICATION_ERROR (-20001, 'Customer must have a name.');
    END IF;
END;
```

This example utilizes the RAISE_APPLICATION_ERROR in a trigger to prevent a user from entering a new customer but not including a name.

Summary

This chapter has focused on cursors and exceptions. In reviewing the processes followed in cursors, the intention is to create ways in which to identify and effectively build error-free cursors. In the second part of this chapter, the focus shifted toward exceptions that occur in PL/SQL. Here the developer should have a more secure grasp of when exceptions should be used and, more importantly, how to use them in an effort to develop stable and trouble-free programs.

IN THIS CHAPTER:

Introducing Trees

Understanding Trees and Hierarchies

Tree Operations

One of the more difficult problems facing SQL programmers is representing data that has a complex internal structure in a SQL database. SQL tables are good for representing related sets of facts. However, what do you do when the facts in a set have relationships with one another that are not easily represented using a collection of columns? For example, you can encounter a table of employees in just about anyone's human resources database. However, all employees are not equal. Some are managers and some are line workers, for example. You can easily distinguish the two using an employee type code. But such a code cannot easily capture the relationships between the managers and the line workers. Each manager has a specific group of line workers to manage. Managers do not share authority over each other's line workers. This relationship between a manager and line workers is hierarchical; that is, the manager is superordinate over a group of line workers. Because columns in a table have difficulty representing such a relationship, you need to do extra work in building this relationship into a table. The type of relationship we are presenting here is a tree. It is a useful example of how to incorporate advanced data relationships into a SQL table.

A clear understanding of what a tree is and how it is used in SQL requires a few preliminarily terms to be defined. First the user needs to understand the meaning of graphs in SQL. *Graphs* are data structures that consist of nodes that are connected by edges—boxes typically represent nodes, and lines with arrowheads represent edges. *Edges* represent a unilateral relationship between two nodes that are connected; the unilateral nature of the relationship is important and can be understood as a parent-child system where the parent is the higher-ranking node and the child is the lower-ranking. The edge points downward from parent to child. Consequently, due to the unidirectional nature of nodes and edges, there is never a circular relationship between parent and child nodes.

Introducing Trees

Trees can be understood in terms of organizational charts—in this chapter, the organization example will be a corporate employee structure. In this corporate structure, each node represents an employee, and each edge connects two nodes to establish a hierarchical relationship within the corporate structure.

The top of the tree is referred to as the *root*. The root holds the greatest importance in the chart; in the example in this chapter, the root node is the CEO of a company. A node's *outdegree* refers to how many edges emerge from it; contrasting with this, a node's *indegree* refers to how many edges point in to it. Organizational charts are understood in terms of parent-child relationships, where the parent is the higher-ranking member. The nodes at the bottom of a tree, with no outdegree edges emerging from them, are called *leaf nodes*. For organizational purposes, most trees are binary. A parent that has at most two children defines a binary tree. Alternatively, it is also possible to have an n-ary tree, which allows an unlimited number of child edges.

Now that you have a better understanding of some of the key terms, a proper definition of a tree can be given. A *tree* is a graph where all nodes other than the root have one indegree and the root has none. In a tree, all nodes can be traced back to the root by following the opposite direction of the arrows that point to any given node. When a function is written for a tree, the purpose is to make a query that resolves uncertainty about sets of nodes defined by hierarchical relationships.

Understanding Trees and Hierarchies

Before the days of SQL, most data was stored in hierarchical databases—this boded well for hierarchies for obvious reasons. However, SQL is not based on a hierarchical arrangement where the data and database have similar structural layouts. In SQL, the data is not hierarchically mapped into tables, since the tables are based on sets instead of graphs. To deal with this, most programmers write code in another language such as C or employ a report writer to handle the tree structures. The point of this is to assure that all of the relationships in the data, for instance the relationship of a CEO to a vice president, are made clear in SQL. The result is that additional columns are often added to correspond to the tree components. Figure 18-1 shows a chart that illustrates an organization's tree.

Frequently, a nesting model is used as an alternative method to display the hierarchical relationships found in trees. Because SQL is a set-oriented language, it is more desirable to use a nested approach when describing trees. Trees displayed as nested sets appear as a group of ovals, which replace the boxes in a chart—the

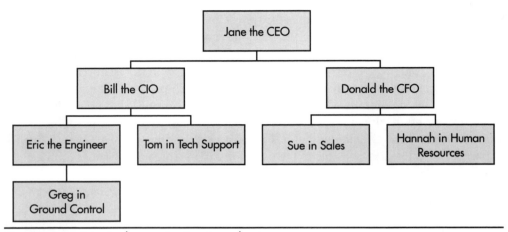

Figure 18-1 *A typical organization tree chart*

smaller, child ovals are subordinate subsets of the larger, parent ovals. An example of a nested tree that mimics the structure of the preceding "node and edge" chart is displayed in Figure 18-2.

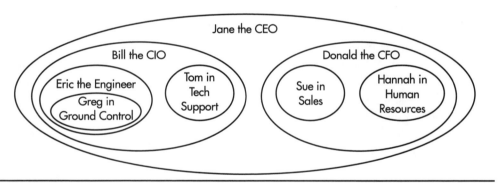

Figure 18-2 *A nested tree that imitates the structure of an organizational chart*

The code that would be used to create the example tree shown in the preceding chart in Oracle would assume this form:

```
CREATE TABLE CorporateChart (
EmployeeID       integer primary key,
ManagerID        integer
Name              varchar(100)
);
insert into CorporateChart values (1, NULL, 'Jane the CEO');
insert into CorporateChart values (2,1, 'Donald the CFO');
insert into CorporateChart values (3,1, 'Bill the CIO');
insert into CorporateChart values (4,2, 'Sue in Sales');
insert into CorporateChart values (5,3, 'Eric the Engineer');
insert into CorporateChart values (6,2, 'Hannah in Human Resources');
insert into CorporateChart values (7,3, 'Tom in Tech Support');
insert into CorporateChart values (8, 5, 'Greg in Ground Control');
```

The following query shows what the table layout looks like when the table is populated with data:

```
SQL> columnname format a20
SQL> Select * from CorporateChart

EmployeeID    ManagerID    NAME
----------    ---------    -----
1             Null    Jane the CEO
2             1       Donald the CFO
3             1       Bill the CIO
4             2       Sue in Sales
5             3       Eric the Engineer
6             2       Hannah in Human Resources
7             3       Tom in Tech Support
8             5       Greg in Ground Control

8 rows selected.
```

The integers used for ManagerID point to rows in the EmployeeID table. Suppose the administrator wanted to display an organizational chart. To do this in Oracle, he could utilize the CONNECT BY clause. CONNECT BY is an operation that retrieves rows hierarchically; using the clause here will produce all of the rows in the chart at one time. This would appear in this way:

```
SELECT name EmployeeID, ManagerID
FROM CorporateChart
CONNECT BY prior EmployeeID = ManagerID
```

Name	EmployeeID	ManagerID
Jane the CEO	1	
Donald the CFO	2	1
Bill the CIO	3	1
Eric the Engineer	4	2
Sue in Sales	5	3
Hannah in Human Resources	6	3
Tom in Tech Support	7	2
Greg in Ground Control	8	4
Donald the CFO	2	1
Bill the CIO	3	1
Eric the Engineer	4	2
Sue in Sales	5	3
Eric the Engineer	4	2
Sue in Sales	5	3
Hannah in Human Resources	6	3
Tom in Tech Support	7	2
Greg in Ground Control	8	4
Tom in Tech Support	7	2
Greg in Ground Control	8	4
Sue in Sales	5	3

```
20 rows selected
```

DESIGN TIP

CONNECT BY syntax is specific to Oracle. You can achieve the same results when querying other databases using a self-join.

Notice that the output of the code has produced every possible tree and subtree combination. To prevent this from happening, a START WITH clause can be used.

```
SELECT name, EmployeeID, ManagerID
FROM CorporateChart
CONNECT BY prior EmployeeID = ManagerID
START WITH EmployeeID in (SELECT EmployeeID
FROM CorporateChart
WHERE ManagerID is null);
```

Name	EmployeeID	ManagerID
Jane the CEO	1	
Donald the CFO	2	1
Bill the CIO	3	1
Eric the Engineer	4	2
Sue in Sales	5	3
Hannah in Human Resources	6	2
Tom in Tech Support	7	3
Greg in Ground Control	8	4

8 rows selected.

If the user wants to know the rankings of each employee—in other words, who each employee reports to—then another column could be added to serve this purpose. This column will show a supervisor's rank in the hierarchy; for instance, Jane the CEO will have a rank of 1, Bill the CIO and Donald the CFO will have ranks of 2, and so on.

To make the output even more readable, a concatenation operator can indent the rank column by adding more spaces before lower-ranking names. The code and output would appear like so:

```
column PadEmployee format a30
SELECT
lpad ( ' ', (rank -1) *2) || name as PadEmployee,
EmployeeID,
ManagerID,
Rank,
FROM CorporateChart
CONNECT BY prior EmployeeID = ManagerID
START WITH EmployeeID = 1;
```

PadEmployee	EmployeeID	ManagerID	Rank
Jane the CEO	1		1
Donald the CFO	2	1	2
Bill the CIO	3	1	2
Eric the Engineer	4	2	3
Sue in Sales	5	3	3
Hannah in Human Resources	6	2	3
Tom in Tech Support	7	3	3
Greg in Ground Control	8	4	4

8 rows selected.

DESIGN TIP

The LPAD function used in the preceding code pads the left side of the first string with spaces, or with copies of the character string specified in subsequent strings.

If the user only wanted to view employees up to a certain rank, then she could insert a WHERE clause and stipulate to which rank she desired to view. For example, if she only wanted to see the first and second levels within the organization, she could add:

```
WHERE rank <= 2
```

For this example, the output would reflect three rows selected, Jane the CEO, Bill the CIO, and Donald the CFO.

Rules for Trees

When representing trees or hierarchies in SQL, it is necessary to have a column that links the node with other nodes. This column shares the same datatype across nodes. For example, Bill the CIO's identification number is 3 and Donald the CFO's identification number is 2. Both report to Jane the CEO, the parent node, whose identification number is 1. All nodes are related via the identification number column, which has the same data type across nodes.

Looking at the ManagerID and finding a null value easily identifies the root of a tree. Because the nature of a SQL database is inherently nonhierarchical, occasionally it is difficult to spot a null value in a crowd of listed values. In this case, the following code can be used to find the root node:

```
SELECT *
FROM CorporateChart
WHERE ManagerID is NULL;
```

On the opposite end of the spectrum, if a user wished to find out the names of all employees who do not have any subordinates, that is, the leaf nodes, the following code would be used:

```
SELECT *
FROM CorporateChart AS EmployeeID
WHERE NOT EXISTS (SELECT *
                    FROM CorporateChart AS ManagerID
                    Where EmployeeID = ManagerID
```

Other uses for trees include enabling users to determine such things as the number of channels that separate one node from another. This is found by tracing the number of levels existing within the hierarchy that must be stepped through in order to get between two nodes. A practical use for this would be, for instance, to find out if Sue in Sales had any authority over Greg in Ground Control.

Finding a one-to-one relationship (e.g., Sue to Greg) is simple enough, but frequently queries are more complex in organizations—say, for instance, a user wants to find out who Greg's boss's boss's boss is. Clearly things can get complicated quickly—especially for organizations with complex structures and hundreds of employees. One drawback to using queries in trees for determining relationships is that most SQL compilers will experience optimization issues. Generally speaking, when queries are written that require the inclusion of five or more tables to be calculated, problems arise, the primary issue of course being extended processing time.

Limits of the CONNECT BY Clause

While it has several important uses, the CONNECT BY clause also has some limitations. An important clause that does not perform optimally when used in conjunction with CONNECT BY is the ORDER BY clause. Since SQL is a set-oriented language, and a CONNECT BY query result's inherent value is its order, it is therefore redundant to include an ORDER BY clause in the same query.

Perhaps an even more pertinent limit when using the CONNECT BY clause is its inability to be used in conjunction with JOIN. A join is used when two or more tables or views are referenced as the target of a SELECT statement. A key function in relational databases is the capacity to merge two or more tables into a single result set by specifying the relations that exist between those tables. Unfortunately, there is a limit in Oracle that raises an error message:

```
ORA-01437: cannot have join with CONNECT BY
```

However, there is a way to avoid this problem. It is a two-step process that involves creating a view:

```
CREATE or REPLACE VIEW ConnectedEmployees
AS
SELECT
     lpad (' ', (level -1) * 2) | | NAME AS PadEmployee,
EmployeeID,
ManagerID,
FROM CorporateChart
CONNECT BY prior EmployeeID = ManagerID
START WITH EmployeeID = 1;
SELECT * FROM ConnectedEmployees;
```

PadEmployee	EmployeeID	ManagerID	Level
Jane the CEO	1		1
Donald the CFO	2	1	2
Bill the CIO	3	1	2
Eric the Engineer	4	2	3
Sue in Sales	5	3	3
Hannah in Human Resources	6	2	3
Tom in Tech Support	7	3	3
Greg in Ground Control	8	4	4

8 rows selected.

With the creation of the ConnectedEmployees view, it is now possible to use a join function:

```
SELECT PadEmployee, CorporateChart.NAME AS ManagerID
FROM ConnectedEmployees, CorporateChart
WHERE ConnectedEmployees.ManagerID = CorporateChart.EmployeeID (+);
```

PadEmployee	ManagerName
Jane the CEO	
Donald the CFO	Jane the CEO
Bill the CIO	Jane the CEO
Eric the Engineer	Bill the CIO
Sue in Sales	Donald the CFO
Hannah in Human Resources	Donald the CFO
Tom in Tech Support	Bill the CIO
Greg in Ground Control	Eric the Engineer

8 rows selected

The result of these two procedures is the same as would have been gained if a join function were to be applied and successfully work without the associated error. While this method is a bit more work, it does achieve the objective by sidestepping the error problem.

Extracting Information Within Trees

Although the problem may not be apparent from the example chart used in this chapter, many organizations grow so large that it can become difficult to determine who works for whom. To alleviate the potential confusion, it is possible to identify those employees who report to a certain individual. For instance, say that a user wishes to know the reporting structure for a specific person or persons employed in an organization. In the example, think of asking the database if Jane the CEO ranks above Greg in Ground Control—a look at the chart makes it clear that the answer to this question is yes, but in terms of actual code, consider the following example:

```
SELECT count (*)
FROM CorporateChart
WHERE EmployeeID = 8
And rank > 1
START WITH Employee = 1
CONNECT BY prior EmployeeID = SupervisorID;


COUNT (*)
    1
```

Conversely, if the user wants to investigate a more finite relationship between two employees (i.e., one that does not involve the root node or CEO), then the following query could be applied:

```
SELECT count (*)
FROM CorporateChart
WHERE EmployeeID = 8
And rank > 1
START WITH Employee = 2
CONNECT BY prior EmployeeID = SupervisorID;


COUNT (*)
    0
```

In this query, the user asks if Greg in Ground Control reports to Bill the CIO. Since the count is zero, we know that there is not a relationship here.

Tree Operations

All organizations experience change throughout their development. Frequently, the change that is experienced occurs internally with promotions and changes in responsibilities. To reflect the changes in the organization, the trees that represent it must also change. Tree operations are used to modify the size and shape of a tree; however, they are not responsible for changing the contents of the nodes. Some operations can be very involved, while others are less complex. The next few pages will deal with some of the more common operations used for modifying trees.

A set of nodes that delineate a hierarchy can have tree function queries applied to them to learn information contained in those nodes. If, for instance, someone in human resources wished to learn how many outstanding vacation days each employee had, he could use a function to find out.

Deleting a Subtree

Subtrees are any parent nodes that exist below the root in a tree; for instance, both Bill the CIO and Donald the CFO plus their subsequent nodes can be considered subtrees beneath the main tree that begins with Jane the CEO. Deleting a subtree can be accomplished by marking the subordinates in a tree and then deleting them, as shown here:

```
BEGIN
UPDATE CorporateChart
     SET ManagerID = 'Get lost'
     WHERE ManagerID = :subtree_root;
WHILE EXISTS (SELECT *
               FROM CorporateChart
WHERE ManagerID = 'Get lost'
AND EmployeeID <> 'Get lost')
LOOP UPDATE CorporateChart
     SET EmployeeID = 'Get lost'
     WHERE ManagerID = 'Get lost';
```

```
        AND EmployeeID <> 'Get lost';
END LOOP;
DELETE FROM CorporateChart
        WHERE ManagerID = 'Get lost';
END;
```

Note that in this example, the parameter :subtree_root refers to the root of the tree (or subtree).

Subtree Incorporation

Inserting a subtree, the reverse of deleting a subtree, is also a frequent part of building and maintaining organizational charts; and compared with deleting a subtree, inserting one is much less involved. The process of adding a new subtree into an organizational chart, for example, inserting a new manager, appears as follows:

```
BEGIN
INSERT INTO CorporateChart
        VALUES (:subtree_root, : NewManagerID, . . . );
INSERT INTO CorporateChart SELECT * FROM Subtree;
END;
```

Summary

This chapter has covered some of the basic elements and uses of trees in SQL as an example of working with complex relationships among data. It discussed the rules for trees and some of the limitations that they have. The chapter also presented some methods that can be used to pull out information that resides inside a tree. It concluded with some tips for adding and eliminating nodes or a subtree from a tree.

Index

INTERNATIONAL CONTACT INFORMATION

AUSTRALIA
McGraw-Hill Book Company Australia Pty. Ltd.
TEL +61-2-9417-9899
FAX +61-2-9417-5687
http://www.mcgraw-hill.com.au
books-it_sydney@mcgraw-hill.com

CANADA
McGraw-Hill Ryerson Ltd.
TEL +905-430-5000
FAX +905-430-5020
http://www.mcgrawhill.ca

**GREECE, MIDDLE EAST,
NORTHERN AFRICA**
McGraw-Hill Hellas
TEL +30-1-656-0990-3-4
FAX +30-1-654-5525

MEXICO (Also serving Latin America)
McGraw-Hill Interamericana Editores S.A. de C.V.
TEL +525-117-1583
FAX +525-117-1589
http://www.mcgraw-hill.com.mx
fernando_castellanos@mcgraw-hill.com

SINGAPORE (Serving Asia)
McGraw-Hill Book Company
TEL +65-863-1580
FAX +65-862-3354
http://www.mcgraw-hill.com.sg
mghasia@mcgraw-hill.com

SOUTH AFRICA
McGraw-Hill South Africa
TEL +27-11-622-7512
FAX +27-11-622-9045
robyn_swanepoel@mcgraw-hill.com

**UNITED KINGDOM & EUROPE
(Excluding Southern Europe)**
McGraw-Hill Education Europe
TEL +44-1-628-502500
FAX +44-1-628-770224
http://www.mcgraw-hill.co.uk
computing_neurope@mcgraw-hill.com

ALL OTHER INQUIRIES Contact:
Osborne/McGraw-Hill
TEL +1-510-549-6600
FAX +1-510-883-7600
http://www.osborne.com
omg_international@mcgraw-hill.com